MW01044762

QUANTUM COMPANIES II

100 MORE CUTTING-EDGE HIGH-GROWTH COMPANIES TO TRACK INTO THE 21ST CENTURY

A. DAVID SILVER

PETERSON'S/PACESETTER BOOKS
PRINCETON, NEW JERSEY

Visit Peterson's on the Internet at
http://www.petersons.com

Copyright © 1996 by A. David Silver

All rights reserved. No part of this book may be reproduced, stored in a
retrieval system, or transmitted, in any form or by any means—electronic,
mechanical, photocopying, recording, or otherwise—without written
permission from Peterson's.

Quantum Companies II is published by Peterson's/Pacesetter books.

Pacesetter Books, Peterson's/Pacesetter Books, and the Pacesetter horse design
are trademarks of Peterson's, A Division of Thomson Information, Inc.

Library of Congress Cataloging-in-Publication Data

Silver, A. David (Aaron David), 1941–
    Quantum companies II : the next 100 / A. David Silver.
      p.   cm.
    Includes indexes.
    ISBN 1-56079-594-8
    1. Corporations—United States—Finance—Directories. 2. High
technology industries—United States—Finance—Directories. I. Title
HG4907.S463   1996
338.7′4′02573—dc20   96-5049
                                       CIP

Editorial direction by Andrea Pedolsky
Production supervision by Bernadette Boylan
Proofreading by Marie Burnett
Composition by Gary Rozmierski

Creative direction by Linda Huber
Jacket design by Kathy Kikkert
Jacket photograph by
   Arthur Tress/Photonica
Interior design by Greg Wozney

Printed in the United States of America

10 9 8 7 6 5 4 3 2 1

CONTENTS

Acknowledgments   v

Introduction   1

PART ONE   The Making of *Quantum Companies II*   3

The Next Great Plays on   The Role of Women   29
  the Internet   9   Best Stock Investments
Internet Zaibatsu   19   for 1996   31
The Means of Selection   23

PART TWO   100 QUANTUM COMPANIES   37

PART THREE   INDEXES

Geographic Index   339
Company Index   341
Industry Index   344

ACKNOWLEDGMENTS

Special thanks for *Quantum Companies II* are due to Andrea Pedolsky, my forward-looking and patient editor at Peterson's/Pacesetter Books, whose friendship has been a fleuralegeum of delight. Ellen Borup and Antone Musick were unflagging in their production and editing work. Carmela Niño, my principal researcher, stayed two steps ahead of me with her output.

To all the venture capitalists who submitted their candidates, I am deeply grateful. Stockbrokers Walter Probst, Michael Hickey, Bob Hill, and Barbara Christian kept the ideas coming, and industry experts Eric R. Markrud, Corey M. Horowitz, and Erik Jansen were generous with their ideas as well. *Quantum Companies II* could not have made it to the starting gate without them.

A. David Silver
Santa Fe, New Mexico

INTRODUCTION

Following the stunning performance in the stock market, and operationally, of approximately three-fourths of the eighty publicly held companies that I profiled in *Quantum Companies* (*QC I*), my editor at Peterson's/Pacesetter books asked me to write a "sequel." I eagerly accepted the challenge to find 100 more rapidly emerging, entrepreneurial companies that are changing the geography of business. Because there are so many, I knew it would be like shooting ducks in a barrel.

Three magnificent new markets are emerging that will delight investors for years to come: client/server software, the Internet, and interactive telecommunications. These three markets were barely touched on in *QC I*, but when I happened to be lucky enough to see their outstanding business plans and heraldic futures, the stock prices of the companies from these three industries in *QC I* outpaced nearly every other company profiled in the book. For instance, Ascend Communications, a manufacturer of network devices for the Internet, had an eightfold price increase. FORE Systems, a similar company, had a sevenfold increase. Asanté Technologies, Bay Networks, Cambridge Technology Partners, Informix, Qualcomm, and 3Com more than doubled in price.

These three markets are in their infancy. It is day one of at least a quarter century of wondrous new enterprises ready to bring efficiencies, pleasure, and money-making opportunities to billions of people all over the planet. For *Quantum Companies II* (*QC II*), I have captured sixty-three of them and thus project an even better batting average this year than last.

QC I had nineteen health-care-delivery companies, some of which suffered from lack of capital to climb the wall erected by the Food and Drug Administration. But had you invested equal money in each of the publicly held health-care-delivery companies in spring 1995, you would have been approximately 14 percent ahead in winter 1995. The overall uptick is largely due to Neurogen's quintuple from 5½ to 26¾, Mitek Surgical Products' acquisition by Johnson & Johnson at a large gain, and Vivus' double in price from 13¾ to 27. There are only eleven health-care-delivery companies in *QC II*, with some tempting "buys" among the four physician-practice management companies profiled.

Although none of the companies I selected for *QC I* went out of business, some of them had a rocky year. Frontier Insurance and Integrated Health Services sustained write-offs and their stocks sold off but have recovered handsomely. Ryka nearly became a fatality when Lands End did not go through with an acquisition. InVision Systems ran out of capital and merged with Connectix to broaden the latter's offerings in desktop videoconferencing.

You would have broken even had you invested equal money in the environmental services company selections in *QC I*, one of which, Molten Metal Technology Corp., tripled from 11⅛ in spring 1995 to 35⅞ in winter 1995 and so carrying the load for the others in the category. The environmental services market did not persuade me of any paradigm shifts this year, and I did not profile any of its companies.

There are some interesting surprises in *QC II*, although it took some digging to find them. Two measurement-instrument manufacturers are profiled—DSP Technology and Zygo—both of which are undervalued stocks; a regional airline, SkyWest, that serves the hot spots in the American economy (Seattle, the Silicon Valley, and Colorado); Virtual I.O. Corporation, a virtual-reality products manufacturer; and a mining equipment distributor—Raleigh Mine & Supply Company.

In some categories, the public companies in *QC II* are overpriced in relation to conventional valuation techniques, such as p/e ratios and market-to-revenue ratios. This is because, in many cases, these companies have strong *validators*: highly successful venture capital funds or strategic partners who have planted kisses worth of megabucks on small companies and turned them from tadpoles into princes, completely passing up the groping-frog stages of their adolescence. Beware the secondary offerings of the stocks of *overvalidated* companies— particularly client/server software and Internet companies—and if you see the validators selling their holdings, don't get left holding yours.

My selection criteria in *QC II* were the same as in *QC I*: dramatically rising sales accompanied by increasing gross profit margins represent the first test. A declining SGA Expenses/Revenues ratio, or at least one that is not rising faster than gross profit margin, is a second filter. A low debt-to-worth ratio is third, and an increase in accounts receivable turnover is the fourth test. Inventories must not be building up, and the footnotes to the financial statements must be clean of any self-dealing. Finally, if a company has been unable to open multiple-marketing channels and relies on sales to original equipment manufacturers (OEMs) to get product to market, this company, notwithstanding other positive inclusion ratios, is not a Quantum Company.

Part One

The Making of Quantum Companies II

To become a Quantum Company, each of the 100 companies profiled herein demonstrated extraordinary economic validity, which translates into having developed an elegant solution for a big and growing problem. By elegant I mean that if the company makes a product, it must be proprietary (unique and, if possible, protected by patents); if the company offers a service, the delivery system must be either too simplistic or too complex to replicate, or the company has statutory or institutional barriers-to-entry that keep out or discourage competition.

The paradigm shift in the information technology market and the concomitant shift from mainframe to client/server computer systems has created a large and growing demand for radically new software. Reflecting this are the twenty-five software companies in *Quantum Companies II*. As a result of the Internet and World Wide Web, the demand for a vast new array of products and services has been set in motion, ranging from service producers to carry the data, devices such as routers and servers to interconnect the communications lines, and enabling technologies to add value to the network and give its users a means to navigate from one site to another. Answering this need are the twenty-three Internet service providers and enabling technology producers and seven network-device manufacturers in *Quantum Companies II*.

INVESTMENT BANKERS' POT O' GOLD

Although not Quantum Companies themselves, the investment banks that have set their caps on Internet company financings and acquisitions— such as Morgan Stanley, Alex Brown, Hambrecht & Quist, and Robertson Stephens, to name the largest—are going to enjoy their best few years ever. Internet service providers (ISPs), for instance, such as Netcom OnLine, consume cash in buckets. If they grow at the rate of 20 percent per month, which is typical, they cannot buy modems fast enough to keep up with demand. This is good news for three Quantum Companies, modem manufacturers all: Diamond Multimedia, Global Village Communications, and U.S. Robotics (which acquired Megahertz, a *QC I* company). When you dial the Internet, your modem connects to an Internet service provider's modem. Busy signals mean that the ISP's modem is tied up. An ISP with only one modem for every ten subscribers is going to have a lot of busy signals and, since the Internet is a free market in every sense of the word, frequent busy signals are reported on Internet news groups and the undercapitalized ISP begins to lose subscribers. Capital and management are the key ingredients at this stage in the build-out of the Internet; certain underwriters' stocks could do as well as those of Internet-related Quantum Companies.

NIETZCHE'S PREDICTION

The medical market is in turmoil and as Freidrich Nietzche reminded us, "It takes a chaos to create a shooting star." Fifteen years ago, hospital managers and physicians could charge their patients any price and buy the fanciest of equipment and the insurers would pay. But those days ended with the birth of health maintenance organizations (HMOs) and their kin in the mid-1980s, now lumped under the sobriquet "managed care." Hospital managers were unprepared to think about costs and cash flow, and many of their jobs were wiped out as their hospitals were merged with major chains and special services were spun-out to doc-in-a-box, store-front operations, a number of which were profiled in *QC I*. Managed-care operations have met up with strong muscle on the defensive line in the form of the provider chains, and the playing field is once again level.

But how have the physicians fared? They are beginning to get it together. One of their solutions is to band together into companies known as physician-practice management groups. A number of these are the brainchild of Russell Carson, a senior partner in the venture capital fund Welsh Carson Anderson & Stowe—a validator in the health-care delivery industry with the power to elevate stock prices only equaled by Kleiner Perkins Caulfield & Byers—a venture capital fund that causes Internet stock prices to levitate when its name is in the prospectus (e.g., Macromedia, NetScape, and Shiva). Four physician-practice management companies are profiled in *QC II*.

Four Outstanding Physician-Practice Management Companies

Name	12/22/95 Stock Price	% Change Revenues 1992–95	Market/ Revenues	Principal Validators
American Oncology	43⅞	+1208	10.4x	Welsh Carson
Occusystems	19⅛	+832	2.2x	Welsh Carson, Sprout
Phycor	44¼	+264	2.7x	First Cent., Massey Burch
Physicians Reliance	39⅝	+152	11.8x	TA Associates, Advent

The disparity in market/revenue ratios is what makes stock selecting an exciting adventure. For instance, Occusystems is growing two-thirds as fast as American Oncology; it has the same venture capital validator, is twice the size, and has a better SGA Expenses/Revenue ratio than American Oncology; it has also slashed this ratio more deeply over the last four years but has a market to revenues ratio one-fifth that of American Oncology.

SOFTWARE ℞

For physicians who seek to maintain their autonomy and gainsay the tempting siren song of the physician-practice management companies, their solution lies in slashing administrative costs. To do this, doctors are increasingly turning to more sophisticated client/server-based software. We spotted CyCare Systems (market/revenues of 2.8x), MedPartners (market/revenues of 3.4x), and Pyxis (market/revenues of 3.2x) as the three most outstanding companies in this category.

Improved medical devices represent another solution to the chaos we know as the health-care-delivery market. We took a look at Incontrol (market/revenues of infinity), Lumisys (market/revenues of 3.9x), Orthopedic Technology (market/revenues of 1.9x), and Perclose (market/revenues of infinity) in this category.

THE BATTLE OF THE BANDWIDTH

The telecommunications marketplace is a pitched battle to bring more options to our communicating needs. The cellular phone got us used to anywhere-anytime calling. The next step is remote access to our databases, remote shopping, and a sharp reduction in long-distance calling via the Internet. Dialing into the Internet costs the price of a local phone call. *Quantum Companies II* profiles Broadband Technology (market/revenues of 17.0x), Data Transmission Network (market/revenues of 1.2x), EZ Communications (market/revenues of 1.7x), GeoWorks (market/revenues of 35.7x), and Interdigital Communications (market/revenues of 2.7x). Keep your eyes on any and all information you can find on privately held Quantum Company International Discount Telecommunications Corp. (IDT), in Hackensack, New Jersey, an emerging phenom in the voice/Internet linkup. The company's beta site is in Finland, where people are using its ISP (Internet Service Provider) to make phone calls. Let's say a 5-minute call from Helsinki to New York costs $15.00. Using a $250/month phone line leased by IDT, the phone call costs about $3.00. Let's say you want to call Helsinki from New York, a $15.00 call via AT&T, MCI, or Sprint. You simply "ping" your contact in Helinski with an inexpensive e-mail asking her to call you via her IDT Internet line. She does so at a steep discount. The giant telecommunications companies are in a tizzy over IDT, because they can't compete with its price.

WATCH QUANTUM'S PRIVATE COMPANIES

Competition will likely come from the Cable TV and wireless companies because they have lots of bandwidth. The Internet is restricted to voice and data, until ISDN pipe is ubiquitous (as it is in Finland, France, Japan, and Atlanta, Georgia). But until then, the cable companies are holding four aces, known as fiber, and they are teaming up with Internet toolmakers to bring the low cost and efficiencies of the Internet to Joe six-pack and his channel changer. TCI invested in Netscape. Sumitomo invested in Xing Technology. Microsoft paid eight times revenue to invest in an ISP called UUNet. Kleiner Perkins Caulfield & Byers has teamed with TCI to launch @Home, a new cable company that intends to use the Internet to carry data, entertainment, and home shopping to the television set through servers bouncing their signals to routers (see CISCO Systems in *QC I*) thence to cable modems (see Bay Networks and Diamond Multimedia in *QC I* and *QC II*, respectively) and thence to the channel changer. The difference from Joe six-pack's point of view is that his options will grow from twenty-four channels today to 5 million or more channels by the end of the decade.

With so many options, keep your eye on Yahoo!, which indexes the Internet. Read all you can about NetCount, which conducts market research on the Net and within a few years will be able to tell advertisers on Fox's NFL games, for instance, the buying habits of their viewers, enabling them to modify their first-quarter advertisement by halftime in order to fit the content to the viewers' demographics.

DIAMONDS IN UNEXPECTED PLACES

One of the largest looming battlefields is content—the entertainment and information that will attract customers to the Internet and hold their attention. CUC International (market/revenues of 2.7x) is moving swiftly to become a dominant content provider on the Net.

The concept of the mobile warehouse, one that we covered in *QC I*, is still very much alive and makes trucking stocks selectively attractive. Just-in-time manufacturing and marketing obviates the need for regional warehouses, where costly inventory is stored and commercial banks at one time thrived on inventory loans. (Note the downsizing and merger mania of banks as their favorite borrower, the distributor, goes the way of the Dodo bird.) We feature trailer manufacturer Featherlite Manufacturing (market/revenues of 1.4x) in *QC II*.

QC II makes some other discoveries, such as DSP Technology (market/revenues of 1.0x), a former defense electronics manufacturer that is remaking itself successfully as a measurement-instruments developer for the auto industry and privately held Best Internet Communications, Inc., which is on an acquisition spree of small Internet service providers.

The Wright Brothers were selling planes to the French government while the American government was asking for more tests. Americans did not take the airplane seriously until Charles Lindbergh flew it across the Atlantic. The U.S. Food and Drug Administration (FDA) continues to stifle the development of biotech companies in America, quintupling the need for venture capital. *QC II* found only two biotech companies that it recommends following closely: Cephalon, an elegantly constructed biotechnology company that may have found an effective therapy against Lou Gehrig's diseas, and Neurex. Our country's leaders have blinders on when it comes to the FDA. Diminish its power and biotech would flourish once again in this country, like the frictionless Internet.

The single best way to find undervalued companies is to read *The New York Times* and the *Wall Street Journal* on a daily basis. They chronicle most of the problems felt by large numbers of people. Problems to some people represent opportunities to entrepreneurs. Once you have found the entrepreneurial companies that are addressing these problems, apply the Quantum Companies evaluation criteria (see The Means of Selection on page 23) to determine if the companies are well managed.

The Next Great Plays on the Internet

ree-flowing information nurtures democracy and democracy is the requisite for capitalism. Dreams are the oil that make the gears of the free-enterprise system turn. And they are turning freely for the first time in China, Chile, and the former members of the Eastern bloc. The Indonesian government prohibits the works of Pramoedya Ananta Toer, whose novels are acclaimed throughout the world, but Indonesians read him freely on the Internet.

When Howard Gordon, the founder and CEO of Xing Technology Corp., was testing StreamWorks in July 1995, a software product that enables radio and TV stations to broadcast their programs over the Internet, his first listener was a personal computer user in Prague. He e-mailed Gordon the following message: "Play the Beach Boys." Freedom is the Internet.

Five months later, Microsoft and NBC announced the formation of a new 24-hour all-news channel, to be streamed over the Internet using Xing's StreamWorks server-plus-software, thence through a cable modem, to our television sets. The Internet thereby was designated as the prime carrier of video signals around the globe. There has never been an innovation of such importance that has changed the societal order as quickly as the Internet. It played a major role in the selection of candidates for *Quantum Companies II*.

WHERE ARE THE INTERNET PLAYS?

Walk through a busy mall in any Pacific Rim country and you'll see people of all ages surfing the World Wide Web—the commercial section of the Internet. They've seen American lifestyle movies for years, heard American music for decades, and they want American products now. Talk about pent-up demand! Levi-Strauss, Nike, Reebok, Calvin Klein, Raybans from Bausch & Lomb—these consumer products are going to sell like blazes via catalogs advertised on the Web. The next great play is consumerism and the stage is the newly emerging democracies.

THE INTERNET FAVORS ENTREPRENEURS

The Internet favors small entrepreneurial companies that are able to quickly adapt new technologies. The giant communications companies are merely rearranging the deck chairs on the Titanic as they announce plans to create 500 new video channels. Then, when they fail to deliver, they will use merger talk to distract the market away from their indecisiveness. The Internet has 5 million channels. Anyone with a personal computer, a modem, and a subscription to an Internet Service Provider (ISP) is a broadcaster.

The rebels in the jungles of Mexico's Chiapas communicate via the Internet. Web sites, or infomercials, are available to everyone—and prospects who contact the Web sites can be counted and their demographics analyzed. There are 35,000 catalog retailers in the United States, and a mere 1 percent have Web sites. They will pay between $1,000 and $15,000 for a design and monthly maintenance fees to manage their domains. The systems integrators—BBN Planet, CIBER, Jack Henry, AmeriData, and the Web-site management division of BEST Internet—will rake in so much money they will have to bail it. Members of a boys' club in Los Angeles are designing Web sites for $50 for small businesses, which indicates that design fees will come down, but site-management fees will rise.

NEW SUPERSTATIONS WILL EMERGE

The people who built the Internet dug no trenches and laid not a foot of cable. They simply lease existing lines, for the Internet is nothing more than routers bouncing signals from one to the other over leased telephone lines. What makes it valuable are the tools and the content. Netscape Communications, Inc., the best-known toolmaker, developed a browser to enable subscribers to search the World Wide Web to find the content they are seeking. Subscribers can order a product, see a TV show, or listen to their favorite football team's game for the cost of a local phone call plus a $20 per month subscription fee. The tollgate to the Internet is so low that it is an example of *frictionless capitalism*. Tiny, local TV stations with nerds in the basement pushing their owners to broadcast over the Internet will emerge as the Turner Broadcasting Systems of the next 20 years. E-Z Communications, Inc., is one of the vanguards of this movement. KOA in Denver is the first station to broadcast an NFL team's games via the Internet.

SOME REAL ESTATE DEVELOPERS WILL PROSPER

In a few years 200 million people will be hooked onto the Internet. Many will find that going to the office no longer makes good sense and will move to the country and download their work to their clients. Thus, there will be a great economic play in real estate developer stocks that build happy Internet communities in remote, low-governance regions.

Communities of geeks and geekettes will demand from their builders the basic requirements of ISDN lines to permit video transmission, satellite antennae for high-quality wireless communication, a library of computer books, magazines like *Wired* and *Web Week*, a community room where software glitches can be worked on collectively, a pizza parlor, swimming pool, and basketball court. Several dozen single-family units will encircle the property and a walking track will be built around the periphery. The developers will be able to earn $675 to $750 per month in rent or mortgage payments versus $450 to $550 for conventional multiunit dwellings. The premium will be in direct proportion to the benefits to computer jocks: bandwidth, maid service, nearby pizza and junk food to pull all-nighters, mostly software engineers as fellow tenants, and minimal governance and regulatory intrusion.

THE EXTREMES

Four blind black teenage girls with voices to die for can't get a record label to produce their first album. A friend hears their tape and goes into a rapturous meltdown. He has a friend who works at KPIG in Santa Cruz, California, which broadcasts on the Internet using Xing Technology Corporation's StreamWorks software. The KPIG engineer hears the tape, loves the songs, and on a lark broadcasts it over the Internet. Listeners in Taiwan, Hoboken, and Belfast hear it and become enslaved by the music and add it to their Web sites. Soon, thousands of Internet radio listeners are tuning in and playing it for friends. Then tens of thousands and finally millions of people are singing along with the girls, who call themselves the Extremes.

Oprah invites them on her show; then Jay Leno debuts them on national TV. The record companies call, fax, and visit. But the Extremes stick to the Internet as their broadcast medium of choice and they develop their own Web site with advertisers who pay them on a per-play basis.

Their success on the Internet is being copied by hundreds of recording artists, who have held onto or never specified contractually the ownership of electronic recording rights to their music. The Internet has become a significant channel for music, and just as home video surpassed the box office, the Net passes CDs in a flash and becomes the medium of choice for recording artists.

You won't find Sony, JVC, Phillips, or RCA in this story. They will still be analyzing the effect on their music distribution system when the Extremes bank their first billion dollars.

Xing Technology Corporation's StreamWorks enables publishers, recording artists, movie studios, radio and television broadcasters, and other content producers to market their content over the Internet, thereby establishing a new commercial channel with unlimited cash flow potential. Similar broadcasts of audio/video content over private enterprise networks for general communications or training are also enabled.

StreamWorks is proprietary and transmits very high quality sound over 28.8 modems and very high quality video at thirty frames per second over double ISDN lines (128 kbps). Radio and television broadcasters have been ordering it at a rapidly increasing rate as they familiarize themselves with its features as an on-ramp, or tuner, to the Internet. These features include:

- the ability to broadcast anywhere so long as the listener/viewer is on the Network;
- the ability to capture the name, gender, address, and other demographic information of all listeners/viewers in real-time;
- the ability to advertise and sell products to listeners/viewers;
- the ability to conduct market research or poll the listeners/viewers about the broadcasters' content;
- the ability to offer games, contests, and other forms of interactive communication with listeners/viewers.

The company's customers include NBC, Reuters, CompuServe, Tribune Companies, Time Warner, E-Z Communications (owner of 21 radio stations and a *QC II* company), Stanford University, Telecom Finland, Swiss News Agency, Bloomberg, CFRA, KOOL-FM, KOA (Denver), MCI, and more. They pay Xing about $16,000 for a complete, ready-to-operate StreamWorks system, including encoders, server, and decoding software.

END-RUNNING GOVERNMENT TOLLGATES

Regulation will eventually slow the growth of Internet-related companies. Elected officials are power-driven and what better tune to sell their constituents than *envy* of the fun and wealth of geeks and geekettes. A good software engineer in her twenties pulls down $100,000 per year before stock options. A voter flipping burgers at McDonalds scrapes along on one-fifth of that. Politicians make hay on economic discrepencies such as these.

The Interstate Commerce Commission (now dismantled) was established in 1887 by the federal government to slow down the rapacious growth of railroads. It eventually bankrupted them. State and local governments sprouted clones of the ICC to regulate highways, pipelines, and power grids on the hypothesis that if something moves it is easy to tax it. Electrons move. They will be taxed.

Consumers and entrepreneurs can outrun a government tollgate. Factories and hospitals cogenerate electricity in their heating plants. They set up private branch telephone exchanges that bypass about one-third of the phone service they would otherwise buy from local phone companies. Landlords erect rooftop satellite dishes on buildings and sell private cable service to tenants. Companies such as Broadband Technologies and Interdigital Systems will thrive.

Wireless phone service is growing unabated, for now, without Federal Communications Commission (FCC) controls. Local-access providers such as MFS Communications and Teleport are expanding under lenient regulation and undercut local phone companies. Direct broadcast satellite service is booming while its competitor, cable TV service, stagnates under the FCC's price regulation. Most software engineers design their data to go over wireless, local-access fiber, and via satellite whenever possible because the transmission costs are lower. The stagnating cable, broadcasting, and Bell system giants are merging and joint venturing with one another in order to control *content*.

THE INTERNET IS A HIGHWAY FOR CONTENT TO ROLL ON

Content is king. The lines can go anywhere. The Web can reach anyone. But if the content is not compelling, people will find ways to amuse themselves other than browsing the Web, flicking their TV channel selector, or roaming the channels on a direct broadcast satellite set-top box. The concept of any movie anytime or any tune anytime sounds good, but the typical consumer does not want 500 options. He likes to know that on Monday nights in the autumn Frank Gifford will be doing Monday Night Football. She likes to know that HBO will offer a feature-length film at 9:00 every evening, and that Big Bird, Bert, and Ernie will teach her children math every morning.

The toolmakers to the Internet were the darlings of the bull market in 1995. But the value of content producers will dwarf those of the enabling technologies. If you think Netscape had a high market value when its sales were $48 million and its market cap was $5.7 billion, you ain't seen nothing yet. The first company to own broadcasting rights to popular Internet programs will command a king's ransom.

THE SOAPS

Sammy Davis Jr. was addicted to the soap operas. Mamie Eisenhower watched the soaps every weekday afternoon. Twenty million Americans followed the O.J. Simpson trial, a live soap opera. Romance novels are the largest-selling trade books category. Clearly the soaps are one of the most popular modalities of entertainment content in the country.

But, they are not on the Internet. A 15-minute daily soap opera segment would be just the ticket for millions of Web surfers who want to take a break with their lunch or afternoon tea. An independent producer could obtain electronic licensing rights to "All My Children" or "General Hospital" or create her own cyberspace-oriented soaps and make them available to romantinets. The possibilites for romantic entanglements between the geekette with her heart set on the separated CEO who is in love with one of the telemarketers, or the geek who finds love in a chat group and then meets the person at InfoNet, provide limitless opportunities to rivet viewers for a few minutes a day.

I should think that Procter & Gamble or Kraft/General Foods would jump through hoops to become the sponsor for "Sylvia of Silicon Valley" or "Writing Code Through the Night." Rupert Murdoch's News Corp. doubtless would be the first to publish an Internet Soap Opera News. Advertisers would flock to it. Actors and actresses would find new outlets for their talent. Agents would have a new cash flow channel.

THE TOOLMAKERS

You will find many toolmakers among the *Quantum Companies II*, because the garden is new and the plebeians require tools to plant their ideas and harvest their rewards. The Internet's toolmakers include server producers, such as Cascade Communications and Cabletron Systems, and software developers, including FTP Software, Netscape, Spyglass, Future Labs, Arbor Software, Shiva, Yahoo!, and more. The great toolmakers serve to give order to a market by introducing standards and efficiencies.

THE HUMBLE PLOW

The first, and perhaps the most significant, invention in the history of man and the one that gave rise to social order is the plow. Prior to the plow, the Egyptians used a digging stick to puncture holes in the soil to drop seeds in. When the Nile flooded their land, the seeds would grow. Everyone was engaged in agriculture. Then around 4000 B.C. it was noticed that the river rose and fell at regular intervals once a year, and the people began to harness the retreating water in basins to be used during the dry season. Ditches were dug from the basins to the fields to carry the water to the growing crops. At about this time, the plow began to replace the digging stick. It became a forward-curving wooden blade for cutting the soil and a backward-curving pair of handles with which the farmer could direct the oxen to pull the plow. Men were replaced as the source of traction power.

The plow enabled the Egyptians to build up a surplus of food beyond the requirements of the community. Thus, for the first time the community could tolerate nonfood producers, and these individuals explored other ways to be productive, which led to the development of bricks to build houses and buildings, the development of government to administer the building and maintenance of irrigation ditches, and the development of the field of mathematics to attempt to predict the growing season more accurately.

Although the plow freed people from being tied to the vagaries of nature, it was the beginning of an umbilical relationship between humanity and its tools. In the fourth quarter of the twentieth century in a portion of the planet known as the United States, we are once again being freed to investigate new means of using our creativity. New operating systems, such as Hot Java, are being developed to enable new applications to be developed on the Internet. Microsoft's dominance is being challenged. Digital video systems, such as those produced by Avid Technology and Advanced Digital Imaging, are sufficiently inexpensive to permit virtually anyone to become a movie producer. Xing Technology's StreamWorks enables anyone to record an album of music and broadcast it over the Internet. IDT enables someone overseas to call a person in the United States via the Internet for the price of a local phone call. Market researchers can imbed their software in Netscape's or Spyglass's browsers and discover a myriad of new dimensions about their customers. Let your fingers do the walking through thousands of Web sites with Yahoo's electronic yellow pages.

Some of the tools of the digital age and the Internet may have an impact on society as extraordinary as the plow. *QC II* attempts to identify those with the most demonstrable economic justification.

SLICE AND DICE

In his seventieth year Robert Whiteman obtained the licensing rights to the Library of Congress, which he is in the process of repackaging for the Internet. Whiteman is one of the grand masters of the slice-and-dice business, having repackaged *Ripley's Believe It or Not* into forty-four museums throughout the world, and in 1996 we'll see Ripley's characters on the Net. The Internet has no barriers to entry, certainly not age.

An at-home way that people will benefit from the Internet is by becoming master chefs. The ingredients are the great indexes, directories, and compilations of data that Internet users, known for their nanosecond needs for data ("I want it, and I want it now"), will pay megabucks for—the U.S. Patent Office could be enticed to license someone its database of patents. The Smithsonian could obviate its need for government support by selling subscriptions to its Web site. The Metropolitan Museum of Art, through an MPEG compression encoder/decoder, can offer live tours. Any number of industry directories, such as *The Dodge Reports* (construction), *The Movie Almanac* (to settle bets on Oscar winners), *The Thomas Registry of Industry*, and the *Guinness Book of World Records*, are licensable.

Then you slice-and-dice the directories. The most propinquitous to revenue-generating goes for a higher price than the less frequently used data. When you have the licensee under contract, you can resell it via your own Web site and OEM it to the Internet service providers that can offer the directories.

THE SUBLIMINAL MESSAGE

It's bound to happen, so why shouldn't you do it: Put subliminal advertising messages on free space on the Internet. Air-space marketing has been popular in retail stores for years. At the check-out counter of most large supermarkets and retail chain stores we are bombarded with impulse-purchase items hung on racks, such as cards, lollipops, razors, tabloids, chewing gum, breath mints, and more. These air-space items, along with buckets placed at the ends of aisles, are nonintrusive, and most of us don't mind them.

Someone is going to sell advertisers on the idea of placing their messages or Internet pages in an inoffensive manner. The ads could brighten the pages of endless text. I can see MasterCard or Visa placing their logos on bank statements, or Nike's logo on a page of sports scores.

Typically there is an entrepreneur who knows how to imbed a visual clip in a browser who puts himself or herself in the middle of this kind of new form of marketing and takes a percentage of the advertiser's fee.

ASSOCIATION-BASED MARKETING

Internet subscribers are hungry for information about how to maximize the benefits of the Net. They meet at computer cafes, a recent development on the American landscape. They read millions of pages of computer magazines. They dial into chat groups to exchange information. They call systems integrators to install their Internet service and train them in its use. Without the information and instruction, an Internet subscription is about as useful to the subscriber as a boat anchor. The marketing opportunity, therefore, is as follows:

1. Sell information
2. Sell instruction
3. Sell add-ons
4. Sell applications
5. Sell memberships to users

The need for these five features is more acute for home-business users who are trying to succeed on their own, because they are operating all alone. There is no PC buff down the road (or if there is, he is there because he has chosen to maximize his privacy and doesn't want to be bothered. Indeed, most of the neighbors are not near and are hermetic). Nearby systems integrators may work on noncompatible systems lines. Thus, the new Internet subscriber is ripe for a club membership.

The way the users group has worked for years in the personal computer industry is that the new customer is offered the opportunity to purchase a membership in the group for an annual fee of, say, $500, which entitles her to attend quarterly users group meetings and advise the manufacturer on the innovations that the customer base needs and wants. She also receives frequent newsletters, fax letters, and e-mail letters that tell her about the applications and solutions to computing gaffs that other users have developed. Users communicate with one another via telephone, e-mail, and fax, and they elect a board of directors and advise the manufacturer on necessary innovations.

The great association-management companies, such as CUC International, are beginning to enter the Internet marketplace. Their marketing skills are imitateable and, when understood, will lead to a second-generation boom in new Internet service companies that offer the benefits of club membership, e.g., insurance, credit, discounts, travel, expos, newsletters, and advance information of innovations.

FLOAT MANY CLUBS

Three words explain why the Internet is easy for entrepreneurs to enter: Float. Many. Clubs. *Float* is capital provided up front by subscribers. *Many* is the large number of people who are searching for solutions to online needs, from inexpensive databases to convenient shopping. *Clubs* represent the privileges offered to association members to encourage their use of a product or service and, more important, their renewal. With few barriers to entry, a large number of entrepreneurs and companies are providing Internet services.

The prepaid subscription is a payment modality that dates back to the fifteenth century and the invention of the printing press by Johannes Gutenberg. When the printing press was invented the most heavily demanded initial publications were how-to books, which propelled the spread of craft techniques throughout Europe. The second most hotly demanded publication was the newspaper, which for convenience was soon offered to readers on a prepaid subscription basis. The idea of asking the customer to prepay soon spread.

At about the same time printing was invented, the concept of insurance was also conceived. As the story goes, the first insurance policy was invented accidentally. There was a storm at sea and a ship laden with many sailors and extremely valuable cargo was being severely tossed about and the captain feared that the ship would soon break in half and sink to the bottom of the sea. He began frantically flashing his signal for help, and the more the ship creaked and groaned, the more vigorously he flashed. Finally, a passing ship saw the flashing light and its captain pulled his ship as near as possible and responded with:

"Do you want us to tow you to safety?"
The captain of the troubled ship flashed back, "Yes."
"How much will you pay me?"

From that point forward, no ship left the harbor to explore for goods without insurers selling safety to the ship captains up front. The cost of paying for property insurance when needed was then and is now prohibitive. Ship captains paid a small percentage of the replacement of their vessels before setting sail, and as the volume of trading vessels increased, the notion of blanket coverage supplanted single-voyage coverage; and from sailing risks, insurance soon spread to cover a multiple of other risks. For example, life insurance was initially burial insurance. Immigrants to the New World wished for a proper burial, which gave rise to burial insurance, much of it offered by upstart burial societies located in new forts chiseled into the wilderness around Milwaukee, Minneapolis, Des Moines, and Kansas City. When the second- and third-generation children of these settlers moved away from home, some of them became sales agents for the insurance policies in the towns where they came to live. But they reframed it as life insurance to appeal to younger, more adventurous people whom they met in remote towns. There was stout competition from the outset due to minimal barriers to entry and the desire by many entrepreneurs to share in the huge float created by the prepaid subscription modality and the future payment of cost of goods sold, indigenous to the insurance business.

Over 1,800 Internet service providers are in business today and perhaps fifty new ones are being formed each month. They charge individuals $20 per month, on average, and $800 to $1,500 per month for corporation subscriptions for access to the Net. The perceived value of their service will erode to a commodity price, however, unless they begin to offer benefits like those provided by the insurance industry, warehouse clubs, and associations. The survivors and thrivers among the Internet service providers must segue into association-based marketing or otherwise go the way of all well-conceived but poorly executed businesses.

Internet Zaibatsu

The *zaibatsu* are Japan's large trading groups that manage hundreds of billions of dollars of assets and have their fingers in dozens of pies—banking, capital equipment, insurance, electronics, lumber, steel, plantations, trading, and more. We know them by their consumer product names—Panasonic, Kirin, JVC, Canon, NEC, Toyota—but the *zaibatsus* are named Dai-Ichi, Sumitmo, Itochu, Mitsui, Mitsubishi, and Toshiba. They can produce goods for many markets, finance their purchase, insure their safe delivery, and sell you a cassette player, camera, or photocopier to record the moment.

In America we are witnessing the development of our own *zaibatsu*, a tightly networked group of extraordinary wealth creators whose new Internet ventures soar in value to undreamed-of heights. At the center of the *zaibatsu* are the major high-technology venture capital funds. The premier fund is Kleiner Perkins Caulfield & Byers. It is followed in rank by Greylock, Sequoia, Hambrecht & Quist, Accel Partners, and several others.* Joined with the venture capitalists through loyalty and the glue of equity are the CEOs of the companies they funded five to ten years ago and launched with venture capital, advice, and contacts and who owe them respect. The third component in the *zaibatsu* are the large corporations, whose research and development departments have been emptied out like Cuban political prisoner camps to start new companies and join the chase. These corporate giants, such as Digital Equipment Corporation (DEC) and Apple Computer, rely on the entrepreneurial companies launched by the venture capital funds to provide them with rights to new and important products. They are willing to invest in the Internet-related portfolio companies of the venture capital funds if that will enable them to gain a flow of new products, a windowsill view of research and development, exclusive territorial or segment marketing rights, or private-label marketing rights. Finally, and fourth, are the senior- and middle-level managers who worked for companies launched by the venture capital funds in a previous incarnation and who are coaxed out of these companies to manage the new start-ups.

FUND MANAGERS AND THE PRESS

The press lords of Silicon Valley praise the skill of Kleiner Perkins in picking winners and further pedestalize the *zaibatsu* fund managers by having them speak at their venture capital conferences. The most important magazine, *The Red Herring*, is published by the son of Tom

---

* In physician-practice management the leading *zaibatsu* is Welsh Carson Anderson & Stowe.

Perkins, who co-founded Kleiner Perkins in 1971. The combination is formidable. The stock market adores the new companies praised by *The Red Herring* and launched by the *zaibatsu* and the market tosses their prices up into the clouds where they trade at multiples of revenues previously considered unthinkable. The mutual fund and pension fund money managers say to one another "We need a few Internet stocks in our portfolios." Their bosses ask, "Which ones?" The money managers, unable to use conventional valuation tools, respond, "Netscape, UUNet, and Ascend. Look at their validators. Observe their endorsers. Behold their sponsors."

NETSCAPE'S MOON SHOT

The validators whom Kleiner Perkins brought into Netscape include Adobe Systems, Times Mirror, Knight-Ridder, The Hearst Corporation, and International Data Group. Netscape's CEO, James H. Clark, had been most recently chairman of the board of Silicon Graphics, Inc., a highly successful computer systems company that he founded in 1981. Netscape was taken public on August 8, 1995, when it was fourteen months of age by the premier major bracket underwriter, Morgan Stanley & Co., at an offering price of $28 per share. There were no earnings. The stock opened that afternoon at $72. Within three months it had doubled to more than $150 per share. At that price, Netscape's market capitalization was $5.7 billion. Its annualized revenues were about $55 million.

Netscape doesn't have a lock on its market. Its browser, called the Navigator, permits marketing on the Internet, but there are other browser manufacturers, including Spry (owned by CompuServe), Spyglass, Booklink Technologies (a subsidiary of America Online), and Quarterdeck Office Systems. In addition, the National Center for Supercomputing Applications (NCSA) at the University of Illinois distributes its product, NCSA Mosaic, for free for noncommercial use; Spyglass has an exclusive right to market it commercially.

SPYGLASS IS A SECOND CHOICE

But Spyglass' market value is one-tenth that of Netscape. It went public on June 26, 1995, at $17 per share, and the stock popped to $44. It recently traded at $120 per share, giving Spyglass a market value of $600 million. Greylock and Venrock are the only validators involved with Spyglass. Its CEO, Douglas P. Colbeth, although obviously capable, had previously risen only to the level of vice president/general manager of a division of Stellar/Stardent Computer Corp., and he was selected by the company's founder, Tim Krauskopf, when he was a student at the University of Illinois. At the time of its IPO, Spyglass' annualized revenues were less than $12 million. Moreover, Spyglass is in Naperville, Illinois, a vacuous area when it comes to silicon and dancing electrons, the current raw materials of wealth.

The stock market requires many validators to give a stock a double-digit market-to-revenues ratio. My own seat-of-the-pants ratio is one validator equals a market/revenues ratio of two times, except for Microsoft and Kleiner Perkins, whose imprimaturs are worth 10x each.

Netscape's OEM, original equipment manufacturers, licensees listed in its prospectus included Apple Computer, Delphi Internet, DEC, MCI, Novell, RSA Data Security, Silicon Graphics, and Sun Microsystems. The linkage of Sun to Kleiner Perkins is through Vinod Khosla, a co-founder of Sun who is now a partner at Kleiner Perkins. Spyglass has a smaller number of licensees—DEC, FTP Software, Microsoft, NEC, and Spry.

UUNET'S VALIDATION

UUNet, one of the three largest Internet service providers, with annualized sales of $50 million (the two others are NetCom and PSINet), has a market value of $1.6 billion (it reached a high of $2.5 billion), and a market-to-revenues ratio (there are no earnings yet) of 32x. Its market-to-revenues ratio is more than three times that of NetCom or PSINet. The biggest validator of them all has $4 million invested in UUNet and owns 15 percent of its stock.

That great validator from the Northwest is none other than Microsoft, which has agreed to provide $26 million to UUNet to finance the purchase of network equipment. Microsoft wants to be certain that a network will be in place to back up its own nascent Internet network, which is in an early stage of development. Other endorsers of UUNet include Mitchell Kapor, the founder of Lotus Development Corp., and three well-known and highly regarded venture capital funds—Accel Partners, Menlo Ventures, and New Enterprise Associates. Microsoft is beginning to form *zaibatsu* relationships to counter the threat of Kleiner Perkins' emerging power. After Kleiner Perkins teamed with TCI to form @Home (a new cable/PC channel), Microsoft teamed with NBC to form a new all-news, cable TV/Internet channel.

THE NET'S GREATEST TOOLMAKER

Ascend Communications is one of the fastest-growing manufacturers and marketers of Internet-related data communications equipment. It is the leader in supplying integrated access units to the Internet service providers. To date, Ascend's capabilities in this area are unmatched and, as a result, the company's equipment is purchased by most Internet Service Providers; for instance, UUNet and PSINet base a significant portion of their network access capabilities on Ascend's product line. The company's double-barrelled *zaibatsu* investors are Kleiner Perkins and Greylock.

The *zaibatsu* effect on Internet toolmakers and Internet service providers can be seen in the following table:

	12/15/95 Stock Price	Annualized Revenues ($mms)	Market Capitalization ($mms)	Market/ Revenues
Zaibatsu Endorsed				
Netscape	135	$48.0	$5,200	108.3x
UUNet	47	48.0	1,400	29.2x
Ascend	74	73.2	2,075	28.3x
Fewer Endorsers				
Spyglass	92	24.0	360	15.0x
PSI Net	19	49.0	569	11.6x
NetCom	46	46.0	410	8.9x

The *zaibatsu* effect is a five to seven times differential in valuations in the Internet market. One can only ponder what will happen to these stocks should they begin to show profits and conventional valuation tools are employed.

THE *ZAIBATSU*'S KISS

When the *zaibatsu* calls on an entrepreneurial company it is not the sweet and loving gesture of Tinkerbell sitting on Peter Pan's shoulder whispering in his ear. It is a bear hug that can mean a loss of autonomy and freedom to carry out the chase, to live the dream. When an entrepreneur has passed the first round of due diligence at Kleiner Perkins, for instance, he is invited to make a 45-minute presentation to the fund's eleven partners at its regular Monday meeting. These individuals aren't your average investor: Vinod Khosla, co-founder of Sun Microsystems; John Doerr, on the boards of Shiva, Netscape, and Ascend, and Will Hearst, who used to run the *San Francisco Chronicle* and is CEO of @Home. When they meet to nail down a vital piece at the Wagon Wheel restaurant in Mountain View, California, boisterous conversations at the other tables become whispers. This *zaibatsu* has done it before; it knows the formula.

When a *zaibatsu* fund selects a company to invest in, the senior management must relocate to within an hour's drive of the fund. It must take in some strategic partners and their capital. It will probably have to replace its founding CEO with a *zaibatsu*-selected CEO, if the founder has never launched and run a successful company. Dare anyone refuse the *zaibatsu*? Some entrepreneurs have done so and they have found certain doors closed to them, access to certain markets sealed off to them, the evil eye upon them.

The *zaibatsu* is not a formal relationship. It is, in economic terms, an informal cartel with continually changing partners. We know that cartels are structurally unsound and eventually fall apart. But at this time and in this place with the bold introduction of something as vast and powerful as the Internet, the *zaibatsu* is an incredible wealth-creator. Will the companies the *zaibatsu* launch actually succeed? Or does a *zaibatsu*-launched company lose its soul when it becomes worth a billion dollars for each $10 million of revenues? Only time will tell.

The Means Of Selection

Quantum Companies must have rising gross profit margins (GPMs) to make the cut. A handful of companies with declining GPMs have been included in *Quantum Companies II*, but they were in the midst of changing their business plans or product lines in order to position themselves for the client/server business model or introducing a new Internet strategy and giving away product to beta sites and early adopters.

But a rising GPM and a falling accounts receivable turnover ratio does not bode well for a company. It could mean that it is able to obtain price increases but only at the expense of giving the customer extended payment terms. For instance, assume that the product sells for $10,000 and costs $5,000 to make (a 50 percent GPM), and that the price is raised to $10,500 (a 55 percent GPM), but the customer is permitted to pay in ninety days rather than forty-five days. Assume the cost of money is 10 percent; then $10,500 for forty-five days costs the company $258.30 for ninety days and $129.15 for the extra forty-five days. Moreover, it establishes a permissive trend, which is hard to break. Further, most customers do not pay on the day due, unless they are offered a discount; hence, in order to actually pull in its accounts receivable, the company may have to offer a 2 percent or 3 percent discount. So much for the benefits of a rising GPM.

A rising GPM can also be a function of declining costs of goods sold. As the company begins shipping greater and greater volumes it can order raw materials and components in greater quantities and give its suppliers longer lead times. This leads to a lowering of costs of goods sold and a rising gross profit margin. Assume costs of goods sold declines to $4,500 and the price remains at $10,000. GPM then rises from 50 percent to 55 percent. An improved accounts receivable turnover ratio from 4.0x, or ninety days, to 5.0x, or seventy-three days, indicates that management is attentive to getting paid for product as soon as possible. This is a very good sign, and one that bodes well for the company's future.

Many of the software companies that have achieved initial public offerings in the second half of 1995 exhibit declining GPMs and a year-to-year extension of their accounts receivable. These companies are probably not going to become highly successful and may fade from the scene via acquisition or bankruptcy court. The ten Quantum Companies with the highest GPMs and the trend of their GPMs over the last four years are listed in the following table:

The Ten Quantum Companies with the Highest GPMs

Name	% 1995 GPM	% Change GPM 1992–95
Cheyenne Software	97.9	+34.9
Arbor Software	96.0	+1.5
Wonderware	95.1	+4.6
Applix	94.8	+16.7
Mercury Interactive	89.1	+6.5
Legato Systems	88.8	+29.8
Inso	87.3	+5.6
Visio	82.2	–2.4
Advent Software	80.7	–0.1
Project Software	73.5	12.2

Only Visio and Advent are facing resistance to their product's prices, although not substantial. Yet, this ratio should be followed closely on a quarter-to-quarter basis.

SGA EXPENSE/REVENUE RATIO

Another grid that a company must pass through in order to make it onto the Quantum Companies chart is a declining selling general & administrative expenses to revenues ratio. A handful of companies with rising SGA Expenses/Revenues ratios were permitted into the book if they had offsetting uptick operating ratios or compelling circumstances. For instance, if their GPMs were rising and their accounts receivable days on hand were declining but the SGA Expenses/Revenues ratio was rising by a relatively small fraction, they made the cut. Or if the utility of the product was not immediately understood by the company's market but seemed apparent to me, I accepted a small rise in this key ratio. High barriers to entry, such as those imposed by the Food and Drug Administration, force many early-stage pharmaceutical and medical devices companies to sell their products in foreign markets. That adds mightily to selling costs, and a rising SGA Expenses/ Revenues ratio is tolerable.

General and administrative expenses encompass a company's operating costs or overhead. A careful management team will guard against rising overhead with zeal. This kind of management has its head under the hood. A management team that permits general and administrative expenses to rise is driving around in new convertibles and watching their companies' stock prices minute by minute.

Now, when you couple rising general and administrative expenses with an extended accounts receivable days outstanding, one must wonder if management is showing up for work or showing up at the first tee. When these ratios were not dispositive, I looked at two other items in the companies' 10-Ks, 10-Qs, and proxy statements. The first is the Certain Transactions section, where companies must admit if they are giving favorable treatment to a member of management or a director. For instance, purchasing a critical component from a company owned by a senior manager is a no-no. Giving the bulk of the company's legal work to a board member, without stating that the work was put out for bid, is a very dubious practice.

The second fail-safe test can be found in the proxy statement. Among other things, the proxy statement informs stockholders if the outside board members are truly objective or mere rubber stamps for management's every wish. If the stockholders are asked to approve pension plans and life insurance policies for board members, you should dump the stock. If the stockholders are asked to approve inexpensive stock option plans for directors, pull your money out. And if the company does not permit the stockholders to vote on the hiring of the company's auditors, an investment in the company is a nonstarter. A rising SGA Expenses/Revenues ratio is chock full of clues that will eventually lead to your discovery that the company will fail.

The ten Quantum Companies that have produced the steepest declines in their SGA Expenses/Revenues ratios are listed as follows:

The Ten Quantum Companies with the Steepest Declines in Their SGA Expenses/Revenues Ratios

Name	% Change SGA Expenses/ Revenues 1992–95	Name	% Change SGA Expenses/ Revenues 1992–95
Network Express	(77.9)	Global Village	(43.2)
Information Storage Devices	(68.9)	DSP Technology	(35.9)
Arbor Software	(63.4)	Edmark	(32.2)
Mercury Interactive	(51.6)	Quickturn Designs	(28.3)
Pediatric Services	(45.2)	Legato Systems	(27.3)

The managements of these companies are penny pinchers, and that is very good for the stockholders.

The ten Quantum Companies that have not controlled their overheads well over the last four years and have the fastest-rising SGA Expenses/ Revenues ratios are listed below.

The Ten Quantum Companies with the Sharpest-Rising SGA Expenses/Revenues Ratios

Name	% Change SGA Expenses/ Revenues 1992 to 1995	Name	% Change SGA Expenses/ Revenues 1992 to 1995
Phoenix Technologies	+51.6	Verity	24.5
Phycor	37.0	FTP Software	18.3
Netcom On-Line	35.0	Diamond Multimedia	17.9
Geoworks	29.6	Applix	17.6
Auspex Systems	27.6	Logic Devices	14.4

Diamond Multimedia competes with Global Village Communications, whose overhead ratio is moving in the other direction. Both companies sell modems and multimedia software, but Global Village appears to be doing it with greater ease. Applix's rising SGA Expenses/Revenues ratio is offset by a rising GPM of about the same percentage. None of the other nine companies with rising overhead ratios are on the Top Ten Rising GPM List. They could become acquisition candidates if they don't get a grip on overhead.

Once a new product is launched there is a period of time when management goes on a press tour to obtain free advertising in the form of articles in trade journals and, hopefully, in the general media. If the budget permits—and it frequently does if there has been a public offering recently—the company then buys a forklift full of advertising, hires and trains dozens of sales persons, and engages a telemarketing firm to prospect for leads.

Naturally the SGA Expenses/Revenues ratio is going to rise under these circumstances. With software producers whose cost-of-goods-sold percentages are in the teens or less, there is a strong temptation on the part of management to spend 70 cents or 80 cents of every sales dollar on marketing. That is blasphemy. If it costs that much to sell a product, then something is basically wrong with the marketing message. Perhaps the utility of the product is difficult to explain to the customer. Perhaps the marketing message is too complicated. Perhaps the barriers to selling are just too high. A declining SGA Expenses/Revenues ratio means that customers are telling prospects how satisfied they are, and they should order the product for themselves.

INVENTORY TURNOVER RATIO

This ratio indicates how carefully the company's management buys raw material and components. To find it, divide ending inventory into annual cost of goods sold. Do not divide it into revenues because that could be misleading. An inventory turnover ratio of 6.0x, for instance, when divided into 365 days produces a days-on-hand figure of sixty-one days. Then when you do that for the year before and the year before that, you can measure the trend. A declining days-on-hand figure is a good sign. It means that management is buying materials with a sharper pencil; perhaps even negotiating just-in-time delivery. That means it is ordering raw materials just-in-time for their manufacture or sale.

This ratio was reviewed as a litmus test before companies were permitted into Quantum Companies. A stretch-out in inventory days-on-hand indicated to me that management was not on top of its suppliers and trying to beat them down on price and declining schedules. An improvement in this ratio made my heart soar like an eagle.

OEM SELLING

OEMs are companies of size and presence with established marketing channels but comparatively weak research and development depart-

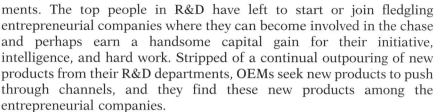

ments. The top people in R&D have left to start or join fledgling entrepreneurial companies where they can become involved in the chase and perhaps earn a handsome capital gain for their initiative, intelligence, and hard work. Stripped of a continual outpouring of new products from their R&D departments, OEMs seek new products to push through channels, and they find these new products among the entrepreneurial companies.

They pay small companies an up-front bear hug fee and a royalty for every unit that they sell. The advance is frequently manna from heaven for the small company. I have been at these companies on the day that six-figure checks arrive from Corel, Apple, IBM, and 3Com and, believe me, the champagne flows. Frequently the up-front payments from OEMs provide the difference between catching up on weeks of unpaid employees' salaries or not keeping the personnel motivated and enthused.

OEM selling can become addictive. It is not particularly difficult for an entrepreneurial company to spot a large corporation that could benefit from a licensing agreement for a market segment, geographical market, or a private label, unrestricted license. The up-front payments are like methadone to a drug addict.

Worse yet, OEM selling shrinks the company's markets. With OEM outdoing the company's selling, the numbers of selling sites that the companies can sell to grows even smaller. Because it took in an up-front payment, the payment per unit is minuscule, perhaps 10 percent of the price they could have received had the sale been made to a distributor, a dealer, or a retailer and perhaps 5 percent of the price had the sale been made directly to an end-user.

The *zaibatsu* that comprises the venture capital, strategic partner, and former successful portfolio company CEO all too frequently encourages extensive OEM selling. In so doing, it helps push a company's sales up over $15 million, at which level the major bracket and second-bracket underwriters take the company public and permit some insider selling, thus replenishing the venture capital funds' bank accounts. This scenario does not a Quantum Company make.

A careful reading of the marketing section of the prospectuses of companies that receive venture capital funding often reveals OEM selling. If there is an excessive amount of this quick-fix for getting product into the marketplace, what kind of bag will the investors be left holding? Empty of opportunity, or full of marketing options and plentiful selling sites? Unfortunately, the former is more likely to be the case.

THE BIOTECH COMPANY TESTS

Throw out the GPM and SGA Expenses/Revenue ratios tests for biotechnology companies. They do not apply. There are generally no sales, and if there is income, it is usually interest income on cash and marketable securities or contract income provided by a pharmaceutical company paying the biotech company for services or new product development.

To determine if a biotech company is a good investment, in addition to investigating its prospective products—the elegance of their solutions—and the size of the problems they are addressing, the other tests are the *zaibatsu* and cash on hand.

In a biotech company the *zaibatsu* is formed by the venture capital funds—the more the better, but five is optimum; the validating scientific advisory board—at least one Nobel laureate helps greatly, but they must each be on the staffs of distinguished teaching hospitals or research institutions; and one or more strategic partners—respected pharmaceutical companies that are paying for marketing rights and that have invested in the company's stock.

The second test is days of cash flow on hand. In this equation you divide the available cash by the company's monthly burn rate. For example, assume the company has $12 million in cash and then take all of the expenses that it incurs in one year and divide by 12. Say that comes to $1.4 million per month. Divide that number, called the "burn rate," into $12 million, and you come up with eight and one-half months of cash on hand. A careful, thorough reading of all of the company's published information should inform you if the company can get its product through the FDA or begin selling product in Europe in eight and one-half months. If the company's product is very close to FDA approval for foreign sales, the *zaibatsu* will surely come up with bridge financing. Or an underwriter well-known to the *zaibatsu* can be persuaded to raise more venture capital from the public.

A case in point is Cephalon, Inc., in West Chester, Pennsylvania, which is developing drugs for treating neurodegenerative disorders, such as amyotrophic lateral sclerosis (ALS), or Lou Gehrig's disease. The company recently completed a successful Phase III trial of Myotrophin in which the results in treating ALS were unprecedented and greater than expected. But the FDA is concerned about recent foreign test results. Cephalon had $62 million in cash on hand at June 30, 1995, and is burning $6 million per month. Revenues are coming in at just under $3 million per month. Thus, the company can run full out toward its destiny for about twenty months.

What level of *zaibatsu* support is behind Cephalon? Its strategic alliance partners are TAP Pharmaceuticals, Smith Kline Beecham, Kyowa Hakko Kogyo, Bristol-Myers Squibb, Schering-Plough, and Chiron. Its venture capital funds include Burr, Egan, Deleage & Company, Hambrecht & Quist Life Science Technology Find, and PCS Health Systems. The company's scientific advisory board members represent Baylor College of Medicine, Vanderbilt University, National Institute of Child Health and Human Development, University of Pittsburgh, University of Minnesota, Yale University School of Medicine, and Princeton University—all outstanding institutions. The pharmaceutical companies are exceptional validators. And the investors are well-known venture capitalists and endorsers. Cephalon bears watching.

The Role of Women

More than half of the three million businesses formed in the United States in each of the past five years were started by women. As we know from Labor Department statistics, the net new job creation in the United States is primarily from small entrepreneurial companies and not from the Fortune 500. Moreover, the workforce in a woman-owned company is typically two-thirds female. By simple arithmetic, one can see that women are being recruited by growth companies more frequently than men.

In a study of the 100 most successful female entrepreneurs of our day,* I found that women were creating employment opportunities by tackling problems that women often face. The sectors that attract them include health, education, child care, information networks, and beauty. What value could men possibly add to Jog-bra Inc., manufacturer of a bra for women runners? Or to *QC I* Pleasant Company, a manufacturer of historical dolls and accompanying books that describe the role of American women in history?

Women represent 55 percent of the employees of biotech companies, of which there are seven in *QC I* and two in *QC II*. Moreover, one in every ten biotech companies has a woman founder and CEO. In the information industries represented in *Quantum Companies II*, 38 percent of the workforce is female. Seven companies in *QC II* were founded or co-founded by women. Linda J. Wachner, founder and CEO of Authentic Fitness Corp., is arguably the best woman manager since Liz Claiborne. Mary Coleman founded Aurum Software, Inc., and has raised more than $6 million in capital. Aurum produces customer-interaction software. Lin Wu Lan is CEO of Pacific Pioneer Corp., the largest insurance underwriter founded and run by a woman. Stephanie G. DiMarco founded and is CEO of Advent Software, Inc., maker of client/server software that solves problems for mutual fund managers. Sally G. Narodick founded and runs Edmark Corp., a leading developer of educational software for children.

Debi Coleman joined Merix Corp., a printed circuit board manufacturer, as its CEO in 1993 after having turned around Apple Computer's failing Macintosh manufacturing plant in Fremont, California, and making it one of the most admired and emulated in the world. She was then promoted to chief financial officer at Apple at the age of 34. Under Coleman's leadership Merix earned $18.2 million on revenues of $106.4 million (annualized) in 1995 and has a market value of $235 million. Not

---

* A. David Silver, *Enterprising Women* (New York: Amacom, 1994).

bad for a two-year-old company. Linden Rhoads co-founded Virtual I.O., Inc., a leading manufacturer of virtual reality headsets for the consumer market, and she raised more than $10 million in venture capital for it She will turn 30 in 1996.

These women entrepreneurs have had no difficulty attracting venture capital, as was the case with women entrepreneurs a decade ago. They think strategically, attract skilled, seasoned veterans to assist them in management, and convey elegant solutions to large and growing problems that are gender neutral.

Best Stock Investments for 1996

The ten Quantum Companies whose stock prices are most likely to triple or better in 1996 are listed in the following table:

**Quantum Companies Whose Stock Prices Are
Most Likely to Triple in 1996**

Name	Type of Business	Stock Price 12/22/95	Market Revenues	% Change '92 to '95		
				Sales	GPM	SGA/ Revenues
AmeriData Technologies	systems integrator	9½	.1x	+1832	(14.2)	(15.2)
Computer Horizons	systems integrator	34¼	.8x	183	6.9	(4.1)
DSP Technology	measurement instruments for autos		1.0x	128	2.3	(35.9)
CISCO Systems	Internet-working devices	76⅝	1.1x	405	0.0	0.0
CIBER Inc.	systems integrator	23¼	1.1x	353	n.a.	(20.4)
Pediatric Services	home care		1.1x	301	n.a.	(45.1)
Orthopedic Tech.	medical devices	6⅞	1.5x	146	2.0	(6.8)
EZ Communications	Internet/radio integrator	17¼	1.7x	160	(8.6)	(8.5)
Quickturn Design	integrated circuits	9⅞	1.8x	297	7.1	(28.3)
Applied Materials	integrated circuits	42⅛	1.9x	279	31.2	(17.9)

These companies were selected on a comparative basis with the best of breed in their markets and based on meeting certain critical financial tests, including:

- low market value-to-revenues ratio
- rapidly rising revenues last four years
- rising gross profit margin last four years
- declining SGA Expenses/Revenue ratio last four years

They are significantly undervalued relative to comparable companies but are growing at very high rates, with solid profitability, rising gross profit margins, and declining overhead ratios. The last two tests are critical. A rising GPM indicates either that a company is able to command higher prices for its products or services or that it is able to squeeze manufacturing and raw materials costs. When these two ratios move in opposite directions over time and not merely for one year, the company's products and services are extremely well received in the market and its management is tightfisted with sales commissions, advertising budgets, health insurance, legal expenses, rent, and the other components of Selling, General & Administrative Expenses.

A final test is to determine if these improvements are being made at the expense of permitting customers to extend payment terms or stockpiling inventory. Case in point: Applied Materials, Inc., a wafer fabricator that has plants throughout the world and is growing at a rate of 40 percent per year with a profitablity ratio of 20.8 percent in 1995. Its GPM has risen 31.2 percent since 1992 while its SGA Expenses/Revenues ratio has declined by 17.9 percent. Accounts receivable turned over 4.2x in 1993, 4.1x in 1994, and then improved to 4.8x in 1995. That is an improvement of thirteen days, and with sales of $2.1 billion this year, Applied Materials has $73.5 million in cash on hand merely by speeding up accounts receivable collections. The stock market values Applied Materials at a low 15.0x p/e ratio and a market/revenues ratio of 1.9x.

Quickturn Design Systems develops and markets verification solutions for the design of integrated circuits. It sells a critical software component to some of the same customers as Applied Materials. Its GPM is 69.3 percent in 1995 and rising. Its SGA Expenses/Revenues ratio is 42.1 percent and falling. Quickturn gives its customers 112 days on average to pay their bills, which should improve by at least a third, because Quickturn Emulation System enables its customers to get their integrated circuits to market at least four to eight months faster. The stock market undervalues Quickturn, with a p/e ratio of 21.9x and a market to revenues ratio of 1.8x.

Three systems integrators made the Top Ten List—AmeriData Technologies, Inc., CIBER, Inc., and Computer Horizons Corp.—because their stock prices are inexpensive relative to the competition, yet their financial and operating ratios are stalwart. The role of the systems integrator is to install and manage computer systems for midsized and large corporations, government agencies, and institutions. With the advent of client/server systems, organizations are relying more than ever on systems integrators to help them through the morass of higher speeds, greater capacities, far more flexibility of information management—which translates into far more information more quickly. But the information technology managers of the client base have billions of dollars invested in mainframes, midsize computers, terminals, printers, and skilled personnel trained to operate these systems.

AmeriData, CIBER, and Computer Horizons provide personnel who are skilled in assisting their clients in migrating to client/server, open-system platforms and frequently manage the installation and training and order (or in the case of AmeriData, sell) the new systems. The systems integration function is nearly thirty years old. Sure, it doesn't have the razzle-dazzle of the Internet, but it does not show any signs of becoming obsolete; indeed it is growing more important. Proof of that is the sales increases of AmeriData, CIBER, and Computer Horizons and, more to the point, their rising GPMs. AmeriData's 1995 acquisitions lowered its GPM, but CIBER's has held steady over the last four years, and Computer Horizons has grown 6.9 percent. The stock market places these three companies in the doldrums area: Their market to revenue ratios are .1x for AmeriData, .8x for Computer Horizons, and 1.1x for CIBER.

CISCO Systems makes the most sought after router among the 1,800-member Internet service provider industry—the CISCO 2511. No competitive router even approaches the popularity of CISCO's. This $1.7 billion (revenues) company has been growing at about 100 percent per annum with an operating profit this year of 34.5 percent. Its GPM is holding steady at 67.1 percent and its SGA Expenses/Revenues ratio is a modest 21.2 percent. When the regional Bell operating companies decide to enter the Internet industry, one of them will try to buy CISCO and a bidding war will develop, because it holds an important key to the kingdom of the Net.

EZ Communications is a rapidly growing, highly leveraged, owner-operator of radio stations that is overlaying Internet broadcasting on its base of stations. EZ's management sees a new advertising channel developing and it is getting ahead of the curve. The stock market is not impressed. Yet EZ's market to revenue ratio is a low 1.7x.

DSP Technology, a former defense electronics firm, has reinvented itself from frog to prince and now sells sophisticated electronics systems to the automotive industry and to national laboratories. With a mere $14.2 million in revenues, the company is largely ignored by investors and its market to revenues ratio is 1.0x. Notwithstanding, GPM is growing and overhead has been slashed 35.9 percent over the last four years.

The medical marketplace has two representatives on the Top Ten: Pediatric Services of America and Orthopedic Technology. The former is an in-home health-care provider for medically fragile children. It is a $100 million (revenues) company whose sales are growing at the rate of 75 percent per annum. It manages its overhead very well in the tightfisted health insurance environment and brings 5 percent to the bottom line. The stock market has fixed a 1.1x market to revenues ratio on Pediatric Services, significantly lower than comparable companies.

Orthopedic Technology makes unique and proprietary orthopedic products for the sports medicine market. Among its economic advantages is its ability to turn around on an order for a custom-fitted knee brace within 48 hours. It is nearly debt-free, has a growing GPM of 51.2 percent and a falling overhead ratio of 37 percent. There are only 3.4 million shares outstanding, which makes it difficult for institutions to buy the stock. Hence, it is a bargain at a market to revenues ratio of 1.5x.

The market forces driving these ten companies are all positive for several years to come. However, for a variety of reasons, these companies are undervalued by the stock market and could triple in price or better within the coming year.

SIGNALS TO DIE FOR

The ten Quantum Companies whose stock prices are least likely to rise in the coming year are the following:

Ten Quantum Companies Whose Stock Prices Are Unrealistically High

Name	Type of Business	Stock Price 12/22/95	Market Revenues
Netscape	Internet software	139½	114.5x
GeoWorks	develop. stage communications	18⅛	35.7x
ParkerVision	video conference device	6⅛	35.1x
Security Dynamics	Internet software	45	25.1x
Verity	Internet software	44¾	22.8x
Arbor Software	software	43	21.8x
Broadband Tech.	telecommunications	18⅛	17.0x
Netcom On-Line	Internet software	59⅜	16.8x
Spyglass	video graphics software	46¾	16.3x
Macromedia	Internet service provider	44⅜	16.8x

Two of these companies have rising gross profit margins and falling SGA Expenses/Revenues ratios: Arbor Software—+1.5% and (63.4%)—and Security Dynamics—+5.9% and (.4%). These trends demonstrate that their products are being very well received in the market and word-of-mouth selling is beginning to move the product. Arbor's gross profit margin is currently 96.0 percent and its sales are growing like a house afire: an average of 380 percent over the last four years. Security Dynamics makes a popular firewall product that enables commerce to occur on the Web without fear of credit card theft. But some industry analysts foresee strong competition from newcomers, such as Quantum Company Network-1. Security Dynamics's SGA Expenses/Revenues ratio is not tumbling, which means that feet on the street are still required to sell its Secure ID product.

Most of these ten companies were recently taken public and had their stock prices bid up to the moon by the existence of their validators. When valuations take a moon shot, such as market to revenue ratios of 15.0x or better and p/e ratios of 100x or better, the explanation usually lies with an Oscar-winning board of directors, including at least three well-known and highly regarded venture capitalists, a handful of strategic partners that open the door to complex distribution channels, and a potpourri of endorsers ranging from a twice-around-the-game CEO to a major-bracket lead underwriter in the IPO. This gaggle of validators, partners, and endorsers cannot, will not, and do not bring in year-to-year sales jumps with concomitant increases in profitability. They give a great first impression, much as does a perfect smile or a delicious first kiss. But they do not guarantee a timeless love affair. Beware the overvalidated small software company. They may not look so beautiful a year from now.

Here are some of the validators, partners, and endorsers that jumped on one end of the teeter-totter of these ten companies and catapulted their stock prices to the rings of Saturn:

**Validators, Partners, and Endorsers of Ten
Levitating Quantum Companies**

Company	% Inside Selling at IPO	Earliest Date of Secondary	Validators, Endorsers
Netscape	0.0	2-96	(m) James H. Clark, ex-CEO Silicon Graphics (m) James L. Barksdale, ex-CEO McCaw Cellular (v) Kleiner Perkins Caulfield & Byers (s) Adobe Systems (s) TCI (s) Times Mirror (s) Knight-Ridder (s) The Hearst Corp. (s) IDG (u) Morgan Stanley
Geoworks	36.1	5-96	(v) Bay Partners (v) Merrill Pickard Anderson & Eyre (s) Nokia Mobile Phones (s) Hewlett-Packard (s) Novell (u) Hambrecht & Quist
Parkervision	n.a.	n.a.	(s) VTEL
Security Dynamics	32.1	2-96	(v) First Analysis/APEX (v) Putnam Investments (s) Sanyo (u) Alex Brown
Verity	24.9	4-96	(m) Philippe F. Courtot, EVP, Lotus (v) Olympic Venture Partners (v) U.S. Venture Partners (s) Advance Decision Systems (s) Adobe Systems (s) Thomson-CSF (u) Hambrecht & Quist
Arbor Software	10.6	5-96	(v) Accel Partners (v) Sequoia Capital (v) Mayfield Fund (v) Hummer Winblad (s) Comshare (s) Microsoft (u) Morgan Stanley
Broadband Tech.	0.0	n.a.	(s) AT&T (s) six RBOCs (s) AMP (s) GTE (v) Advent (v) Accel (v) BEA

Company	% Inside Selling at IPO	Earliest Date of Secondary	Validators, Endorsers
			(v) St. Paul Fire & Marine
			(v) Allstate
			(v) TA Associates
			(v) Abacus Ventures
			(u) Bear, Stearns & Co.
NetCom Online	20.0	11-95	(v) Geo Capital
			(v) Chancellor Capital Management
			(v) Hancock Venture Partners
			(u) Alex Brown
Spyglass	11.1	12-95	(s) Microsoft
			(v) Greylock
			(v) Venrock
			(u) Alex Brown
Macromedia	n.a.	n.a.	(s) Netscape
			(v) Kleiner Perkins Caulfield & Byers
			(v) New Enterprise Associates

(m) Management
(v) Venture Capitalist
(s) Strategic Plan
(u) Underwriters

TOO MUCH OF A GOOD THING

An excessive amount of bailing out by early backers in the IPO—the first opportunity they have to sell stock—is a flashing red light that some smart, early money is not firmly convinced of a company's future. Underwriters do not like to see a large percentage bailout at the IPO, but they must be competitive and allow it to occur. The "caution" sign is out for Geoworks, Security Dynamics, and Verity.

Typically, six months after the IPO, insiders can sell stock in a secondary offering, and that generally occurs if the stock has run up from the date of the IPO. If a good number of key managers sell a large percentage of their holdings in the secondary offering, the stock could be one to die for. Let it die without you.

Obviously, there is demonstrable economic validity that underpins each of these companies, and for seven of them it is spelled Internet. For Geoworks and Broadband Technologies, it is giant steps in interactive telecommunications. And with Parker Vision it is a small, profitable, inexpensive video teleconferencing product that could dramatically alter the distance learning business.

PART TWO

---

100 QUANTUM COMPANIES

ADAPTEC, INC.

Have you dialed into a network recently and waited 15 minutes for the data to boot up? Most of us have at one time or another. Well, don't curse the network; use that 15 minutes profitably to phone your broker and buy stock in Adaptec. The company develops input/output solutions in software and burned into silicon.

Software advances, such as enterprise computing, networking via LANs and WANs, and E-mail have come rapidly, and many of our PCs can't handle the traffic. Think of Adaptec as a builder of on- and off-ramps to frontage roads that quickly move us off the bottleneck expressways onto faster roads.

Every PC is shipped with inexpensive mass storage devices that are required to store vast amounts of information and data: CD-ROMs, tape drives, and hard disk drives. These devices are inadequate to handle the traffic.

Adaptec makes host-adapter products based on the Small Computer Systems Interface (SCSI) standard which interfaces with all PCs and peripherals. Adaptec's SCSI devices are used in data backup and archiving for tape drives and storage needed for multimedia programs where video, text, graphics, and sound are stored on a CD-ROM. Through strategic alliances with IBM, Microsoft, and Novell, the company's software is embedded within their operating systems. Adaptec also sells through distributors. Nearly two-thirds of all sales are made to foreign customers.

Adaptec is a brilliantly managed company. Its gross profit margin has grown 30.9 percent over the last four years—a remarkable achievement in the dog-eat-dog world of enabling technologies. Its ratio of SGA expenses/revenues to sales in 1995 was 17.2 percent, up only slightly over the last four years. Net Profits/Sales was running at a ratio of 27.0 percent in 1995, up 34.3 percent since 1992.

With $276 million in the bank, 69 percent of its net worth is in cash. One might expect listless indolence on the part of Adaptec's management with a market value of $2.1 billion and rapid sales growth. On the contrary: Receivables were being collected faster in 1995 than in 1994—48 days versus 54 days—and both of these ratios exceeded the industry average of 63 days and 72 days. Profitability ratios are rising on a year-to-year basis. And net profits per employee were $79,238 in 1995.

The stock market is not sanguine about Adaptec's future, giving the company a paltry 21.0x p/e ratio. Perhaps traders and brokers aren't

ADAPTEC, INC.

Chief Executive Officer:	F. Grant Saviers
Principal Location:	691 Milipitas Blvd. Milipitas, CA 95035
Telephone:	408-945-8600
Fax:	408-262-2533
E-mail:	vicki-robinson@corp.adaptec.com
Web site:	http://www.adaptec.com
Satellite Locations:	Singapore; Munich, Germany; Waterloo, Belgium; Tokyo, Japan
Date Founded:	1981
Description of Business:	Designs, develops, and manufactures input/output hardware and software including board-based solutions and proprietary software that increase data transmission rates and eliminates bottlenecks in multiple PC environments.
# Employees Current:	1,100
% Female Employees:	34%
# Employees Projected 9/30/96:	1,500
Revenues 1995*:	$498,025,000
Gross Profit Margin (GPM):	57.6%
SGA Expenses/Revenues:	17.4%
% Sales Increase 1992 to 1995:	+160.1%
% Change GPM 1992 to 1995:	+30.9%
% Change SGA Expenses/Revenues 1992 to 1995:	+12.9%
Total Debt/Net Worth:	19.2%
Net Profits Before Taxes 1995*:	$134,466,750
Net Profits Before Taxes/Revenues:	27.0%
Market Value/1995 Revenues*:	4.3X
Traded On:	NASDAQ (ADPT)
Opportunity Company Addresses:	The enterprise computing market is increasingly more sophisticated, including such things as network management software and multimedia applications that eat up hard drives and increase delay times in data transfer.
Elegance of Company's Solution:	The company's products enhance data transmission rates and eliminate bottlenecks.

*Annualized.

multitasking on massively networked PCs waiting for their data to come up on the screen. If they were, they would surely know that Adaptec is to clogged networks as STP oil additive is to automobiles.

ADVANCED DIGITAL IMAGING, INC.

Advanced Digital Imaging (ADI) is the maker of three principal products for desktop digital postproduction. Digital Magic, its signature product, is a microprocessing accelerator board that provides a modular and expandable system for video editing on desktop nonlinear-editing systems that are Macintosh-based. Because of its power—it has a 32-bit data bus "videobahn" that is extremely fast and loaded with memory capabilities—Digital Magic is a very valuable tool for digital postproduction because it allows for fast compression of video and real-time feedback when editing video clips. Digital postproduction that is desktop-based has traditionally been very slow because of the time it takes for digitization and compression of video images. Furthermore, it usually takes most desktop editing systems a long time to process or render video effects such as multilayer dissolves and animation. Digital Magic solves these problems because of its power, speed, and memory capacity. Editors can process all the effects they want up to 28 gigs, render their animations, and rotoscope (move objects from one environment to the next) seamlessly in half the time. This saves time and money for everyone involved.

There are no well-known competitors to Digital Magic, because it is truly an enhancer of full-service nonlinear-editing systems such as AVID and Media 100. Both AVID and Media 100 have their own "Digital Magics" in them, but they are not as powerful or fast. Since AVID and Media 100 have their own proprietary processing busses, they can be considered competitors.

ADI's MacVac is an animation controller for the Macintosh that provides multilayer compositing of images. MacVac makes it possible to place up to fourteen layers of object images in front of or in back of one another on the screen. It takes the normal confines of the screen or frame (two-dimensional) and makes it three-dimensional and manipulatable. MacVac is only useful if you have a fast, powerful processor in your desktop editing system that can handle all the layering. Hence Digital Magic.

X-Matte, ADI's newest product, is a key or matte-producing software that provides bluescreening capabilities. It is also Macintosh-based. This is a very important software that is revolutionizing the way movies are being made today. Instead of expensive set construction and make-it-or-break-it studio takes, X-Matte allows moviemakers to film actors separately from the action and then layer them perfectly and seamlessly

ADVANCED DIGITAL IMAGING, INC.

Chief Executive Officer:	Cliff Auchmoody
Principal Location:	1250 N. Lakeview Ave. Anaheim, CA 92807
Telephone:	714-779-7772
Fax:	714-779-7773
E-mail:	not available
Web site:	not available
Satellite Locations:	none
Date Founded:	1992
Description of Business:	An emerging developer of enhancement systems for digital video editors that materially shorten postproduction time.
# Employees Current:	9
% Female Employees:	not available
# Employees Projected 9/30/96:	not available
Revenues 1995*:	$3,000,000
Gross Profit Margin (GPM):	The company is privately held and is not required to publish its financial statements.
SGA Expenses/Revenues:	not available
% Sales Increase 1992 to 1995:	not available
% Change GPM 1992 to 1995:	not available
% Change SGA Expenses/Revenues 1992 to 1995:	not available
Total Debt/Net Worth:	not available
Net Profits Before Taxes 1995*:	not available
Net Profits Before Taxes/Revenues:	not available
Market Value/1995 Revenues*:	not available
Opportunity Company Addresses:	Time is money for video producers working in postproduction.
Elegance of Company's Solution:	Digital Magic shortens their editing time fivefold or more.

*Annualized.

into a scene later. It also allows moviemakers to experiment with different takes without destroying the set and having to build it back up for the next take. Other companies make this matting software, but the prices are incredibly high and the process is very slow. X-Matte is remarkably affordable, and its turnaround time is very fast. However, X-Matte is as fast as it is because of Digital Magic.

In essence, ADI makes some very important products that are valuable to digital, nonlinear postproduction houses. But none are more important than Digital Magic, which is the vehicle that the rest of ADI's products ride on. X-Matte and MacVac are only as good as Digital Magic allows them to be. Since ADI's products are so affordable, it shouldn't take much coaxing for a postproduction facility to invest in all their products and give their facility a jump start. That is, unless, the studio has already spent $100,000 on an AVID system or dropped $200,000 into a HENRY, which a lot of them do because of track record, reputation, and industry cross-compatibility.

Since ADI's strength is its ability to enhance Mac-based digital postproduction, the company markets itself that way. Its marketing strategy stresses speed and memory, not control. Control is achieved through software, but the market for digital postproduction software is saturated with a lot of companies making the same claim: "Personal Control." Watch for ADI's print advertisements that say, "Do you feel the need for speed?" with a picture of an editor sweating in the studio looking at the clock while the computer screen flickers in its meager attempts to render. The "Rolaids" approach worked for FedEx. Why not for ADI?

ADVENT SOFTWARE, INC.

Low interest rates are impelling savers to move their money into mutual funds and mutual fund managers arc driven to seek the highest return on investment, which compels the appetite for new issues, growth stocks, and complex financial instruments. These dynamics have increased the volume and intricacy of data flows within mutual funds and outside the organizations between the funds and brokerage firms, custodians, banks, pricing services, and other data providers. Accordingly, mutual fund managers seek more sophisticated software to manage the data flow.

Historically, mutual funds have relied on internally developed systems, time-sharing services, or simple spreadsheet-based systems to manage information flows. Try running a slick, PC-based spreadsheet from a dumb terminal hooked to a big, expensive mainframe. It's a kluge. The mainframe may be more valuable as a boat anchor for the customers' yachts.

Into the breech leapt Advent, armed with $7.5 million in venture capital from Mayfield Fund and others. It's growing at a torrid pace. In fact, as daily volumes rise on the NYSE and NASDAQ, you can literally see the coins fall into Advent's tollbooth.

Advent offers six primary products including Axys Advantage, investment-decision support software; Moxy, trade order management; Qube, client contact and management; and the brand new Geneva, portfolio accounting for international-account management. Axys Advantage, introduced in 1994, is a portfolio management system tailored to the needs of the growing number of smaller financial planners and individual brokers. Currently licensed to more than 350 clients, it provides Windows-based sophisticated portfolio accounting, portfolio valuations, and portfolio performance measurement. Axys Advantage offers high-quality graphics and more than 70 standard reports that support investment decision making, client communication, performance measurement, and billing. It can be linked with several brokerage firms using Advent's proprietary interfaces to streamline pricing and transaction processing. As the company's clients grow and require additional functionality, Axys Advantage allows for a smooth upgrade path that avoids the problems associated with data conversion.

Advent's clients are many and top drawer. They include Fidelity Investment Advisor Group, State Street Bank and Trust, and T-Rowe Price. But the market has well-funded competitors, including Shaw

ADVENT SOFTWARE, INC.

Chief Executive Officer:	Stephanie G. DiMarco
Principal Location:	301 Brannan St. San Francisco, CA 94107
Telephone:	415-543-7696
Fax:	415-543-5070
E-mail:	gosulliv@advent.com
Web site:	not available
Satellite Locations:	New York, New York; Boston, Massachusetts
Date Founded:	1983
Description of Business:	Leading provider of stand-alone and client/server software products and services that automate and integrate mission-critical functions of investment management firms.
# Employees Current:	201
% Female Employees:	46%
# Employees Projected 9/30/96:	255
Revenues 1995*:	$24,145,000
Gross Profit Margin (GPM):	80.7%
SGA Expenses/Revenues:	50.1%
% Sales Increase 1992 to 1995:	+227.8%
% Change GPM 1992 to 1995:	(.1%)
% Change SGA Expenses/Revenues 1992 to 1995:	(13.6%)
Total Debt/Net Worth:	25.9%
Net Profits Before Taxes 1995*:	$2,360,000
Net Profits Before Taxes/Revenues:	9.8%
Market Value/1995 Revenues*:	6.6x
Traded On:	NASDAQ (ADVS)
Opportunity Company Addresses:	Annual net cash inflows into U.S. mutual funds increased from $60 billion in 1990 to $154 billion in 1994 and currently clock in at $1.5 trillion. With the flood of dollars has come a deluge of complex financial instruments and evolving regulations.
Elegance of Company's Solution:	New software systems are needed to solve the problems of rapid growth and complexities, and the company is right on the mark with its line of products.
*Annualized.	

Data, Thomason Financial, and Performance Technologies, Inc., a subsidiary of the Charles Schwab Corp. But we can tell when a product begins to sell itself: Advent's SGA Expenses/Revenues ratio has fallen 13.6 percent since 1992, and its accounts receivable days on hand have shrunk from a pay-me-when-you-feel-like-it 96 days in 1993 to a respectable 54 days in 1995. That kind and degree of improvement is nontrivial. Someone in senior management probably told the sales staff that they would receive their commissions when the customers' checks arrived, versus the 1992 system of paying commissions when the sale was made. GPM has held fairly firm, and probably cannot move up until the company introduces new upgrades.

With a mere 6.1 million shares outstanding, the stock price may become volatile. Look for management to make a handful of acquisitions using its stock and then splitting it. If that sucking sound you hear is money leaving the savings passbooks and wooshing into mutual funds, use your ears and catch a ride on this rocket.

ALTERA CORPORATION

A ltera designs, develops, and markets CMOS (complimentary-metal-oxide-semiconductor) programmable logic integrated circuits and associated computer-aided engineering development software and hardware. The company's semiconductor products, which are generally known as CPLDs (Complex Programmable Logic Devices), are standard logic chips that customers configure for specific end-use applications using the company's proprietary software. Altera's customers enjoy the benefits of low development costs, short lead times, and standard product inventories when compared to Application Specific Integrated Circuits (ASICs).

In the 1980s, ASICs gained popularity as a solution to the high-density-related problems caused by building more logic functions into chips. ASICs include a variety of custom and semicustom alternatives, such as gate arrays, cell libraries, and silicon compilers. Using computer-aided engineering software tools, ASIC designers are able to combine sections of standard logic and generate unique tooling, which can then be used to fabricate a unique custom chip in the manufacturing process. Although ASICs achieved the goal of higher density and more integration by combining a variety of low-density parts into a single chip, they do so by introducing several compromises, resulting from the customized manufacturing process, that are undesirable to users of standard low-density chips. These compromises can include longer lead time to the marketplace, non-recurring engineering (NRE) fees, dedicated custom product inventory, lack of control over sources of supply, and inflexibility of design iteration.

An alternative, historically, has been the bipolar Programmable Logic Device (PLD), introduced in the late 1970s. Bipolar PLDs are standard products that are sold by the vendor as blank circuits. By blowing fuses on the chip, the user customizes it to a specific logic application. This addresses some of the ASIC compromises eliminating the up-front design fees, production lead-time, and custom inventory. Bipolar PLDs, however, have been limited to relatively low densities (under 500 gates) due to the significant power consumption and heat dissipation inherent in bipolar technology.

Altera, along with Quantum Company Xilinx, is the fastest-growing company in one of the fastest-growing semiconductor segments: CPLDs. The CPLD market is growing at about 50 percent per year, while Altera is growing at 57 percent per annum.

ALTERA CORPORATION

Chief Executive Officer:	Rodney Smith
Principal Location:	2610 Orchard Parkway San Jose, CA 95134-2020
Telephone:	408-894-7000
Fax:	408-428-0463
E-Mail:	lindaj@altera.com
Web site:	http://www.altera.com
Satellite Locations:	Sales offices in several U.S. cities plus the United Kingdom; France; Germany; Italy; Korea; Canada; Hong Kong; Japan
Date Founded:	1984
Description of Business:	Designs, develops, produces, and markets one of the most tightly packed programmable logic integrated circuits.
# Employees Current:	850
% Female Employees:	55%
# Employees Projected 9/30/96:	1,700
Revenues 1995*:	$275,428,000
Gross Profit Margin (GPM):	60.0%
SGA Expenses/Revenues:	20.7%
% Sales Increase 1992 to 1995:	+271.4%
% Change GPM 1992 to 1995:	+6.0%
% Change SGA Expenses/Revenues 1992 to 1995:	(16.2)%
Total Debt/Net Worth:	35.4%
Net Profits Before Taxes 1995*:	$61,305,000
Net Profits Before Taxes/Revenues:	22.2%
Market Value/1995 Revenues*:	4.9x
Traded On:	NASDAQ (ALTR)
Opportunity Company Addresses:	The need among electronics and PC manufacturers to lower their development costs and shorten product to market lead times.
Elegance of Company's Solution:	Programmable logic integrated circuits are programmed during manufacture to save time and money.

*Annualized.

The acceleration in growth of the CPLD market is coming largely at the expense of the gate array market as CPLD pricing closes the gap. Gate array sales are growing at 30 percent per annum in 1995, below the overall semiconductor market's worldwide growth of 40 percent. The cost per function of high-density CPLDs (several thousand gates or more) has decreased 100-fold in the past 10 years. As the following examples show, the cost decline accelerated in 1994-95 as Altera has moved to the same process (0.5- and 0.6-micron triple layer metal) technology generation as sub-100,000 gate mask programmable gate arrays and as innovative new architectures have been introduced.

Altera is particularly well positioned in the high-density CPLD market because of the rapid product development and strong software support the company provides. As the largest supplier of CPLDs in Japan, Altera is taking advantage of the move from gate arrays in that region. Altera achieved the highest operating margins (22.2 percent in 1995) in the CPLD industry, more than two percentage points higher than those of the nearest competitor, while growing at the fastest rate. Its GPM improves each year; in 1992 it was 56.6 percent and in 1995 60 percent.

Although known for its sound technical capability, Altera must stay a step ahead of and anticipate the needs of its markets—telecommunications and PCs. High-level software is needed to design CPLDs, and Altera will need to maintain its high level of software support. With a market capitalization of $1.3 billion and $100 million cash in the bank, these investments are very affordable.

AMERICA ONLINE, INC.

Bill Von Miester has started some of the more unique and interesting online telecommunications services in the last 20 years, but none has better legs than America Online. Over the last few years, the variety of online services and the number of subscribers to these services has grown dramatically. It was estimated that by the end of 1995, there would be approximately 9.6 million subscriptions to online services in the United States. This represents a 46 percent annual growth rate from the 1992 total of 3.1 million subscribers. Further growth will be fueled by a confluence of factors: 1) an increase in the population of household PCs with modems as prices fall, and an increased penetration of that market; 2) increasing prevalence of the home office with online services becoming the required tool of communication; 3) faster and cheaper communications options; 4) user-friendly operating systems making systems more usable; 5) content providers actively pursuing online distribution; and 6) expansion and marketing of the Internet by online services. The overall consumer online market is expected to grow as vendors create demand, online services acquire compelling new content, and new online technologies emerge. It is projected that the market will grow to almost $4 billion by the end of the century, with one out of every two U.S. households having access to at least one online service.

America Online's shopping mall hosts Oldsmobile, Hallmark, Tower Records, 1-800-Flowers, and Hanes. Six companies currently share the market, and their revenues, number of subscribers, service costs, and features (see page 53).

Internet access providers are similar to consumer online service providers but offer little proprietary content. Access providers compete based on their front-end Internet access interface, price, and service. Netcom is the largest Internet access provider; PSInet is second, and UUnet is third.

America Online is engaged in one of the most intensive marketing campaigns ever seen in the software services industry. It is reminiscent of dropping diskettes from thousands of airplanes flying over the United States daily. The company's ads are captivating, funny, and appealing. Its 1995 report states that it is adding upwards of 250,000 new subscribers per month. Sure, it's losing 25 percent or more to Internet access providers, but its growth of subscribers is so stunning that Netscape is seeking a joint venture. Moreover, the company is beating out some of

AMERICA ONLINE, INC.

Chief Executive Officer:	Stephen M. Case
Principal Location:	8619 Westwood Center Dr. Vienna, VA 22182
Telephone:	703-448-8700
Fax:	703-918-1107
E-mail:	amerir@aol.com
Web site:	http://www.aol.com
Satellite Locations:	none
Date Founded:	1991
Description of Business:	A leader in offering online services including the Internet, multimedia, shopping malls, and other services.
# Employees Current:	2,481
% Female Employees:	not available
# Employees Projected 9/30/96:	not available
Revenues 1995*:	$394,290,000
Gross Profit Margin (GPM):	41.7%
SGA Expenses/Revenues:	30.2%
% Sales Increase 1992 to 1995:	+101.7%
% Change GPM 1993 to 1995:	(6.5%)
% Change SGA Expenses/Revenues 1993 to 1995:	(14.2%)
Total Debt/Net Worth:	86.5%
Net Profits Before Taxes 1995*:	deficit
Net Profits Before Taxes/Revenues:	deficit
Market Value/1995 Revenues*:	5.8x
Traded On:	NASDAQ (AMER)
Opportunity Company Addresses:	Home-shopping access to games, entertainment, information channels, and stock market quotes are just a point and click away to millions of homes, if the price is low enough.
Elegance of Company's Solution:	America Online offers the most value-added features at competitive prices among the online service providers.

*Annualized.

the heaviest hitters in the country—IBM, GE, News Corp., and H&R Block—which is testament to the ability of entrepreneurial companies to create and continue to dominate an industry.

COMPARATIVE ONLINE SERVICES

Online Service	Subscribers	Revenues[b]	Service Price	Target Market
America Online	3,200	$394,000	$9.95/month 5 free hours, $2.95/hour	Home/HomeOffice
CompuServe[a]	2,600	$430,000	$9.95/month 5 free hours, $2.95/hour	Business/Professional
Prodigy	1,700	$230,000	$9.95/month 5 free hours $2.95/hour or $30.00/month 30 free hours	Family/Internet
Delphi	160	$ 12,000	$10.00/month 4 free hours $4.00/hour or $20.00/month 20 free hours $1.80/hour	Internet
eWorld	100	$ 12,000	$8.95/month 4 free hours, $3.00/hour	Macintosh
GEnie	100	$ 10,000	$8.95/month 4 free hours, $3.00/hour	Games

Source: Company filings & analyst reports.
[a] Does not include an estimated 800,000 subscribers in Japan.
[b] Revenues for 1995 are derived as follows: America Online from most recent 10-K, CompuServe from most recent H&R Block 10-K, Prodigy from estimates, Delphi Internet Services from estimates, eWorld from estimates, GEnie from estimates.

AMERICAN ONCOLOGY RESOURCES, INC.

I t used to be that shrewd investors would follow John Foster's health care deals and make small fortunes on them—InSpeech, Foster Medical—but the mantle has clearly passed to Russ Carson of Welsh Carson Anderson & Stowe. He is following a terrific buildout in Occusystems and a half-dozen other health-care companies with American Oncology Resources, a gem of a company. The Carson concept is to make money in complexity and chaos by offering order and a clear direction. Nothing is more complex or chaotic than delivery of cancer care. Enter Carson.

American Oncology Resources is a leading physician-practice-management company providing cancer treatment through 90 physicians in 49 sites in 10 major markets in 9 states. In 1994, 1.2 million cases of cancer were diagnosed in the United States, and direct medical costs associated with cancer totaled $35 billion. Management of oncology practices is a desirable market sector for three reasons. 1) It is a large niche with few competitors; 2) It is an under-penetrated market niche; only approximately 250 of the estimated 6,000–7,000 oncologists in private practice have chosen a corporate partner; and 3) Oncologists have extraordinary leverage and power. One oncologist can account for $1.2 to $1.5 million of annual direct billing revenue; 10 to 15 physicians can establish a leading position in large urban markets.

Physician services account for approximately $200 billion of the nearly $1 trillion in health-care expenditures in 1994. In addition, physicians control 75 to 80 percent of the $1 trillion total by deciding patients' treatment regimens, which drugs are prescribed, which hospital or facility is used, etc. Despite the desirable market characteristics, in general physicians have remained in private practice and are just now beginning to associate with physician-practice-management companies to access capital markets, make more informed purchasing decisions, improve strategic planning, and negotiate more effectively with managed care entities. All five publicly held physician practice management companies—Med Partners, Occusystems, PhyCor, and Physician Reliance Network, along with AORI, have been selected as Quantum Companies. They address huge problems with elegant solutions and bring skilled management into a chaotic marketplace.

The treatment of cancer has developed into a multidisciplinary approach involving a combination of four methodologies—chemotherapy, radiation, surgery, and immunology. Through the years,

AMERICAN ONCOLOGY RESOURCES,INC.

Chief Executive Officer:	R. Dale Ross
Principal Location:	16825 Northchase Dr. Houston, TX 77060
Telephone:	713-873-2674
Fax:	713-873-7762
E-mail:	not available
Web site:	not available
Satellite Locations:	none
Date Founded:	1992
Description of Business:	An emerging leader in the oncology-specific physician-practice-management market.
# Employees Current:	1,100
% Female Employees:	75%
# Employees Projected 9/30/96:	2,200
Revenues 1995*:	$53,159,000
Gross Profit Margin (GPM):	not available
SGA Expenses/Revenues:	12.3%
% Sales Increase 1992 to 1995:	1208.4%
% Change GPM 1992 to 1995:	not available
% Change SGA Expenses/Revenues 1992 to 1995:	(25.5%)
Total Debt/Net Worth:	23.1%
Net Profits Before Taxes 1995*:	6,485,000
Net Profits Before Taxes/Revenues:	12.2%
Market Value/1995 Revenues*:	10.4x
Traded On:	NASDAQ (AORI)
Opportunity Company Addresses:	Direct cancer costs are $35 billion per year and the disease hits 1.2 million Americans per year. Oncologists are overwhelmed with patients, along with greater complexity of billing and collecting, more sophisticated medical equipment, and pressures from managed care groups.
Elegance of Company's Solution:	The company provides oncologists with the opportunity to partner with experienced managers and off-load the administrative parts of their jobs.

*Annualized.

as the new methodologies were developed, they were administered in new and different treatment settings. As a result, a patient would seek care through different specialists in different locations. The different treatment settings and multiple, unaffiliated specialties often led to frustration and confusion for the patient and family members. At the same time, the uncoordinated system created inefficient and uncoordinated care for the patient.

Over the past five years, the market has been moving to comprehensive, integrated oncology group practices that deliver a full range of services in one outpatient facility. The results are higher quality, more focused, more convenient, and less frustrating. At the same time, services are delivered at a lower cost. As a result, treatment is also shifting to outpatient service sites. Although the incidence of cancer has increased consistently over the past 30 years, the number of inpatient hospital admissions has begun to decrease over the past several years. For example, the number of admissions from 1989 to 1994 decreased 11.5 percent from 243,000 to 215,000, according to the National Cancer Institute.

Oncologists traditionally operated a solo practice or formed groups of two to five physicians and, in general, offered a limited range of services. However, market forces have altered the business and operational dynamics of running a practice, and oncologists are forming larger, comprehensive group practices that provide a wider range of outpatient services primarily driven by four market factors: cost containment pressures; technological advances that make more outpatient treatments feasible; convenience for the patient; and increased awareness and acceptance of outpatient treatment.

However, the specific management talent, capital requirements, and corporate structure needed to operate a multidisciplinary clinic in a changing market environment are not in place at or readily available to most groups. Although physicians are highly intelligent people, in general, they lack the time, focus, and management skills needed to operate in today's more organized, cost-sensitive, result-oriented health-care environment. In addition, although groups are lucrative practices, they do not usually have a retained earnings base. Earnings are generally distributed as income.

What Russ Carson and others who have harnessed these kinds of markets have found is that they can make capital gains with the skills of strategic planning, raising capital for expansion, more efficient purchasing, information management, improved physician recruitment, and outcomes measurement.

AMERIDATA TECHNOLOGIES, INC.

Nietzche wrote: "It takes chaos to create a shooting star." Nothing is more chaotic than the personal computer industry and the solution, an environment filled with vaporware and a cacophonous effluvia of claims of better-faster-cheaper from hardware, software, and systems vendors alike. Into the breech leaps the systems integrator, and quickly becoming the best of that breed is AmeriData Technologies.

Co-founder Leonard J. Fassler has been-there-done-that. He co-founded TIE/Communications, Inc., one of the first entrepreneurial companies to challenge the interconnect domain in the early 1970s. TIE, MCI, and Sprint beat AT&T in the courtrooms and in the marketplace with better-more-efficient-less expensive handsets and PBX systems. A bet on AmeriData, Fassler's second company, is a can't miss. This gem of a company is trading at a p/e ratio of 13.0x and a market to revenue ratio of .14x. Its competitors' stock prices are 5x to 10x higher.

AmeriData's substantial growth from 1992 to 1995 (sales were $6.4 million in 1992) can be attributed to the company's Computer Systems and Services group, which provides personal computer and networking products, integration, and networking and support services. Its newly formed and growing consulting organization is capitalizing on the increasing need for business performance improvement services, software design and development capabilities, and sophisticated information technology (IT) department support services. For those organizations that have short-term requirements, AmeriData's computer rental business provides personal computers, networks and workstations, and related peripherals. In addition, the company is meeting the needs of the government marketplace, helping it achieve new levels of productivity and performance by providing PC-based products and services. Together, these business units comprise AmeriData Technologies, the only provider in the industry capable of addressing this multibillion-dollar market opportunity with three solutions. I look for the company to acquire a staffing and/or employee leasing company to provide software engineers to its clients when they wish to take their systems integration work in-house.

Acquisitions are getting to be a habit at AmeriData. In April 1995, the company acquired the assets of the Whitlock Computer Group of Virginia for $3.6 million, plus assumption of liabilities. Whitlock is a provider of computer products and services predominantly in Virginia. Estimated revenues for this entity approximate $56 million per year.

AMERIDATA TECHNOLOGIES, INC.

Chief Executive Officer:	Gerald A. Poch
Principal Location:	700 Canal St. Stamford, CT 06902
Telephone:	203-357-1464
Fax:	203-357-1531
E-mail:	lfassler@sage.ameridata.com
Web site:	not available
Satellite Locations:	Minneapolis, Minnesota; Gaithersburg, Maryland; Fairfax, Virginia; Woburn and Framingham, Massachusetts; Birmingham, Alabama; St. Louis, Missouri; Irvine, California; Blue Bell, Pennsylvania; and elsewhere
Date Founded:	1990
Description of Business:	Distributes and rents computer products and provides systems-integration services to corporate and government users.
# Employees Current:	28,073
% Female Employees:	35.7%
# Employees Projected 9/30/96:	not available
Revenues 1995*:	$1,172,600,000
Gross Profit Margin (GPM):	13.9%
SGA Expenses/Revenues:	8.9%
% Sales Increase 1992 to 1995:	+1832.2%
% Change GPM 1992 to 1995:	(14.2%)
% Change SGA Expenses/Revenues 1993 to 1995:	(15.2%)
Total Debt/Net Worth:	198.1%
Net Profits Before Taxes 1995*:	$22,236,000
Net Profits Before Taxes/Revenues:	1.9%
Market Value/1995 Revenues*:	.14x
Traded On:	NYSE (ADA)
Opportunity Company Addresses:	Government agencies and corporate information technologies divisions seek answers to their puzzlement regarding which is the best and most cost-effective solution to their needs.
Elegance of Company's Solution:	AmeriData is a leader in the systems-integration field and is able to rent, lease, or sell the systems that it recommends.

*Annualized.

AmeriData also acquired the assets of the Abacus Group, Inc., dba Entre' Computer Centers, for a combination of cash, stock, and assumption of liabilities in 1995. Headquartered in New Orleans, Louisiana, Abacus, too, is a provider of computer products and services. The purchase price for this transaction was approximately $1.4 million consisting of $1.1 million in cash and $.3 million of the company's common stock. Estimated 1994 revenues of the Abacus Group were approximately $23 million.

The pattern of acquisitions is both regional and horizontal markets. How will AmeriData make a statement in the Internet market? It could enter that business through the vehicle of Web site design and facilities management.

APPLIED MATERIALS, INC.

I n 1967, when the Silicon Valley was still just the Santa Clara Valley with more fruit orchards than semiconductors, the MOS transistor was developed by Fairchild Industries. Applied Materials was founded that year and achieved revenues of $110,000 and lost $300,000. It spent $70,000 on research and development that year in pursuit of gas-flow panels for the emerging chip companies. Over the next five years, Applied Materials grew at the rate of 40 percent per year and by 1972, with sales of $8.2 million and earnings of $800,000, the company went public. Its market share of semiconductor equipment was 6.5 percent at the time.

In 1981 the semiconductor industry was hard hit by the worldwide recession. Applied Materials, however, fared better than many other equipment suppliers during the recession, largely due to the introduction of the AME 8100 plasma etch system in May, 1981. Besides diversifying Applied Materials' product line into a large new market, this leading-edge technology virtually revolutionized etching of semiconductors, solving many of the control problems inherent in other approaches that were delaying development of very large scale integration (VLSI) devices. The AME 8100 gained rapid market acceptance, accounting for more than 50 percent of all dry plasma etch systems purchased by semiconductor manufacturers for VLSI production. Sales of these systems enabled the company to continue to grow through the 1980-82 recession.

The company's sales in 1990 were $70.8 million and its earnings were $6.4 million. The next year the numbers were $79.3 million and $4.3 million respectively. Applied Materials continued to increase its participation in the Japanese semiconductor market, with more than 30 percent of its 1983 corporate sales coming from Japan. That same year, Applied Materials Japan began construction of a Japan Technology Center in Narita, which opened in October 1984. The Technology Center was built at a cost of $9.2 million, $3.4 million of which was provided by a loan from the Japan Development Bank, an agency of the Japanese government. It was the first such loan by the bank for a facility that is 100 percent owned by an American corporation.

In September 1993, Applied Materials and Komatsu, Ltd. formed a new company—Applied Komatsu Technology, Inc. (AKT)—whose global plan was to develop, manufacture, and market systems used to produce Flat Panel Displays (FPDs). Komatsu has made an equity investment in

APPLIED MATERIALS, INC.

Chief Executive Officer:	James C. Morgan
Principal Location:	3050 Bowers Ave. Santa Clara, CA 95054
Telephone:	408-727-5555
Fax:	408-748-9943
E-mail:	not available
Web site:	http://morganjames.com
Satellite Locations:	Austin, Texas; Horsham, United Kingdom; Narita, Japan; Tel Aviv, Israel; Edinburgh, Scotland; Paris and Grenoble, France; Milan, Italy; Berlin, Munich, and Stuttgart, Germany; plus many in the United States
Date Founded:	1967
Description of Business:	World's largest supplier of wafer fabrication systems, processes, and services to the global semiconductor industry.
# Employees Current:	6,500+
% Female Employees:	not available
# Employees Projected 9/30/96:	not available
Revenues 1995*:	$2,090,000,000
Gross Profit Margin (GPM):	53.8%
SGA Expenses/Revenues:	13.8%
% Sales Increase 1992 to 1995:	+279.0%
% Change GPM 1992 to 1995:	+31.2%
% Change SGA Expenses/Revenues 1992 to 1995:	(17.9%)
Total Debt/Net Worth:	78.4%
Net Profits Before Taxes 1995*:	$433,900,000
Net Profits Before Taxes/Revenues:	20.8%
Market Value/1995 Revenues*:	1.9x
Traded On:	NASDAQ (AMAT)
Opportunity Company Addresses:	Semiconductors are being used in an ever-widening array of products, and reliable, global manufacturers of semiconductor production equipment are a necessity.
Elegance of Company's Solution:	Applied Materials is the explosively growing omnipresent manufacturer of the equipment that the semiconductor producer relies on.

*Annualized.

Applied Materials' subsidiary, Applied Display Technology, Inc., resulting in a 50-50 ownership of the renamed company. It is based in the United States and Japan, with its headquarters in Japan, and has a global reach to support the emerging flat panel display manufacturing industry worldwide. In October 1993, the company introduced its first product, the AKT 1600 PECVD, for chemical vapor deposition of the thin films used to make the Thin Film Transistor (TFT) structures in Active Matrix Flat Panel Displays.

Ending its 1993 fiscal year on a positive note, Applied Materials reached a long-awaited milestone—it became the first independent company in the semiconductor equipment industry to surpass $1 billion in revenue.

By the end of calendar year 1993 more than 1,500 of the company's single-wafer, multichamber systems had been shipped worldwide. Endura PVD shipments had exceeded 150 and the system had gained clear worldwide market leadership in PVD; more than 1,000 Precision 5000 Etch chambers were in use; the Precision 5000 WCVD had shipped more than 125 systems; the Precision Implant 9500 had broken all sales records for the company's implant technology; and the Precision 5000 CVD system continued as the global market leader.

Annualized sales for 1995 exceeded $2 billion with NPBT of more than $433 million. Applied Materials is benefiting from the shift to eight-inch wafers from six-inch wafers as the raw material of chips. This process means more individual chips can be made from a single wafer, but it also increases the chance that chips will have errors. The trend could help Applied Materials, because its machines are among the industry's most dependable.

Applied Materials, which currently controls more than 17 percent of the total semiconductor equipment market, has the largest installed base of any chip-equipment manufacturer. Its wafer-fabrication business is more than double the size of its nearest competitor, Tokyo Electron Ltd.

To assure customer responsiveness, the company maintains 54 customer service and sales offices around the world, including 15 in Japan, nine in Europe and eight in the Asia/Pacific region. Applied Materials' reputation for innovation is so stellar that it is one of the few equipment companies to have captured the Japanese market, which last year accounted for 27 percent of its sales; Europe and the Asia/Pacific region each accounted for 18 percent of sales.

The company's GPM is rising and its SGA Expenses/Revenues ratio is declining to a very small number: 13.8 percent. This kind of close attention to operations puts 20.8 percent of Applied Materials' sales on the bottom line. Does its stock price reflect its capabilities and effluvial future? Not at all. The company has a P/E ratio of 15.0x, about as dull as this ratio ever gets for a company that consistently grows in profitability. It is selling at approximately Netscape's market value, another producer of enabling products, whose annualized sales are about $50 million or 2.5 percent of Applied Materials' sales.

APPLIX, INC.

W hen toolmakers (think of Black & Decker as an example) sell a tool to a customer, they shrink their market by one customer. I like Black & Decker's electric drills, but after I buy one, I probably will not be a customer of the company for another five years. In the software industry there are many toolmakers, generally known by the more elevating title of makers of enabling technology. But this is their dilemma.

Applix makes tools. The tools enhance the functionality of spreadsheet software and permit users to rapidly and efficiently analyze data that changes in seconds. The financial markets adore Real Time, Applix's lead product, because it helps users make money. But one product for one market a major company does not make. Acknowledging this, Jit Saxena, the company's CEO, is diversifying rapidly and well. One of his moves is to make its products available on the Internet, and, one would trust, collect continuous per-use fees from Internet subscribers.

At the Sun Microsystems Inc. Java Day at its Menlo Park, California, campus in November 1995, Applix demonstrated one of its first products for the Internet, code-named "Espresso," highlighting the potential for utilizing the Java language and the Internet to support interactive client/server business applications securely and efficiently.

Java, Sun Microsystem's revolutionary new object-oriented programming language for the Internet, gives users the responsiveness and infinite extensibility of the Internet. Applix's presentation is the first to show how users can interact with spreadsheets using Java. In Applix's implementation, associates in any location worldwide accomplish virtually anything available to an enterprise-systems user at headquarters. Users can develop custom reports, drill down to data sources in new ways, initiate new queries of databases, drop information into compound documents, e-mail or fax reports, and the like.

Java-enabled applications may be accessed by any hardware device enabled with Java run time. For example, the much-discussed "Internet appliance," a new concept in hardware devices, would be able to run Java, as can a large variety of workstations and computers. Access to up-to-the-minute customer information, order entry or inventory applications, e-mail—even the actual spreadsheet models available on headquarters workstations and desktops—will all be available via the Internet.

APPLIX, INC.

Chief Executive Officer:	Jitendra S. Saxena
Principal Location:	112 Turnpike Rd. Westboro, MA 01581
Telephone:	508-870-0300
Fax:	508-366-9313
E-Mail:	jitsaxena@applix.com
Web site:	http://www.aplix.com
Satellite Locations:	none
Date Founded:	1983
Description of Business:	Leading developer and producer of software for real-time decision support and groupware.
# Employees Current:	140
% Female Employees:	not available
# Employees Projected 9/30/96:	not available
Revenues 1995*:	$18,792,000
Gross Profit Margin (GPM):	94.8%
SGA Expenses/Revenues:	65.3%
% Sales Increase 1992 to 1995:	+160.0%
% Change GPM 1992 to 1995:	+16.7%
% Change SGA Expenses/Revenues 1992 to 1995:	+17.6%
Total Debt/Net Worth:	53.6%
Net Profits Before Taxes 1995*:	$2,965,000
Net Profits Before Taxes/Revenues:	15.8%
Market Value/1995 Revenues*:	8.2x
Traded On:	NASDAQ (APLX)
Opportunity Company Addresses:	Lotus 1-2-3 and Excel put spreadsheet capability in everyone's hands, but the ability to rapidly change the data creates another need.
Elegance of Company's Solution:	Applix provides software that enables the user to retrieve, analyze, and communicate rapidly changing information such as stock market data.

*Annualized.

With Applix's implementation, for example, a traveling businessperson could connect directly and securely into the headquarters' enterprise-information systems and utilize the extensive applications and data there. A bank could provide clients with up-to-the-minute snapshots of client portfolios. A CFO on the road could check the company's financial position, directly and fully up-to-date.

Currently, Applix is very well-run. Its GPM has improved 16.7 percent since 1992, and its Operating Ratio has more than doubled. But the product requires 65 cents of every sales dollar to sell and monitor. To finance its necessary diversification, Saxena will need to slash SGA costs and use its stunningly priced stock to acquire other toolmakers—hopefully, toll booths and not electric drills.

ARBOR SOFTWARE CORPORATION

Accountability. Some of the recent innovations in remote computing software and systems have the happy effect of having managers in an enterprise put a drop of their blood on every document or piece of data that they sign off on. Gone are the days when a manager can avoid being accountable for a decision, an estimate, a sentence of text, or a buy order based on the sales department's projections. And no single client/server-plus software system brings so intense a level of accountability into an organization as does Arbor Software's Essbase System.

Speed. The second benefit of Essbase is speed. In the past the analyst who was asked to work up a spreadsheet had to gather inputs from different departments via telephone or fax or by walking around. Now he or she can do it by collaborating on the Essbase System.

Essbase is online analytical processing software. Its proprietary sparse matrix-computation engine enables users to rapidly calculate data relationships and analyze a division's sales by channel, geography, customer, fiscal period, or budget versus actual, among other dimensions. Essbase supports large databases of information and provides robust aggregation and drill-down capabilities for trend analysis, time comparisons, and statistical analyses. Essbase's high-performance analytical capabilities allow users to perform planning and analysis functions at the "speed of thought," running multiple iterations and scenarios with immediate feedback.

Users access the Essbase Server seamlessly through familiar Microsoft Excel and Lotus 1-2-3 spreadsheets or other popular front-end applications, eliminating the need to learn a new user-interface or query or programming language. Essbase allows users to populate spreadsheets with summarized or computed data and to recognize, pivot, drill-down, or navigate through such information using simple mouse-based operations. These factors are designed to result in quick customer adoption, repeated use, and rapid proliferation throughout the organization.

Essbase allows users to easily move, realign, and add new categories of data for scenario analysis and to change analytical calculations or modify data relationships. These capabilities enable users to easily and quickly adapt their planning and analysis requirements to dynamic business and organizational conditions requiring little, if any, utilization of MIS resources.

ARBOR SOFTWARE CORPORATION

Chief Executive Officer:	James A. Dorrian
Principal Location:	1325 Chesapeake Terrace Sunnyvale, CA 94089
Telephone:	408-727-5800
Fax:	408-727-7140
E-mail:	not available
Web site:	http://www.arborsoft.com
Satellite Locations:	none
Date Founded:	1991
Description of Business:	Leading provider of client/server multidimensional database software for business planning and analysis.
# Employees Current:	135
% Female Employees:	32%
# Employees Projected 9/30/96:	Approx. 190
Revenues 1995*:	$16,809,000
Gross Profit Margin (GPM):	96.0%
SGA Expenses/Revenues:	83.7%
% Sales Increase 1992 to 1995:	+1519.8%
% Change GPM 1992 to 1995:	+1.5%
% Change SGA Expenses/Revenues 1992 to 1995:	(63.4%)
Total Debt/Net Worth:	24.5%
Net Profits Before Taxes 1995*:	$1,328,000
Net Profits Before Taxes/Revenues:	7.9%
Market Value/1995 Revenues*:	21.8x
Traded On:	NASDAQ(ARSW)
Opportunity Company Addresses:	The need for various related departments within an enterprise to collaborate on an analytical project.
Elegance of Company's Solution:	The company's Essbase Server-plus software permits seamless collaboration on spreadsheets.

*Annualized.

Arbor Software is essentially a single-product company with sales of approximately $16 million. It recently became profitable. It takes a lot of marketing muscle to sell Essbase: The SGA Expenses/Revenues is about 84 percent, which means that a ton of money from investors is being transferred over to Madison Avenue and into salesmen's commission. At some level of the SGA Expenses/Revenues ratio, a company becomes a switch for passing money through it. But the wild and woolly stock market of 1995 bid Arbor's market value up to a quarter of a billion dollars. I don't see it staying there for long because the company is too unproven. That may be a plateau for Arbor management to strive for; but with these kinds of platinum chips to toss around, look for Arbor to acquire some other product lines for stock.

ASPEN TECHNOLOGY, INC.

tudies of the effect of environmental regulations on the chemical-process manufacturing industries might as well be labeled coroners' reports. The costs of bringing new plants online and then dealing with their waste have skyrocketed. The opportunity to mitigate some of these problems was seized by Lawrence B. Evans and his team at Aspen Technology, Inc., and the company has created a quarter-billion-dollar capital gain and a near monopoly position. Moreover, it has penetrated a mere 15 percent of its market, giving it a future of perhaps six times its current revenue size and market value.

Don't let the name fool you. Aspen is not hobnobbing on the slopes with Hollywood starlets. Its name comes from an Energy Department acronym, and its facilities are in the hardworking towns of Boston, Houston, and Brussels, among others. Its products are getting better with time. Witness its 13 percent improvement in GPM over the last four years. Attention to detail at Aspen Tech is demonstrated by a steadily improving accounts receivable turnover ratio from 74 days outstanding in 1994 to 65 days in 1995. The costs of selling the product line are beginning to level off at just under 50 percent of sales; as this ratio comes down, earnings will grow, and cash for acquisitions and new product development will be so plentiful that Evans will have to bail it.

Aspen Tech has a dominant position in the chemicals segment of the process-manufacturing industry, with a market share of approximately 50 percent. The company is also an important supplier to other process-manufacturing industries. Its more than 450 commercial customers throughout the world include DuPont, Dow, Eastman Chemical, Union Carbide, and BASF in the chemicals industry; Phillips and Citgo in petroleum; Merck, Abbott, and Ciba Geigy in pharmaceuticals; and Procter & Gamble, 3M, and Unilever in consumer products. Aspen Tech profits from a beneficial product-licensing strategy in which customers sign noncancellable three- to five-year-term licenses. The result has been very close customer relationships—which address all of the major aspects of process manufacturing today, including steady-state and dynamic simulation, modeling, optimization, and analysis.

The flagship ASPEN PLUS product allows customers to simulate and analyze steady-state process-manufacturing operations. It is the most widely used and proven product of its type in the market and has been used to simulate hundreds of manufacturing operations. Release 9, a

ASPEN TECHNOLOGY, INC.

Chief Executive Officer:	Lawrence B. Evans
Principal Location:	10 Canal Park Cambridge, MA 02141
Telephone:	617-577-0100
Fax:	617-577-0303
E-mail:	info@aspentec.com
Web site:	not available
Satellite Locations:	Houston, Texas; Cambridge, United Kingdom; Brussels, Belgium; Tokyo, Japan; and Hong Kong
Date Founded:	1981
Description of Business:	A leading provider of computer-aided chemical-engineering software products to the process manufacturing industries.
# Employees Current:	413
% Female Employees:	29%
# Employees Projected 9/30/96:	not available
Revenues 1995*:	$61,065,000
Gross Profit Margin (GPM):	83.3%
SGA Expenses/Revenues:	49.3%
% Sales Increase 1992 to 1995:	180.3%
% Change GPM 1992 to 1995:	+13.0%
% Change SGA Expenses/Revenues 1992 to 1995:	+2.7%
Total Debt/Net Worth:	53.6%
Net Profits Before Taxes 1995*:	$10,563,000
Net Profits Before Taxes/Revenues:	17.3%
Market Value/1995 Revenues*:	3.8x
Traded On:	NASDAQ (AZPN)
Opportunity Company Addresses:	The need to predict the performance and efficiency of a process manufacturing plant before it is built.
Elegance of Company's Solution:	Software to mathematically model the chemical process that occurs during production, reducing raw materials, waste, and energy costs.

*Annualized.

new version released in June 1994, allows the user to point and click its mouse—an enhanced user-friendly innovation.

The steady-state products are complemented by SPEEDUP. It enables the simulation of dynamic chemical processes, allowing chemical engineers to analyze chemical-manufacturing processes in which significant process changes are occurring but have not reached steady-state equilibrium, such as the start-up and shutdown of a manufacturing plant or major operational changes in the manufacturing process. SPEEDUP is integrated with ASPEN PLUS, which saves users substantial time and effort.

Aspen Tech's products frequently provide a return on investment that far exceeds the combined cost of the software and the engineers that use it by revealing ways to reduce the cost of building a new software manufacturing plant or to improve the efficiency of an existing plant. The significant savings arise because process manufacturing has a very high ratio of capital investment and raw materials costs to labor costs. As a result, significant improvements in profitability can be achieved through a more optimal use of plant, equipment, and raw materials. Aspen Tech's products are among the most critical tools for improving profitability in the chemical and other process manufacturing industries.

@HOME

Based in Mountain View, California, @Home is conceived as a high-speed network that provides real-time multimedia news, information, entertainment, advertising content, access to the Internet, E-mail, and other services to consumers via cable systems and their personal computers. The company is a joint venture between Telecommunications Inc. and Kleiner Perkins Caulfield & Byers venture capital firm.

The @Home network will provide consumers with a significant increase in speed and quality over current online connections, using a customized version of the popular Netscape browser that will run on most Microsoft Windows 95, Macintosh OS, and UNIX personal computers. Employing an open-platform architecture that will make its features available to the widest possible number of users and content providers, @Home network will operate over a high-speed backbone and existing cable systems and will be linked to home computers via cable modems and standard Ethernet connections.

@Home will include a wide variety of content. In addition to providing connections to the global Internet, the World Wide Web, and E-mail, the service will enable content providers to create movies, home-shopping services, ticket purchasing, travel planning, and other interactive services that take advantage of the high-speed network, as well as extensive local news and information.

Deployment of the @Home service began in early 1996 in select national markets, starting with Sunnyvale, California. The monthly charge for @Home is expected to be $30 to $50 for unlimited use of basic services.

The growing interest in the Internet and online services has created demand for a faster, easier means of accessing information than standard telephone lines. Bottlenecks caused by relatively slow telephone modems and network tie-ups are frustrating to most Internet and online users. Today's challenge is to create a high-speed global network that provides low-cost and ubiquitous access to all Internet and commercial online services.

The immense bandwidth of cable offers the potential to build such a network. Cable is most commonly known for its television services, but when used for data transmission, the broadband pipeline of cable offers benefits unmatched by current dial-up systems. Cable modems are 700 times faster than today's telephone modems and nearly 80 times faster

@HOME

Chief Executive Officer:	William Randolph Hearst III
Principal Location:	385 Ravendale Mountain View, CA 94043
Telephone:	415-833-4950
Fax:	415-833-4955
E-mail:	not available
Web site:	http://www.home.net
Satellite Locations:	none
Date Founded:	1995
Description of Business:	Plans to offer cable TV customers Internet-like services such as movies-on-demand, banking, and shopping.
# Employees Current:	40
% Female Employees:	35%
# Employees Projected 9/30/96:	80
Revenues 1995*:	not available
Gross Profit Margin (GPM):	The company is privately held and is not required to publish its financial statements.
SGA Expenses/Revenues:	not available
% Sales Increase 1992 to 1995:	not available
% Change GPM 1992 to 1995:	not available
% Change SGA Expenses/Revenues 1992 to 1995:	not available
Total Debt/Net Worth:	not available
Net Profits Before Taxes 1995*:	not available
Net Profits Before Taxes/Revenues:	not available
Market Value/1995 Revenues*:	not available
Opportunity Company Addresses:	Forrester Research predicts that annual Internet revenues will grow from $123 million today to $4 billion by the year 2000. But how does the industry reach the couch potato?
Elegance of Company's Solution:	For the non-PC user, @Home will bring the interactivity of the Internet to a set-top box on the cable TV set, accessible via a channel changer.

*Annualized.

than ISDN connections. They do not require an extra phone line and eliminate the time and potential trouble involved in dialing a service. Cable-based Internet services offer an even richer multimedia experience than CD-ROM technology, including real-time delivery and updating of content. And cable offers a direct connection to the online world—when you turn on the computer, you are on the network.

@Home's network is based on a distributed model that makes extensive use of caching and replication to minimize traffic on the system's backbone and maintain high levels of speed. @Home will operate its own global network infrastructure connecting to the Internet at multiple locations. Its backbone will connect regional data centers together via a multimegabit switched-data system. These regional centers would serve limited geographic areas, such as individual cities, and would be connected to local servers located at cable system headends. @Home users would be connected to the headends via local area networks over the cable system, which is a two-way hybrid fiber-optic/coaxial cable configured asymmetrically. Many cable companies have upgraded their systems to handle such two-way connections or are in the process of doing so.

In the home, the service would arrive over the same cable that delivers television signals, which would not be affected by the addition of data services. The cable modem, supplied by the cable company, would be connected to the subscriber's computer with a standard 10-Base-T Ethernet cable. Many computers now include Ethernet connections or can easily be upgraded. The software required to use the service would be provided to the subscriber by @Home and will include a TCP/IP stack and Internet browser software with built-in e-mail and multimedia capabilities.

@Home will be facing competition from TimeWarner Cable, which has launched a cable modem pilot in Elmira, New York. To provide the best scientific foundation it can, Hearst and John Doerr, partners at Kleiner Perkins, lured Milo Medin, 32, one of the developers of the Internet, to become vice president and chief technical officer of @Home. He immediately changed their business plan. @Home will create its own national high-speed data backbone network running Internet protocols by purchasing bandwidth from providers such as MCI, AT&T, and Sprint and attaching replicators throughout the system. This, Medin believes, will eliminate Internet failures and time delays. Kleiner Perkins, the IPO market's favorite validator, once again has plucked the singular straw out of the hay bale to stir its intoxicating new drink: @Home.

AURUM SOFTWARE, INC.

In order to deliver on its enterprise integration mission, Aurum has developed strong partnerships with companies such as Avalon Software and Oracle. Aurum's customer asset management product line has been integrated with Avalon's CIIM package for order entry and inventory control, as well as Oracle's financial, manufacturing, and distribution applications.

Aurum has also devoted significant resources to building a team of expert professionals able to use information systems to implement business-process reengineering initiatives. Its enterprise integration focus and the in-house expertise of its developers and professional services personnel are an important market advantage.

IBM has selected SalesTrak, Aurum's sales-force-automation software. Another company that is in the process of implementing an integrated enterprise-wide system is NCCI, Inc., a Florida-based provider of information services. NCCI is working to integrate Aurum's SupportTrak with the order-entry module of Oracle Financials. NCCI plans to have a single database, accessible by both SupportTrak and Oracle Financials, that contains both product and customer information. Service representatives will first log a call in SupportTrak. Aurum's applications will be used to resolve customer issues and provide information with Oracle Financials immediately accessible for placing new orders and checking the status of existing orders.

With revenue growth of 100 percent in the last year, Aurum Software's focus on strategic partnerships has clearly paid off. The company's new partners—among them, Cambridge Technology Partners (a Quantum Company), Deloitte & Touche, Ernst & Young, and IBM—are gaining widespread expertise in SalesTrak. Working in tandem with Aurum, the new partners are customizing their clients' information systems and, as needed, are incorporating Aurum's applications: the shortening of sales cycles; reduction in sales costs; and improved customer interaction.

By partnering with large customers, Aurum has expanded its field operations to include 28 countries around the world. In a recent win, MCI chose Aurum to provide information systems to its 5,000 sales representatives as part of a $60-million sales force automation program.

If Aurum succeeds, you and I will be able to place orders by phone or fax, get a customer tracking number (like FedEx gives us), receive rapid

AURUM SOFTWARE, INC.

Chief Executive Officer:	Mary E. Coleman
Principal Location:	3385 Scott Blvd. Santa Clara, CA 95054
Telephone:	408-986-8100
Fax:	408-654-3400
E-mail:	mary@aurum.com
Web site:	http://www.aurum.com
Satellite Locations:	Atlanta, Georgia; Chicago, Illinois; Ocean City, New Jersey; Boston, Massachusetts; Dallas, Texas; Phoenix, Arizona
Date Founded:	1990
Description of Business:	A leading developer and supplier of customer-interaction software.
# Employees Current:	88
% Female Employees:	31%
# Employees Projected 9/30/96:	130
Revenues 1995*:	$10,000,000 est.
Gross Profit Margin (GPM):	The company is privately held and is not required to publish its financial statements.
SGA Expenses/Revenues:	not available
% Sales Increase 1992 to 1995:	not available
% Change GPM 1992 to 1995:	not available
% Change SGA Expenses/Revenues 1992 to 1995:	not available
Total Debt/Net Worth:	The company recently completed $6 million venture capital financing.
Net Profits Before Taxes 1995*:	not available
Net Profits Before Taxes/Revenues:	not available
Market Value/1995 Revenues*:	not available
Opportunity Company Addresses:	To truly reengineer a corporation means beginning with the customer and analyzing the information link-up from there to the shipping room, then efficiently automating the flow of information.
Elegance of Company's Solution:	Not an easy task, but someone has to do it. Mary Coleman and her team are.

*Annualized.

delivery, and receive a customer service follow-up call in a week or two. Prices may come down a little also, because Aurum's software reduces its client's cost of goods sold.

Morgan Stanley Ventures is the company's principal backer. A recent $6 million funding is the next step prior to an IPO.

AUSPEX SYSTEMS, INC.

pproximately 60 million PCs were shipped worldwide in 1995, compared with 48.5 million in 1994 and 38.2 million in 1993. The percentage of PCs that are tied into enterprise networks as opposed to public networks and stand-alone was roughly 25 percent in 1994 and 34 percent in 1995. Clearly the PC is becoming the communications medium of choice among corporations, institutions, and government agencies. But it isn't as simple to operate as the telephone. Just as we hear a dial tone every time we lift a telephone handset to our ear, we want to be able to click and point our mouses onto a network.

In today's world of distributed computing, which translates as *distributed decision making*, data must be available across our enterprise networks—day in and out. The era when only a select portion of our corporate data warranted a highly reliable, high-availability computing solution is fast giving way to a new era where all of our information must be available on demand. As a result, we are under increasing pressure to move vast quantities of data quickly and reliably over enterprise networks. Everything is critical; everything is strategic. And instant access to information has become a key competitive weapon in every business large or small.

Auspex understands these needs. It has spent nearly a decade focused on the challenge of securely storing, managing, and rapidly distributing its customers' data over networked computing environments around the world. Through the design, manufacture, and support of high-performance data servers for networks of workstations and personal computers, Auspex helps its customers store, manage, and distribute critical information among employees and customers on a global basis.

Unlike traditional servers designed to compute and process applications, Auspex pioneered a whole new class of server—the network data server—optimized to manage and move network data. Unique in approach, its NetServer family has proven itself time and again as the highest performance, most reliable solution for moving and managing network data. It has installed NetServers on the networks of Los Alamos National Laboratories, Loral Space Systems, CS First Boston, Bear Stearns, Cabletron, and Dassault, among others. Most of the company's installations are international.

The NetServer line is symbiotic with network servers and routers manufactured by CISCO, Bay Networks, Chipcom, and Cabletron all Quantum Companies. With each sale they make to an enterprise that

AUSPEX SYSTEMS, INC.

Chief Executive Officer:	Bruce N. Moore
Principal Location:	5200 Great American Pkwy. Santa Clara, CA 95110
Telephone:	408-986-2000
Fax:	408-986-2020
E-mail:	info@auspex.com
Web site:	http://www.auspex.com
Satellite Locations:	France, Germany, Japan, United Kingdom
Date Founded:	1986
Description of Business:	Designs, develops, manufactures, and supports high-performance servers that assure businesses that move large amounts of data at high rates of through-put of the rapid distribution of critical information.
# Employees Current:	400
% Female Employees:	27%
# Employees Projected 9/30/96:	520
Revenues 1995*:	$101,437,000
Gross Profit Margin (GPM):	53.5%
SGA Expenses/Revenues:	32.8%
% Sales Increase 1992 to 1995:	+97.1%
% Change GPM 1992 to 1995:	+15.5%
% Change SGA Expenses/Revenues 1992 to 1995:	27.6%
Total Debt/Net Worth:	27.4%
Net Profits Before Taxes 1995*:	$9,985,000
Net Profits Before Taxes/Revenues:	9.8%
Market Value/1995 Revenues*:	3.8x
Traded On:	NASDAQ (ASPX)
Opportunity Company Addresses:	The need to have critical information distributed to employees on a global basis.
Elegance of Company's Solution:	High-performance servers for distributed networks of PCs and workstations.

*Annualized.

moves critical information globally, a light should go on at the vice president of sales' desk at Auspex and he should dispatch a salesperson to the scene. Although it doesn't work quite that way the personal networking at Auspex is beginning to take effect. Bay Networks' CFO recently joined Auspex's board of directors. Auspex's founder and former CEO, Laurence B. Boucher, is a member of Adaptec's (a Quantum Company) board of directors. Plus, there are three venture capital investors on Auspex's board of directors, including David F. Marquardt of Technology Venture Investors, Microsoft's early backer. Clearly, at Auspex, networking has spread to the person-to-person level.

Auspex turned in an excellent quarter ended December 31, 1995. Revenues leapt 44 percent to $38 million over the same quarter in the prior year and operating ratio grew to 12.3 percent from 9.7 percent.

Prior to the new CEO, Bruce N. Moore, coming on board, Auspex had not been delivering year-to-year sales leaps either. Sales grew a mere 97.1 percent from 1992 to 1995, not very much in this league, where many companies double their size each year. And accounts receivable that used to be collected in 78 days just a few years ago were being collected in 91 days in mid-1995.

Auspex could be a takeover candidate unless second quarter 1996 results can't be replicated. Moore's task is to earn more.

AUTHENTIC FITNESS CORP.

Pick your top 100 entrepreneurs of the last decade, give them each the same amount of money to start a new company, and it's even money that Linda J. Wachner will finish ahead of most of the pack. She took over Warnaco in a leveraged buyout in 1991, then spun out Authentic Fitness, which owned the Speedo line of swimwear and swim accessories. Speedo is a competition brand, and the company has many Olympians, like Summer Sanders, among its endorsers.

Wachner also has acquired other well-known swimwear consumer brands, including Cole of California ($42.6 million acquisition); entered the skiwear business with White Stag, a 100-year old brand name; and created a new line of skiwear, Skiing Passport. The company's channel for the skiwear line includes mass merchandisers such as WalMart.

Borrowing a page from the marketing bible of Quantum Company Just For Feet, Inc., Authentic Fitness entered the event marketing retail business in 1992. Event marketing is turning a retail store into an action-oriented place whose consumers can try on and try out products while being bombarded with sound and videos related to the products they see around them. Authentic Fitness' "happening dude" stores now account for $20.4 million of the company's $266.1 million in annual revenues. Their growth rate is more than 500 percent since 1994.

In November 1992, the company opened its first retail store in Los Angeles and since has opened 73 more (as of August 31, 1995) in major metropolitan areas of the United States. The retail stores are a model for innovative retailing of the company's products and a proving ground for new products and marketing and merchandising techniques. They are designed to appeal to participants in water- and land-based fitness activities, offering a complete line of Speedo and Speedo Authentic Fitness products for year-round activities.

The stores have been operating ahead of the company's expectations, with annualized gross revenues in excess of $425 per square foot. Same-store sales for the sixteen stores open for the full 1995 fiscal year increased 4.6 percent. The stores are unlike retail apparel shops: They are happy, enthusiastic expo-like venues that celebrate swimming and fitness. Wachner believes that the success of its retail stores evidences substantial consumer interest in innovative channels of distribution for fitness apparel.

The stores average approximately 1,200 square feet in size. Capital expenditures for each store of this size average approximately $250,000 and require approximately $60,000 of working capital.

AUTHENTIC FITNESS CORP.

Chief Executive Officer:	Linda J. Wachner
Principal Location:	6040 Bandini Blvd. Commerce, CA 90040
Telephone:	213-726-1262
Fax:	213-724-2256
E-mail:	not available
Web site:	not available
Satellite Locations:	New York, New York; Santa Monica and Van Nuys, California
Date Founded:	1990
Description of Business:	Designs, manufactures, and markets swimwear, swim accessories, and active fitness apparel under the Speedo, Catalina, Cole of California, and other strong brand names.
# Employees Current:	1,915
% Female Employees:	not available
# Employees Projected 9/30/96:	not available
Revenues 1995*:	$266,133,000
Gross Profit Margin (GPM):	36.7%
SGA Expenses/Revenues:	11.9%
% Sales Increase 1992 to 1995:	+262.5%
% Change GPM 1992 to 1995:	(2.9%)
% Change SGA Expenses/Revenues 1992 to 1995:	+8.2%
Total Debt/Net Worth:	69.5%
Net Profits Before Taxes 1995*:	$31,592,000
Net Profits Before Taxes/Revenues:	11.9%
Market Value/1995 Revenues*:	1.7x
Opportunity Company Addresses:	The strategies for marketing swimwear have been the same for years.
Elegance of Company's Solution:	Authentic Fitness is making swimwear purchasing an event. It has brought the concept of the happy expo to the "occasion" of buying a swimsuit.

*Annualized.

Although the data aren't publicly available, one would think the average purchase is larger in this environment than in the swimwear section of a typical department store. People buy more when their eyes are excited by events and graphics around them, when they are happy and strolling, and when people around them are in a similarly enthusiastic mood. Flea markets have proven this hypothesis: a relaxed consumer surrounded by entertaining chaos buys more than he or she does in an orderly antiseptic retail environment.

Authentic Fitness did not meet my critical test of rising GPM and falling SGA Expenses/Revenues ratio, but the company is laying pipe for the future. Retail margins generally are higher than manufacturing margins, its GPM should kick into higher gear in 1996 and beyond. The bottom-line profit margin is a terrific 11.9 percent, up steadily over the last four years.

Receivables collections improved from 122 days on hand in 1994 to 98 days on hand in 1995. Inventory turnover got a bit out of hand in 1995, ballooning to nearly 6 months from 121 days. That means foolishly high interest costs, an area that the inimitable Ms. Wachner is certainly not one to suffer lightly.

AVID TECHNOLOGY, INC.

The knock on toolmakers is that with every sale, their market shrinks. Once the customer is satisfied the toolmaker may never sell him another thing. That is why many tool distributors encourage us to join their "users groups" to convert us from occasional to frequent fliers/buyers.

Avid Technology is the leading toolmaker in the professional film, video, and audio postproduction business. Its gross profit margin has been steadily declining, which normally would eliminate a company from inclusion in *Quantum Companies II*. But the decline is relatively small and arguably has more to do with Avid's spate of acquisitions and attempts to integrate these disparate companies than with a need to lower prices to find customers. Moreover, SGA Expenses/Revenues declined from a nosebleed 36.2 percent in 1992 to 30.0 percent in 1995. That is a positive trend. Coupled with an improved accounts receivable collection trend—94 days in 1994 and 89 days in 1995—Avid made the cut.

What will really get Avid's management moving and shaking is a strong competitor. A relatively new, privately held company called Play, with a better, faster, and less expensive digital editing machine is apparently stirring things up in Avid's pasture. Play's product is apparently so popular in Hollywood that customer prepayments have obviated the need for venture capital. The year 1996 will be pivotal for Avid, and additional horizontal acquisitions may be its strategic plan.

Since Avid introduced its first digital nonlinear editing systems in 1989, Avid Media Composer systems have led the industry; the demand for these products has continued to grow. In fact, the company sold more Media Composers in 1994 than in the previous five years combined!

While Media Composer Systems remained the product of choice in television and commercial production communities, Avid's Film Composer system, with nearly 200 feature films to its credit, was selected by the Academy of Motion Picture Arts and Sciences to receive a 1994 Scientific and Engineering Achievement Award. At the same time, prestigious audio facilities worldwide purchased Avid's AudioVision and AudioStation digital audio systems for feature film, television, and commercial work.

A key component of Avid's strategy for the '90s has been to leverage core technology and distribution into new markets, and 1994 saw the successful realization of this strategy in both broadcast and desktop

AVID TECHNOLOGY, INC.

Chief Executive Officer:	Curt A. Rawley
Principal Location:	One Park West Tewksbury, MA 01876
Telephone:	508-640-3033
Fax:	508-851-7216
E-mail:	info@avid.com
Web site:	not available
Satellite Locations:	Iver, Bucks, United Kingdom; Tokyo, Japan; plus 15 other foreign locations
Date Founded:	1988
Description of Business:	The leading toolmaker in the professional film, video, and audio postproduction business.
# Employees Current:	1,200
% Female Employees:	28%
# Employees Projected 9/30/96:	not available
Revenues 1995*:	$289,142,000
Gross Profit Margin (GPM):	50.5%
SGA Expenses/Revenues:	30.0%
% Sales Increase 1992 to 1995:	+556.7%
% Change GPM 1992 to 1995:	(7.2%)
% Change SGA Expenses/Revenues 1992 to 1995:	(17.1%)
Total Debt/Net Worth:	48.8%
Net Profits Before Taxes 1995*:	$17,114,000
Net Profits Before Taxes/Revenues:	5.9%
Market Value/1995 Revenues*:	3.1x
Traded On:	NASDAQ (AVID)
Opportunity Company Addresses:	As the communications industry converts from analog to digital, the need arises for toolmakers to effect the conversion.
Elegance of Company's Solution:	Avid makes the most important digital conversion-enabling technology for the movie and television industries.

*Annualized.

businesses. First, television stations around the world began to adopt Avid's "lens-to-transmitter" solutions. Using Avid's AirPlay system, broadcasters aired commercials and newscasts directly from hard drives, bypassing tape completely. Then the company began installing its first AvidNet/ATM networking and server solutions; wrote its first million-dollar, multisite broadcast order; and shipped its first multichannel AirPlay systems. Its NewsCutter editing systems also made strong inroads into newsrooms worldwide. Further providing broadcasters with integrated solutions, Avid acquired two leading developers of newsroom automation technology—Basys Automation Systems and SoftTECH Systems, Inc.

In March 1995, Avid acquired The Parallax Software Group of London, England, a leading developer of paint and compositing technology, and Elastic Reality, Inc., of Madison, Wisconsin, a leading developer of special effects software, including morphing and film restoration tools. Avid issued the aggregate 1.5 million shares of common stock, valued at approximately $12 million. Avid can now offer morphing solutions for the home, small office, and educational markets.

So tight a grasp has Avid on its market that its name has become a verb, more like "Fed/Ex" and "Xerox," but as Joseph A. Shumpeter wrote, "entrepreneurship is the act of creative destruction," and companies like Play, Advance Digital Imaging (a Quantum Company), and Apple Computer are nipping at Avid's heels.

BBN CORPORATION

The footprints of BBN appear at many datapoints of the Internet, from its origin and out into its future. Like the child in the Edward Albee play "Who's Afraid of Virginia Woolf," it is the direct object of conversations between geeks and geekettes, but rarely the verb. It appears not to be a protagonist of the action in the play entitled "Grow the Internet," yet virtually every key player regards its potential with awe.

Why this veneration? Why did AT&T team up with BBN, invest $8 million in its stock, and agree to sell BBN's Internet service (BBN Planet) through its sales force for the next three years? The answer lies in the step-by-step, 45-year construction of one of the most elegant remote-computing systems-development companies in the world. It is definitely the tortoise of the Internet, but we know how that story ends.

BBN created the Internet's forerunner, the ARPANET, twenty-six years ago. Today, BBN Planet is the nation's fourth-largest provider of Internet services for businesses and organizations. It provides the reliable and responsive Internet access that organizations need and complete service packages that make it simple to take full advantage of the business potential of the Internet. Consumers need not apply for a BBN dial-up service.

BBN Planet expanded nationwide in 1995 by acquiring two of the premier national Internet access networks in the country: BARRNET in Silicon Valley and SURAnet covering 13 southeastern states and the District of Columbia. In addition, BBN has created a nationwide service-delivery network that enables it to hook up organizations to the Internet at over 500 local access points. BBN's customers include Apple Computer, CISCO Systems, DuPont, General Cinema, Hale and Dorr, Hewlett-Packard, International Data Corporation, Lotus Development Corporation, Lockheed Martin, The New York Stock Exchange, Oracle, Polaroid Corporation, Raytheon, Stratus Computer, The Boston Globe, Westinghouse, and Ziff-Davis Publishing Company.

These customers are accustomed to excellent service from their communications providers. BBN Planet provides dedicated leased-line connections from their premises to its nationwide access network, and it provides 24-hour, 7-day-a-week, end-to-end monitoring and problem resolution.

The company currently consists of four operating units: BBN Systems and Technologies Division, BBN Domain, BBN Planet, and BBN

BBN CORPORATION

Chief Executive Officer:	George H. Conrades
Principal Location:	150 Cambridge Park Dr. Cambridge, MA 02140
Telephone:	617-873-2000
Fax:	617-873-6023
E-mail:	not available
Web site:	not available
Satellite Locations:	Australia, China, France, Germany, Italy, Japan, The Netherlands, Singapore, United Kingdom, and many cities in the United States
Date Founded:	1950
Description of Business:	Fourth-largest Internet-service provider and manufacturer of software and hardware products that facilitate remote computing.
# Employees Current:	1,700
% Female Employees:	not available
# Employees Projected 9/30/96:	not available
Revenues 1995*:	$224,414,000
Gross Profit Margin (GPM):	64.5%
SGA Expenses/Revenues:	37.0%
% Sales Increase 1993 to 1996:	(3.9%)**
% Change GPM 1993 to 1996:	+1.4%
% Change SGA Expenses/Revenues 1993 to 1996:	+37.5%
Total Debt/Net Worth:	190.8%
Net Profits Before Taxes 1996*:	($36,864,000)
Net Profits Before Taxes/Revenues:	deficit
Market Value/1995 Revenues*:	3.4x
Traded On:	NYSE (BBN)
Opportunity the Company Addresses:	It is inevitable that the major long-distance telephone carriers will get into the Internet market.
Elegance of Company's Solution:	BBN was tapped on the shoulder by AT&T and asked to dance the Internet two-step.

*Annualized
**The company sold its LightStream subsidiary to CISCO Systems, Inc.

HARK Systems. The BBN Systems and Technologies Division includes Internet-working services and products, and collaborative systems and acoustic technologies for both the government and commercial markets. BBN Domain focuses its business on networked data analysis and process optimization software products for pharmaceutical and manufacturing applications. BBN HARK is an early-stage company that develops and markets commercial speech recognition software products.

A significant portion of BBN's revenue is derived from its business with the U.S. government and its agencies, particularly the Department of Defense (DOD). BBN provides network systems and services to the DOD, including the Defense Data Network, a common-user data network servicing the DOD.

BBN currently loses money and has been losing money at the operating level for a number of years. Being a DOD vendor hasn't been a good place to be since Perestroika. The company is segueing into Internet services and has more than $100 million of deployable cash available to it. At a market to revenues ratio of 3.4x, BBN is the least expensive investment opportunity in the market. The question remains: Can BBN think like the consumer of its services and take business from UUNet, PSINet, NetCom, and its other competitors?

BEST INTERNET COMMUNICATIONS, INC.

Best Internet Communications, Inc., incorporated under the laws of the state of California in November 1994, is a rapidly emerging Internet Access Provider currently serving the San Francisco Bay Area. The company has 50 employees and a high-quality and low-latency Wide Area Network (WAN) that services a 100-mile radius with local toll-free access from the company's headquarters in Mountain View, California.

Best has fiber-optic lines from Pacific Bell (PacBell) and Metropolitan Fiber Systems (MFS) and is capable of offering all of PacBell's Intra-LATA services and MFS's national and international connectivity options to its customers. Best also has a T3 connection to MAE-West, a West Coast peering point where large WANs touch and exchange data directly.

Best services corporate clientele. There is less pressure on price and more demand for bandwidth and high-quality linkups in the corporate niche. As testament to its high-quality lines, the company has attracted more Web site domains in the last several months than any competitor.

Best presently operates nine points of presence, or POPs, and it intends to expand by creating new POPs in regions east of its present market and contiguous to existing POPs, by acquisition or de novo expansion. The company has the opportunity to acquire four ISPs with 18 POPs ranging from Orange County, California, to Tigard, Oregon.

The Internet has an estimated 37 million users and it is projected by International Data Corp., and others, that it will grow to 200 million worldwide by the turn of the century. The commercial part of the Internet—the World Wide Web (WWW)—offers "frictionless capitalism" to buyers and sellers. The advantages to buyers on the WWW include low search cost, low transaction cost (i.e., a local phone call), considerable product information easily accessible and payment by credit card, followed by product delivery. The advantages to the seller include maintenance of less inventory, lower advertising costs, ease of locating prospects, lower market research costs, and rapid modification of the Web site (or infomercial) to be more responsive to the demographics of prospective customers who visit the Web site.

The commercial reasons for providers and consumers moving to the WWW are considerable, but they are only a portion of the factors driving Internet usage. The many other reasons include lower cost long-distance communications, user-friendliness, and communications system at your

BEST INTERNET COMMUNICATIONS, INC.

Chief Exec. Officer:	Alan D. Mutter
Principal Location:	345 E. Middlefield Rd. Mountain View, CA 94043
Telephone:	415-964-2378
Fax:	415-940-6464
E-mail:	buzby@best.com
Web site:	http://www.info@best.com
Satellite Locations:	none
Date Founded:	1994
Description of Business:	A value-added Internet service provider.
# Employees Current:	50
% Female Employees:	15%
# Employees Projected 9/30/96:	100
Revenues 1995*:	$7,500,000
Gross Profit Margin (GPM):	The company is privately held and is not required to publish its financial statements.
SGA Expenses/Revenues:	not available
% Sales Increase 1992 to 1995:	not available
% Change GPM 1992 to 1995:	not available
% Change SGA Expenses/Revenues 1992 to 1995:	not available
Total Debt/Net Worth:	not available
Net Profits Before Taxes 1995*:	not available
Net Profits Before Taxes/Revenues:	not available
Market Value/1995 Revenues*:	not available
Opportunity Company Addresses:	Getting a busy signal when you dial your Internet Service Provider can be frustrating and costly.
Elegance of the Company's Solution:	Best has architected its backbone in a manner that guarantees immediate access to the Net. The company has attracted more Web site domains in 1995 than any of its competitors.

*Annualized.

fingertips (for PC users), and enhanced collaboration with co-workers; ease of checking incoming calls or faxes when traveling; moving files from one office to another; placing a classified advertisement inexpensively; and publishing a poem, short story, book, record album, or movie. For these and other reasons, the Internet is expected to become one of the two or three largest communications and entertainment channels in the world. It will need service providers that offer exceptional service.

Alan Mutter was brought in to Best by the company's board of directors because he had built a cable TV station conglomerate via multiple acquisitions to revenues of $200 million. Mutter's goal is to consolidate the Internet service provider industry via acquisition of the best of breed in each of two doze markets. Mutter brings a newspaperman's experience to the Internet market. He was senior editor of the *San Francisco Chronicle* before entering the cable TV busines. One of Best's early investors, Robert Leppo, is a founding investor of another Quantum Company, Information America. Can lightning strike twice for Leppo?

BROADBAND TECHNOLOGIES, INC.

I f the Internet has a defect, it's that the pipe isn't very wide. Video cannot be sent down twisted pairs of copper wire, the primary conduit of information into the home. AT&T is betting on switched digital video (SDV), a technology developed by Broadband Technologies, Inc. The Telecommunications Act of 1995 deregulates the communications industry and permits long-line carriers such as MCI, Sprint, and AT&T to offer local services. A free-for-all is about to occur—musical chairs with elephants tiptoeing around gnats such as the Internet access providers and SDV developers.

Who will win? Does the consumer want to shop and see unlimited sports events on cable TV (the Sprint venture with TeleCommunications and Comcast Cox), on their personal computers (CompuServe's strategic alliance with Xing), or on a new AT&T box—the SDV play? Most of us cannot imagine multiple video-on-demand and interactive services. Is it VHS vs. Beta all over again? You bet it is. Good luck to the runners. On your mark, get set, go . . . !

Here is how SDV works. The heart of the platform comprises two elements—the Host Digital Terminal (HDT) and the Optical Network Unit (ONU). These elements integrate the proven digital video transport capabilities of BroadBand Technologies' GLX System with the wide range of capabilities of AT&T's SLC-2000 Access System. This product delivers the full spectrum of information/communication services including interactive video and multimedia services. These service capabilities enable the access-network operator to differentiate itself and surpass the competition in breadth of service and ease of use.

The baseband architecture of the SLC-2000 Access System with GLX SDV brings a fiber-optic network closer than ever to the end-user. The key elements in this architecture are the HDT, housed in a central location as far as 36 kilofeet away from the subscriber, and the ONU, connected by fiber optics to the HDT, and placed at or near the end-user's location. These elements combine to deliver a full range of switched telephony services, as well as broadcast and interactive video services. To provide these services, the system has interfaces to the digital head-end, the analog head-end, and the telephony system.

The digital head-end receives compressed digital signals in the form of Asynchronous Transfer Mode (ATM) cells at the AT&T GlobeView™-2000 Switch. The service-independent ATM format will handle any standard. The system complies with existing standards including

BROADBAND TECHNOLOGIES, INC.

Chief Executive Officer:	Salem A.L. Bhatia
Principal Location:	Two Park Center 3908 Patriot Dr. Research Triangle Park, NC 27709-3737
Telephone:	919-544-0015
Fax:	919-544-3459
E-mail:	not available
Web site:	not available
Satellite Locations:	none
Date Founded:	1988
Description of Business:	Leader in the fields of broadband digital technology and fiber-in-the-loop transmission systems.
# Employees Current:	296
% Female Employees:	25%
# Employees Projected 9/30/96:	380
Revenues 1995*:	$20,383,000
Gross Profit Margin (GPM):	(10.0%)
SGA Expenses/Revenues:	57.6%
% Sales Increase 1992 to 1995:	+381.5%
% Change GPM 1992 to 1995:	0.0%
% Change SGA Expenses/Revenues 1992 to 1995:	(49.2%)
Total Debt/Net Worth:	0.0%
Net Profits Before Taxes 1995*:	($28,000,000)
Net Profits Before Taxes/Revenues:	not available
Market Value/1995 Revenues*:	17.0x
Traded On:	NASDAQ (BBTK)
Opportunity Company Addresses:	AT&T and U.S. West are betting on switched digital video as the de facto standard to bring interactive services into the home.
Elegance of Company's Solution:	Broadband has developed the technology that its large partners believe will compete with the Internet.

*Annualized.

MPEG1 and MPEG2, along with future standards like digital HDTV. The ATM switch then maps encoded programming onto a SONET-compliant signal for downstream transport to the HDT. The HDT and ATM edge switch route the programming out to the appropriate ONU close to the customer. From there, the video programming goes directly over twisted pair and coax cable drops into the house wiring to a set-top box. The ATM cells continue all the way to the user's TV set-top, PC, or integrated appliance. The result is the flexibility of ATM to the customer providing bandwidth-on-demand for multiple services.

This same infrastructure transmits the subscriber's upstream signal to select and order programming, to order and pay for merchandise, to communicate each player's moves in video game applications, and to respond to other interactive situations. The use of ATM transport for upstream communication provides for a very flexible and powerful network. In words of one syllable, if SDV becomes the de facto standard communications system in our homes and offices, then Broadband Technologies' stock price will soar like the eagles.

CABLETRON SYSTEMS, INC.

Founded in 1984, Cabletron has experienced tremendous growth and success in a highly competitive industry. This upward spiral is even more remarkable when you consider the company's modest beginning.

Robert Levine and Craig Benson began their small yet ambitious operation out of a tiny garage in Ashland, Massachusetts, selling Ethernet cable and accessories to the computer industry. Both men soon realized that there was an untapped, unlimited market for Local Area Network (LAN) products. With that in mind, they moved their business to a textile mill in Rochester, New Hampshire, where they were able to broaden and diversify their product line to meet the increasing demands of LAN users. Once settled into its new surroundings, Cabletron quickly established itself as a driving force in networking, first on a national level and then on a global scale.

Still headquartered in Rochester, Cabletron has six manufacturing sites, four research and development facilities, and sixty-nine regional offices worldwide. Of its more than 53,000 customers, more than eighty are Fortune 100 companies and many more are Fortune 500 companies. Cabletron's products are being used in virtually every work environment, from insurance and financial institutions to federal and state agencies to industrial and manufacturing companies and academic institutions.

Cabletron dukes it out with rugged competitors such as Bay Networks, Cascade Communications, CISCO Systems, Newbridge Networks, 3 Com—Quantum Companies all—and others.

Cabletron's p/e ratio and market value to revenues ratios are relatively low in relation to its competitors, as can be seen below.

Computer Networking

Equipment Manufacturers	Trailing p/e ratio	Market Value to Revenues
Bay Networks	43.2x	4.5x
Cabletron Systems	21.7	3.1
Cascade Communications	96.0	14.4
CISCO Systems	43.2	10.4
Newbridge Networks	12.9	4.1
3 Com	45.3	4.2
6-Company Average (a)	43.7x	6.8x

(a) Source: *Red Herring*, Technology Digest, November, 1995, p. 118.

CABLETRON SYSTEMS, INC.

Chief Executive Officer:	S. Robert Levine
Principal Location:	35 Industrial Way Rochester, NH 03867-0505
Telephone:	603-332-9400
Fax:	603-332-8007
E-mail:	sales@ctron.com
Web site:	not available
Satellite Locations:	Sales offices throughout the United States, Europe, Latin America, the Middle East, and the Pacific Rim
Date Founded:	1983
Description of Business:	Develops, manufactures, markets, and supports a line of standards-based LAN and WAN connectivity hardware and software.
# Employees Current:	4,456
% Female Employees:	36%
# Employees Projected 9/30/96:	not available
Revenues 1995*:	$870,800,000
Gross Profit Margin (GPM):	59.3% SGA Expenses/Revenues: 19.5%
% Sales Increase 1992 to 1995:	+199.8%
% Change GPM 1992 to 1995:	+.01%
% Change SGA Expenses/Revenues 1992 to 1995:	(1.0%)
Total Debt/Net Worth:	14.8%
Net Profits Before Taxes 1995*:	$266,100,000
Net Profits Before Taxes/Revenues:	30.6%
Market Value/1995 Revenues*:	3.1x
Traded On:	NYSE (CS)
Opportunity Company Addresses:	There are myriad computers and operating systems within an organization that need to cooperate with each other.
Elegance of Company's Solution:	The company's multiprotocol routers permit disparate computers to interconnect.

* Annualized.

The company is significantly undervalued relative to its competitors, notwithstanding its stunning operating ratios, including a 30.6 percent operating ratio, rising GPM, falling SGA Expenses/Revenues ratio, and minuscule (14.8 percent) debt-to-worth ratio.

Cabletron and its competitors have the most impact on the network infrastructure market, and they whip each others' hip and thigh to define their product lines as the most novel and leading edge. Cabletron can offer virtual LAN support and highly manageable support, all of it flexible and proprietary, as well as the widest backbone, deployable from the desktop to the WAN, which can fit it into many existing client/server systems.

If Bay Networks buys Xylogics and Cabletron is shut out from a source of supply for remote access devices, it may have to do some scurrying about for an alternative source, such as Netmatics, Inc., but that problem appears solvable. With an SGA Expenses/Revenues ratio of 19.5 percent, relatively low for a competitive market, Cabletron does not have a bitch of a time selling product. A fair amount of it is done by word of mouth. This is a beautifully managed company with an elegant product line.

CASCADE COMMUNICATIONS CORP.

Data communications is generally accomplished by organizing digitally encoded information into packets of "frames" or "cells." Frames consist of three parts: a header that identifies the sender, the destination, the type of information contained in the frame, and the size of the frame; the actual information; and a trailer indicating the end of the frame. The term "cell" refers to a specialized form of frame that has fixed length. Fixed-length cells can be switched faster than variable-length frames. Frame Relay, SMDS DXI, and ATM DXI are frame-based services; SMDS and ATM are cell-based services.

Packet-based data communications technologies are further subdivided between connection-oriented services, which are similar to telephone services in that a connection between end points must occur prior to the transmission of information, and connectionless services, which are similar to courier services in that information is addressed and transmitted without a preestablished path.

Public carriers, including Regional Bell Operating Companies (RBOCs), Interexchange Carriers (IXCs), Local Exchange Carriers (LECs), cable, TV operators, and wireless networks, are actively competing to deliver data communications services. And why not! The market for data communications services is growing at more than 50 percent per year, according to International Data Corporation, and is more than $1 billion in size currently. The trend is catalyzed by a downsizing from centralized mainframes to standards-based distributed networks linked with PCs.

Cascade has pioneered the concept of utilizing a single, powerful switching platform designed to support simultaneously the major high-speed packet data communications services: Frame Relay, SMDS, and ATM. Cascade's multiservice, standards-based products enable network providers to select the transmission services with the cost and performance attributes that best fit the end-user's requirements, without requiring network providers to build multiple specialized data networks. Cascade's family of switch products can be displayed in a wide variety of configurations to suit customers' specific needs for capacity, functionality, and cost-effectiveness.

When reflecting upon Cascade Communications, think of a football player who plays 60 minutes of every game as both an offensive and a defensive player. Cascade's switches serve the explosive Internet industry and the private network (WAN) market on a single platform. A user of a

CASCADE COMMUNICATIONS CORP.

Chief Executive Officer:	Daniel E. Smith
Principal Location:	5 Carlisle Rd. Westford, MA 01886
Telephone:	508-692-2600
Fax:	508-692-5052
E-mail:	mktg@case.com
Web site:	http://www.case.com
Satellite Locations:	none
Date Founded:	1990
Description of Business:	Designs, develops, manufactures, markets, and supports a family of high-performance, multiservice WAN switches.
# Employees Current:	384
% Female Employees:	84%
# Employees Projected 9/30/96:	600
Revenues 1995*:	$71,047,000
Gross Profit Margin (GPM):	62.8%
SGA Expenses/Revenues:	23.9%
% Sales Increase 1992 to 1995:	+870.7%
% Change GPM 1992 to 1995:	+75.9%
% Change SGA Expenses/Revenues 1992 to 1995:	(89%)
Total Debt/Net Worth:	27.9%
Net Profits Before Taxes 1995*:	$18,441,000
Net Profits Before Taxes/Revenues:	26%
Market Value/1995 Revenues*:	33.2x
Traded On:	NASDAQ (CSCC)
Opportunity Company Addresses:	Traditional switched WAN architectures, optimized for voice, are not well-suited for high-through-put data communications.
Elegance of Company's Solution:	Packet-switched networks permit capacity to be allocated where required, thus improving utilization and performance.

*Annualized.

private network can migrate seamlessly to the Internet. The company's technology is considered so vital that Quantum Company CISCO Systems not only entered into a joint marketing agreement with Cascade in December 1993, but it licensed source code to the company for development and support of symbiotic products. CISCO Systems is an early investor in the company's common stock as well.

Cascade is one of the fastest-growing companies in the Quantum 200. Since 1992, it has grown eight-fold whiles its GPM improved nearly 76 percent and its SGA Expenses/Revenues ratio declined 89 percent. Cascade spends a mere 15 cents of every sales dollar on sales. Its products are the Deion Sanders of the remote-computing market, and the company is destined for continued growth.

CEPHALON, INC.

I t was on the Internet on June 12, 1995, that victims of amyotrophic lateral sclerosis (ALS, or Lou Gehrig's disease) learned that 266 ALS patients who received Myotrophin (recombinant human insulin-like growth factor-1, or rhIGF-1) in a Phase III study experienced less disease severity, slower progression of disease, and better functional ability compared to patients who received a placebo. The effects from Myotrophin administration were dose-related and consistent across primary and secondary measures, and benefits of Myotrophin were evident as early as the first few months of drug therapy.

People with terminal illnesses discuss therapies and other common issues on chat lines. If a victim of a broadly infectious disease treated it successfully by ingesting a mixture of vinegar and shoe polish, others would be experimenting with that concoction within the hour. And so it was with Myotrophin.

"Demand pull" the economists call it. Cephalon, the developer, was saved the expense of creating product awareness—a task usually assigned to advertising—courtesy of the Internet. ALS is a fatal neuromuscular disease characterized by the chronic, progressive degeneration of motor neurons. The term amyotrophic refers to muscle wasting or atrophy; lateral sclerosis refers to the scarring or degeneration of motor neurons that project from the lateral columns of the spinal cord to muscle tissue. It is the loss of these motor neurons that leads to muscle weakness, muscle atrophy, and eventually death from respiratory failure.

There are several heroes in this profile. Lou Gehrig played in 5,200 consecutive games and batted .300 over a fifteen-year career. He fell down rounding first base several times toward the end of his career. It is believed that he may have played more than twenty years had he not had ALS.

IGF-1 is a naturally occurring protein found in muscle and other tissue, which mediates regeneration of the peripheral nervous system and its recovery from injury. In preclinical studies, IGF-1 has been shown to support the survival of motor neurons and accelerate the regeneration of damaged motor neurons. Preclinical studies have also shown that IGF-1 promotes sprouting and function of peripheral nerves and induces skeletal muscle hypertrophy, or enlargement of muscle cells, in the presence of neurodegenerative conditions. Neuronal sprouting is the natural process by which neurons generate additional branches,

CEPHALON, INC.

Chief Executive Officer	Frank Baldino Jr., Ph.D.
Principal Location:	145 Brandywine West Chester, PA 19380
Telephone:	610-344-0200
Fax:	610-344-0065
E-mail:	not available
Web site:	not available
Satellite Locations:	Beltsville, Maryland, and Guilford, United Kingdom
Date Founded:	1987
Description of Business:	Researches, develops, and markets products to treat neurological disorders.
# Employees Current:	325
% Female Employees:	45%
# Employees Projected 9/30/96:	not available
Revenues 1995*:	$28,675,000
Gross Profit Margin (GPM):	not available
SGA Expenses/Revenues:	not available
% Sales Increase 1992 to 1995:	+316.7%
% Change GPM 1992 to 1995:	not available
% Change SGA Expenses/Revenues 1992 to 1995:	not available
Total Debt/Net Worth:	46.1%
Net Profits Before Taxes '95*:	($38,601,000)
Net Profits Before Taxes/Revenues:	deficit
Market Value/1995 Revenues*:	not available
Traded On:	NASDAQ (CEPH)
Opportunity Company Addresses:	An estimated 60,000 victims of Lou Gehrig's disease worldwide watch their bodies deteriorate while their minds remain intact.
Elegance of Company's Solution:	Cephalon is developing neurotrophic factors that may treat neurodegenerative diseases of the peripheral nervous system.

*Annualized.

enabling them to establish functional contacts with muscle fibers whose original nerve contacts have been lost as a result of neuronal death. These multiple actions of IGF-1 may explain the effects of Myotrophin demonstrated in this Phase III study.

Cephalon was founded in 1987 by Frank Baldino Jr., with the venture capital backing of Bill Egan of BEDCO, to discover and develop drugs for treating neurological disorders. The company's specific focus during its initial years was on neurodegenerative disorders—conditions caused by the progressive death of cells in the nervous system. Such conditions include Alzheimer's disease, Lou Gehrig's disease, Parkinson's disease, and stroke. Although neuroscientists have obtained detailed pictures of the cell death patterns associated with neurodegenerative diseases, the causes of neuronal cell death are not well understood, and the development of new treatments is grounded in apparently reasonable theories supported by relatively thin preclinical data. Thus, the risks associated with Phase III trials may be higher than for drugs designed to treat better-understood diseases.

In addition to its success with Myotrophin, Cephalon also has active programs to develop small-molecule variants of Myotrophin, an Alzheimer's disease program with Schering-Plough, a stroke project based on small-molecule research, candidates for head and spinal trauma, and a program to develop other recombinant-growth factors. Although several of these projects have evolved or been dropped, the company has retained a consistent product development focus.

Baldino and his team decided to offset the inherent risks of its ALS/Myotrophin endeavor and the early stage of its work in neurotrophic drug development. As a partial solution, the company in-licensed two products, Stadol NS and Modafinil. Stadol is a Bristol-Myers Squibb drug that is approved in the United States for acute pain. Cephalon has obtained rights to co-promote Stadol NS to neurologists. The revenues from Stadol sales are not sufficient to buoy Cephalon into profitability, but the sales effort is establishing the Cephalon name among neurologists. Cephalon has also acquired the U.S. rights to Modafinil—a drug to treat narcolepsy—from Laboratoire L. Lafon, a midsize French company, and is running major Phase III trials on the drug.

In January 1996 the U.S. Food and Drug Administration (FDA) put a roadblock in front of Cephalon's plans to expand patient tests of Myotrophin. Relying on European test results which showed that patients using the drug died at twice the rate of patients taking a placebo, the FDA expressed concern. Baldino said the European test results were not statistically significant. The debate will rage for months. Meantime, Cephalon's market value plunged by one third.

CHEYENNE SOFTWARE, INC.

You can count on the fingers of one hand the number of companies that have achieved initial public offerings as start-ups and then gone on to become successful. Cheyenne Software is one of the unique species to raise its launch capital from the public before its business plan was written. Today it sits on top of approximately $125 million in tangible net worth, of which more than $40 million is in cash and short-term investments.

Cheyenne's launch plan was to develop software products under OEM agreements and live off of the upfront payments and future royalty streams. Throughout the 1980s it wrote software for medical office management, hospitality, litigation support for attorneys, debt collection, and income tax preparation. No marketing skills were needed. The company was purely technology driven, living from contract to contract.

In 1990, Cheyenne discovered that it had developed a superior software product for the LAN market at just the point in time when corporations were installing LANs in droves. It elected to market its initial proprietary product, NetBack, through distributors and by hiring and training a captive sales force.

A year later, Cheyenne developed and launched what would become its flagship product—ARCserve—a backup utility for NetWare services, DOS, Windows, OS/2, UNIX, Macintosh, and Windows NT workstations, as well as database services. Sales shot up to $22.4 million for the company's fiscal year ended June 30, 1992. They have quadrupled in the three years since then.

Software is somewhat akin to the "hits" business. Software developers are like the artisans in Plato's cave, trying to determine who and what are casting the shadows on the wall of the cavern without being permitted to turn and see the shadow casters. They project the software needs of the next five years and try to develop elegant solutions to fill those needs. When they are unable to produce hit after hit, if their war chest is large enough, software companies acquire promising untested software products. Lately, that has been Cheyenne's route. It is seeking another ARCserve.

The company acquired Applied Programming Technologies, Inc., in 1993 to gain a skill set in network imaging technology. In 1994 it acquired Bit Software, Inc., to obtain entry into the group computing market with Bit's fax, data, and voice software packages. In 1995, the

CHEYENNE SOFTWARE, INC.

Chief Executive Officer:	ReiJane Huai
Principal Location:	3 Expressway Plaza Roslyn Heights, NY 11577
Telephone:	516-484-5110
Fax:	516-484-7106
E-mail:	hr@cheyenne.com
Web site:	http://www.cheyenne.com
Satellite Locations:	none
Date Founded:	1983
Description of Business:	Design, development, production, and marketing of software for local area networks (LANs) and wide area networks (WANs).
# Employees Current:	650
% Female Employees:	40%
# Employees Projected 9/30/96:	775
Revenues 1995*:	$112,034,000
Gross Profit Margin (GPM):	97.9%
SGA Expenses/Revenues:	32.8%
% Sales Increase 1992 to 1995:	+401.2%
% Change GPM 1992 to 1995:	+34.9%
% Change SGA Expenses/Revenues 1992 to 1995:	(19.6%)
Total Debt/Net Worth:	10.4%
Net Profits Before Taxes 1995*:	$49,156,000
Net Profits Before Taxes/Revenues:	29.8%
Market Value/1995 Revenues*:	7.1X
Traded On:	AMEX (CYE)
Opportunity Company Addresses:	Software developers are like the artisans in Plato's cave, trying to determine who and what are casting the shadows on the wall of the cavern without being permitted to turn and see the shadow casters. They project the software needs of the next five years and try to develop elegant solutions to fill those needs.
Elegance of Company's Solution:	With a large "war chest," Cheyenne is able to acquire promising, untested software products.

*Annualized.

company acquired the DataJET product line for its image-based, high-performance software-backup product for NetWare file servers.

Not straying too far from its chosen path of corporate LANs and WANs, Cheyenne doubled its sales force from 85 in 1993 to 153 in 1994 and to 650 in September 1995. Its sales outside the United States have grown from $620,000 in 1991 to $42 million in 1994.

Although the company's GPM increased more than 10 percent in the last four years to 97.9 percent, Cheyenne's ratio of selling expenses to sales is moving in an unattractive direction: from a tolerable 24.3 percent in 1994 to a worrisome 32.8 percent in 1995. That means that there is significantly more competition for the company's product, and selling it has become more of a challenge.

However, Cheyenne has an extremely strong and liquid balance sheet and its management knows how to make and consolidate acquisitions, as well as strategic alliances. Cheyenne will become a billion dollar (revenues) company by the end of the decade.

CIBER, INC.

W e park in driveways and drive on parkways. A similar kind of semantic confusion confronts senior management of thousands of companies when they encounter the words and phrases brought about by the Internet, LANs, WANs, and ATM. "Do we throw out what we've got? Can we integrate distributed information processing into our IBM System 36?" These are just two of the questions that CEOs are asking. Enter the systems integrator.

CIBER, Inc., is one of the nation's largest providers of computer-related information technology consulting and services. The company's nearly 1,500—and growing—employees help clients design, program, implement, maintain, and evolve custom-application software systems. From mainframe to micro-PC platforms, services are generally provided on-site to large corporate clients that have complex information processing requirements. CIBER also provides related advanced technology support to clients migrating to client/server, open system platforms, as well as outsourcing and technical training services. Business Information Technology, Inc. (BIT), a subsidiary of CIBER, is an implementor of packaged application Human Resource and Financial software systems.

CIBER serves clients, principally throughout the United States, through a network of branch offices. The company has demonstrated consistent growth in revenues, while its ratio of SGA Expenses/Revenues has declined. CIBER began in the oil patch, in the Houston/Denver marketplaces; fifteen years ago its customer-base was very heavily dominated by the auto and oil and gas industries. Today it is very much telecommunications oriented, with clients including AT&T, MCI, Sprint, GTE, and the Baby Bells—U.S. West and Ameritech.

The systems integrator industry is several billion dollars in size. The largest competitor in the industry segment has revenues of $300 million, and CIBER is at roughly $100 million and growing very rapidly.

CIBER recently announced its acquisition of Business Information Technology, Inc. (BIT), a private, California-based, system integration company specializing in human resource applications developed by PeopleSoft. Since then PeopleSoft has added financial packages and is in the process of including manufacturing and procurement modules. Gartner Group credits PeopleSoft with over 50 percent of the client/server human resources software market. PeopleSoft software is

CIBER, INC.

Chief Executive Officer:	Bob G. Stevenson
Principal Location:	1200 17th St. Denver, CO 80202
Telephone:	303-220-0100
Fax:	303-220-7100
E-mail:	not available
Web site:	not available
Satellite Locations:	Atlanta, Georgia; Buffalo, New York; Charlotte, North Carolina; Cleveland, Ohio; Dallas, Texas; Dearborn, Michigan; Edison, New Jersey; Houston, Texas; Kansas City, Missouri; Melbourne and Orlando, Florida; Phoenix, Arizona; Pittsburgh, Pennsylvania; Reston, Virginia; Rochester, New York; Sacramento, California; Tampa, Florida
Date Founded:	1974
Description of Business:	A leading systems integrator of computers to corporate America.
# Employees Current:	1,495
% Female Employees:	28.4%
# Employees Projected 9/30/96:	approx. 2,000
Revenues 1995*:	$109,069,000
Gross Profit Margin (GPM):	not available
SGA Expenses/Revenues:	19.5%
% Sales Increase 1992 to 1995:	+353.1%
% Change GPM 1992 to 1995:	not available
% Change SGA Expenses/Revenues 1992 to 1995:	(20.4%)
Total Debt/Net Worth:	45.3%
Net Profits Before Taxes 1995*:	$8,783,000
Net Profits Before Taxes/Revenues:	8.1%
Market Value/1995 Revenues*:	1.1x
Traded On:	NASDAQ (CIBR)
Opportunity Company Addresses:	The remote computing paradigm is evolving extremely fast and CEOs need help understanding what the changes mean to them.
Elegance of Company's Solution:	It's a good bet that CEOs will rely on well-known, highly regarded systems integrators to smooth the transition.
*Annualized.	

particularly well known for its ability to provide for international operations through multiple languages and automatic currency conversions.

BIT is very well positioned as a PeopleSoft implementation partner. Demand is strong and companies are having difficulty finding qualified assistance for PeopleSoft implementations. Further, PeopleSoft does not generally provide consulting support for implementations. Rather, they prefer to team with implementation providers, such as BIT, and are in fact a continuous source of client referrals.

BIT's current revenue run rate of $24 million annually resulted in a purchase price of approximately fifty cents per annual revenue dollar. CIBER got good value for the dollar.

The merger's primary leverage comes from an extension of CIBER's services. BIT is currently profitable and growing in a new services segment. CIBER will be able to leverage this activity through additional internal growth and future acquisitions. As a consequence, BIT will generate immediate bottom-line value for CIBER shareholders.

With revenues growing at about 80 percent per year and overhead falling 20.4 percent over the last four years, CIBER earned 8.1 percent on annualized 1995 sales of $110 million. The stock market values the company at a little more than 1.1x revenues. That seems low for a company so well positioned in so many markets.

CISCO SYSTEMS, INC.

Imagine that you wish to make a telephone call from New York to Los Angeles without paying the long distance cost. If you had the right kind of telephone and had enough patient friends across the country, you could call someone at the western edge of your local zone, who could call someone at the western limit of their local zone and patch you through, and so forth all across the country. This may be an impractical way to make a telephone call, but it is the method by which the Internet works. The friends at the edges of the zones are routers and servers, depending on traffic demands, and more than likely they are made by CISCO. Routers and servers are dedicated computers at the connection points.

The Internet has little physical substance. There is no central computer. Indeed, there is no center. The Internet is more like a spider's web. It uses the telephone networks as its hosts and lets them carry the cost. Thus, it is a virtual network running on top of a physical network in a frictionless manner. And, the cost to access a Los Angeles Web site from a New York computer is still a local phone call.

The Internet as it exists today, and its need for connectivity, were envisioned by a husband-and-wife team, Leonard Bozeck and Sandra Lerner, a decade ago. Bozeck was director of Stanford University's Computer Science computer facility. Lerner managed computer services for Stanford's Graduate School of Business. They conceived of a primitive multiprotocol internetwork to link disparate systems and networks spread across the university's campus. They combined bits and pieces of various hardware and software technologies to solve the thorny connectivity problems that confronted them.

Soon word of the fledgling internetwork capability spread to other universities and organizations. Sensing opportunity, the Stanford group led by Bozeck and Lerner founded CISCO in December 1984. It wasn't until 1986 that they left Stanford to run the business out of their living room in nearby Atherton. By year's end, the company introduced its first commercial network router.

Two years later, the need for routers became increasingly apparent and demand leapt ahead of supply. Bozeck and Lerner stepped aside as John Morgridge arrived to enable CISCO to capitalize on its opportunities and raise venture capital to build and sell product. By 1989, sales had reached $27 million. Sales grew to more than $1 billion five years later.

CISCO SYSTEMS, INC.

Chief Executive Officer:	John P. Morgridge
Principal Location:	170 West Tasman Dr. San Jose, CA 95134
Telephone:	408-526-4000
Fax:	408-526-4545
E-mail:	mthurber@cisco.com
Web site:	http://www.cisco.com
Satellite Locations:	24 U.S. locations plus Sydney, Australia; Paris, France; Toronto, Ontario; and Tokyo, Japan
Date Founded:	1984
Description of Business:	Designs, develops, manufactures, markets, and services highly reliable internet-working systems to enable its customers to build large-scale integrated computer networks and gain access to global as well as local networks.
# Employees Current:	4,408
% Female Employees:	not available
# Employees Projected 9/30/96:	not available
Revenues 1995*:	$1,718,000,000
Gross Profit Margin (GPM):	67.1%
SGA Expenses/Revenues:	21.2%
% Sales Increase 1992 to 1995:	+405.3%
% Change GPM 1992 to 1995:	-0-
% Change SGA Expenses/Revenues 1992 to 1995:	-0-
Total Debt/Net Worth:	26.8%
Net Profits Before Taxes 1995*:	$592,163,000
Net Profits Before Taxes/Revenues:	34.5%
Market Value/1995 Revenues*:	1.06x
Traded On:	NASDAQ (CSCO)
Opportunity Company Addresses:	The Internet operates on the telephone companies' lines, which were never built to handle multiple networks of computer-generated data, images, sound, music, and graphics.
Elegance of Company's Solution:	CISCO is the de facto standard for high-quality, reliable internet-working systems.

*Annualized.

Bozeck and Lerner left CISCO in the early 1990s. They gave a large percentage of their wealth to charitable and environmental causes. CISCO continues to serve its marketplace. Its GPM hasn't budged since 1992—remaining at a stalwart 67.1 percent of sales—evidence of strong demand. Its ratio of SGA Expenses/Revenues is the same in 1995 as it was in 1992: 21.2 percent. Routers as good as CISCO's are not hard to sell. Receivable turnover is 5.0x, about where it was in 1992, which means that customers must pay their bills in 73 days or they don't get shipped again.

The stock market gave CISCO a negligible P/E ratio of 48.0x in December 1995 and a paltry 1.06x market/revenue ratio. At a relatively small valuation of $1.8 billion, we can expect to see at least six Regional Bell operating companies (RBOCs) try to buy CISCO, to put them four-square in the Internet business, once the telecommunications industry's regulations are liberalized. Then, CISCO's valuation will be bid up to more than $3 billion in a takeover battle.

CLARIFY, INC.

Organizations and consumers today value service as an important distinguishing factor in the selection of products and the firms with which they choose to do business. At the same time, customers' overall expectations regarding service levels have increased, whether related to products or services. Companies in a variety of industries recognize that excellent service leads to customer loyalty. Businesses that can address service demands with fast, accurate responses and incorporate resulting customer input into future products can achieve a competitive advantage in their marketplaces.

Consumers are no longer satisfied with basic product information and warranty service. They expect value: 24-hour, 7-day-a-week priority service, guaranteed response times, and custom service contracts. At the same time, businesses are increasingly challenged to meet these demands as product offerings have become more complex, more products have become integrated with and dependent upon third-party products, and cost-reduction pressures have intensified. In addition, customer support can generate important information, including customer descriptions and usage, requested product enhancements, or new product or market opportunities. This information can be a valuable resource if it is quickly and easily available on an enterprise-wide basis. Businesses facing increasingly shortened product life cycles, and development cycles place a premium upon the ability to easily and cost-effectively retain, analyze, and use information acquired through interactions with customers.

Historically, businesses have used software applications developed by third-party vendors to automate and integrate certain business processes, such as accounting, manufacturing, and human resources. They have attempted to keep up with the demand for increased customer support by increasing staffing in telephone support and service technician organizations and creating internally developed systems to track customer issues. However, as businesses grow, customer-service demands increase and staffing often cannot keep up with customer demands. Furthermore, as customer service costs rise and companies move from providing free support to fee-based support, most internally developed systems are often not designed to track costs and manage customer service as a profit center.

Similarly, there is an increased need for internal support or "help desk" solutions to support increasingly large, geographically distributed

CLARIFY, INC.

Chief Executive Officer:	David A. Stamm
Principal Location:	2702 Orchard Pkwy. San Jose, CA 95134
Telephone:	408-428-2000
Fax:	408-428-0633
E-mail:	dstamm@clarify.com
Web site:	http://www.clarify.com
Satellite Locations:	none
Date Founded:	1990
Description of Business:	Leading provider of client/server application software for the customer-support market.
# Employees Current:	150
% Female Employees:	not available
# Employees Projected 9/30/96:	272
Revenues 1995*:	$17,607,000
Gross Profit Margin (GPM):	74.8%
SGA Expenses/Revenues:	40.9%
% Sales Increase 1992 to 1995:	+7622.0%
% Change GPM 1994 to 1995:	+2.6%
% Change SGA Expenses/Revenues 1993 to 1995:	(56.5%)
Total Debt/Net Worth:	24.1%
Net Profits Before Taxes 1995*:	$755,000 (9 months)
Net Profits Before Taxes/Revenues:	5.4%
Market Value/1995 Revenues*:	12.2x
Traded On:	NASDAQ (CLFY)
Opportunity Company Addresses:	Customers are more demanding than ever, and "help desks" at the end of 800-service phone numbers are swamped with requests.
Elegance of Company's Solution:	The company has developed servers that "learn" with each call for service and enable the enterprise to respond to the most complex customer requests for help.

*Annualized.

and technology-dependent organizations and to disseminate problem-solving information. The trend of combining hardware and software from multiple vendors greatly increases the complexity of management and support functions. By necessity, organizations are setting up internal help desks to identify the source of a problem and resolve it or work with the external support department of one or more product vendors. Like external customer support organizations, these internal help desks can consist of hundreds of employees responding to thousands of inquiries daily.

External customer support and internal help desk organizations have similar requirements for software solutions. Delivering customer support is a complex group activity requiring sophisticated software to track customer commitments, disseminate problem-solving information throughout a geographically dispersed organization, dispatch field engineers and manage their expense, control service inventory, and report on related costs on a real-time basis. Furthermore, because support has rapidly changing requirements, such as work-flow practices, terminology, and policies and procedures, solutions must be flexible and adaptable to accommodate the highly dynamic support environment. Increasingly, organizations need support and help desk solutions that serve the entire enterprise as opposed to discrete departmental solutions. In addition, many calls to support centers frequently relate to common usage problems or other common inquiries. To maximize response efficiency, it is important for support systems to have the capability to "learn" by accumulating and reusing previously developed responses to similar fact patterns rather than requiring experts to solve the same problems repeatedly.

Clarify has resolved this challenging paradigm by developing support systems that learn by accumulating and reusing previously developed responses to similar fact patterns. Thus, customer-service costs are reduced as the staff is saved the trouble of solving the same problems repeatedly. It has sold its Customer Support Management System (CSM) to customers as diverse as 3 Com (a Quantum Company), Amoco, GE Medical Systems, Norand, and Teradyne.

The company was founded by David A. Stamm, a co-founder of Daisy System Corp. He attracted $12.6 million of venture capital and had a first generation product in beta in 24 months. Sales have grown Homerically to $17.6 million, with a solid GPM of about 75 percent. The company's SGA Expenses/Revenues ratio has dropped from 94 percent in 1993 to 40.9 percent in 1995, a sure sign that word-of-mouth marketing is kicking in. Clarify is a well-named company, providing clear solutions to a large and growing need.

CMG INFORMATION SERVICES, INC.

In 1986 CMG Information Services, Inc., was formed through the acquisition of the College Marketing Group, Inc., which had been in operation since 1968. Since its origin, the company has expanded the breadth and depth of its product and service offerings to the direct marketing industry: completing and introducing the College List database in 1973; diversifying its mailing list product offerings in 1982 through the introduction of the Information Buyers List database; and introducing its Elementary/High School List database in 1992. In the course of creating and developing these databases and lists, the company also developed expertise in servicing and managing customer and prospect lists compiled by its clients, leading to the establishment of its ListLab and ListLine services in 1987 and 1989, respectively. In 1989, CMG also completed the acquisition of SalesLink, which provides fulfillment services including sales lead/inquiry management, product and literature fulfillment, and business-to-business telemarketing services.

In 1994, CMG formed a new subsidiary, BookLink Technologies, Inc., which develops software that provides online access to information electronically. BookLink has developed InternetWorks, a PC-based viewer/browser for the Internet, and is developing electronic libraries that could improve speed and accessibility to published information on the Internet by providing new and existing customers the opportunity to speed the delivery of published materials to their respective markets.

CMG recognizes revenue from the sale of mailing lists when the labels for a list order are produced for shipment. Each order is custom processed for the company's clients upon receipt of the request. Revenue from the company's services is recognized upon completion of the service. This is conservative accounting. Approximately 3,000 customers purchase CMG's products or services. For each of the last three years, approximately 80 percent of the company's net sales were provided by existing customers.

Before it was one year old, BookLink was acquired by America Online, Inc,, for 710,000 of its shares of common stock, a value of more than $47 million. With the proceeds of the sale of BookLink, CMG is making venture capital investments in the Internet industry through a new subsidiary, CMG@Ventures.

In June 1995 CMG@Ventures purchased the exclusive rights to the Lycos Spider Technology, source of the largest catalog of sites on the

CMG INFORMATION SERVICES, INC.

Chief Executive Officer:	David S. Wetherell
Principal Location:	187 Ballardvale St. Wilmington, MA 01887-7000
Telephone:	508-657-7000
Fax:	508-988-0046
E-mail:	cmgi.com
Web site:	http://www.lycos.com
Satellite Locations:	Chicago, Illinois
Date Founded:	1986
Description of Business:	Develops and markets mailing lists and other information-based products to publishers, mutual funds, and other direct mail marketers.
# Employees Current:	202
% Female Employees:	40.0%
# Employees Projected 9/30/96:	not available
Revenues 1995*:	$22,280,000
Gross Profit Margin (GPM):	44.8%
SGA Expenses/Revenues:	27.4%
% Sales Increase 1992 to 1995:	+55.9%
% Change GPM 1992 to 1995:	-0-
% Change SGA Expenses/Revenues 1992 to 1995:	-0-
Total Debt/Net Worth:	50.8%
Net Profits Before Taxes 1995*:	$8,048,000**
Net Profits Before Taxes/Revenues:	36.1%
Market Value/1995 Revenues*:	6.0x
Traded On:	NASDAQ (CMGI)
Opportunity Company Addresses:	In every new market, particularly fast moving ones like the Internet, road maps, flashlights, and yellow pages are desperately needed to measure demand.
Elegance of Company's Solution:	With deep experience in creating lists, CMG jumped in early as a Diogenes of the Internet.

*Annualized.
**Of which $4,781,250 is from sales of BookLink.

Internet, from Carnegie Mellon University, Pittsburgh, Pennsylvania. With nearly 3.5 million hits from an estimated 500,000 users per week, Lycos is the preeminent Internet catalog and one of the most popular sites on the World Wide Web.

"The Lycos catalog is built weekly by dozens of software robots, or agents, 'which we call spiders,'" explained its developer, Dr. Fuzzy Mauldin. "Each day these spiders roam the web, finding and downloading web pages, creating abstracts of those pages. Each week, the resulting lists of abstracts are merged, older versions are discarded, and the new catalog is distributed to 11 Lycos servers, as well as the licensees."

Lycos, Inc., will offer advertising space on its site and will also license key technology components. With the number of users visiting the site growing rapidly, Lycos is one of the premier advertising locations on the Web; it plans to develop a number of other related products and services all built on the Lycos catalog.

Catalog and search technology is key to the growth of the Internet. "Anything on the Lycos home page will be seen by hundreds of thousands of Internet users a week," said Dave Wetherell, @Ventures' managing partner and CEO of CMG Information Services. "There is no better way to publicize the products and services of our other investments."

Subsequent ventures investments of CMG appear less stellar than Lycos but include the acquisition of Nice Technologies, Inc., a Web site design and management firm (i.e., an advertising agency for Internet advertisers); an investment in Product View Interactive, which also creates ads for the Internet; an investment in Ikonic Interactive, Inc., a software developer that intends to make tools to update large volumes of multimedia content; and an investment in Black Sun Interactive, Inc., which is developing tools that allow Internet users to interact with one another in three dimensions. Will CMG be able to pull off another BookLink? Or will its best investment be its first? Buy the stock if you think the best is yet to come.

COMPUTER HORIZONS CORP.

In analyzing this systems integrator, I am reminded of President Harry S. Truman's plea for a one-handed economist. "They're forever saying on the one hand, and on the other hand," said Truman. Computer Horizons meets all of the key financial ratios that warrant inclusion as a Quantum Company save one. Its accounts receivable days are growing rather than shrinking. While on the other hand, in light of the dynamic growth of the information technology industry, the company's sales are growing relatively slowly and its bottom line profitability is a relatively small 7.9 percent of sales. It would seem that the price of integrating client/server systems for clients such as Eli Lilly, RR Donnelly, AT&T, and Florida Power & Light should warrant the healthier margins of other systems integrators in *Quantum Companies II*. The stock market keeps the p/e ratio on Computer Horizons pretty close to 20.0x, or in the vicinity of its annual sales growth rate.

With the technical ability of corporations to define themselves anew in a plethora of cyber-identities has also come the common understanding that intellectual ability is needed to make the conversions. Systems integrators such as Computer Horizons possess the intellect to advise the iron-hugging giant computer-users on how to reengineer themselves on a path of internet-working key information hubs.

The growth in the company's revenues is coming primarily from a strong demand for contract programming personnel and rapid growth in its value-added information technology solutions in such areas as mainframe applications reengineering, client/server development and migration, and outsourcing of such functions as applications development, maintenance and network, and facility management.

With 75 percent of its revenues from contract programming services, providing skilled software development professionals to supplement the internal information technology staffs of its customers remains Computer Horizon's core business. The company is committed to expanding this business in order to leverage its branch marketing and recruiting infrastructure. (It has 33 branch offices throughout the United States.) In addition, through its professional services operation, Computer Horizons builds relationships with information technology management and an understanding of its customers' information technology operations, a factor which aids Computer Horizons in marketing its solutions services to its client base. The company has

COMPUTER HORIZONS CORP.

Chief Executive Officer:	John J. Cassese
Principal Location:	49 Old Bloomfield Ave. Mountain Lakes, NJ 07046
Telephone:	201-402-7400
Fax:	201-402-7985
E-mail:	not available
Web site:	not available
Satellite Locations:	Cincinnati, Ohio; Detroit, Michigan; Clark, New Jersey; and 30 other locations in the United States
Date Founded:	1969
Description of Business:	A leading systems integrator that assists clients with their computer system innovations and upgrades.
# Employees Current:	2,150
% Female Employees:	not available
# Employees Projected 9/30/96:	not available
Revenues 1995*:	$187,338,000
Gross Profit Margin (GPM):	29.4%
SGA Expenses/Revenues:	21.3%
% Sales Increase 1992 to 1995:	+183.3%
% Change GPM 1992 to 1995:	+6.9%
% Change SGA Expenses/Revenues 1992 to 1995:	(4.1%)
Total Debt/Net Worth:	64.3%
Net Profits Before Taxes 1995*:	$14,787,000
Net Profits Before Taxes/Revenues:	7.9%
Market Value/1995 Revenues*:	84.7%
Traded On:	NASDAQ (CHRZ)
Opportunity Company Addresses:	In the land of the blind, the one- eyed man is king. The task of integrating client/server systems into corporations that operate on mainframes falls to systems integrators.
Elegance of Company's Solution:	Computer Horizons solves information-technology problems for large corporations that are overwhelmed with the prospect of replacing big obsolete iron with smaller, faster, and more efficient client/servers.

*Annualized.

generated significant loyalty from its clients, with more than 90 percent of its revenues in 1995 derived from customers with which it did business in the prior year.

An extremely important strategic move in 1995 was the company's 50/50 joint venture with the Birla Group of India, one of that country's largest companies. The joint venture, Birla Horizons International, will allow Computer Horizons clients to take advantage of the lower cost of technical talent in India for applications maintenance, program design, and coding. The joint venture maintains a state-of-the-art software "factory" in India. Birla Horizons also can provide technical resources to Computer Horizons in the United States, where appropriate, to meet a customer's needs.

Now, if the company could leap tall buildings like its Quantum Companies competitors Cambridge Technology Partners or Gartner Group, Inc., its stock would double in a flash.

CUC INTERNATIONAL, INC.

UC has slowly and carefully built a membership services company over 30-plus years (its market value is roughly equal to that of Quantum Company Netscape), and along came the Internet. Talk about being in the right place at the right time! What Internet service provider or online service company would not like to tap into CUC's 40 million members? Knowing CEO Walter Forbes' tenacity and intelligence, look to him to acquire and joint-venture his way onto the Internet, while adding high-income, frequent shopping members.

Recognizing the growing strategic importance of the Internet, CUC acquired NetMarket Company in early 1995, an Internet software and marketing company, which processed the first secure transaction through the Internet. Notably, in 1995 CUC launched its core shopping service on the Internet. It is the largest online "store," including access to a vendor information database containing more than 250,000 brand name products and an extensive customer service and support operation with more than 4,000 highly trained customer service representatives.

CUC's long-term strategy is to become the preeminent provider of quality content and back-end fulfillment services, irrespective of the platform, i.e., through catalogs, telephones, PCs (commercial online, Internet), and cable TV. Today, CUC has more than 185,000 members who gain access to its core products and services on an interactive basis from their PCs, primarily through online networks such as America Online and CompuServe. While currently only a fraction of CUC's total base of members, this channel could lead to a significant ramp up in the company's membership base, particularly with CUC's recent launch on the Web. CUC is destined to become a major shopkeeper on the Web.

CUC is expanding abroad with the acquisition of Advance Ross Corporation, whose primary business is the operation of a value-added tax (VAT) refund system serving travelers shopping in Europe. This business is conducted through Advance Ross's wholly owned subsidiary, Europe Tax-free Shopping AB (ETS), and operates under the log "Tax-free for Tourists." ETS is the largest VAT-refund service in Europe.

The VAT is a vital component of the tax policy of most European (and many other) countries. ETS's business is based upon serving travelers by making purchases less expensive through ETS's convenient, efficient, and reliable VAT refunds and serving retailers by promoting the benefits of tax-free shopping, thereby relieving the retailers' administrative burden. ETS has established affiliations with over 90,000 retail outlets in

CUC INTERNATIONAL, INC.

Chief Executive Officer:	Walter A. Forbes
Principal Location:	707 Summer St. Stamford, CT 06904-2049
Telephone:	203-324-9261
Fax:	203-977-8501
E-mail:	not available
Web site:	not available
Satellite Locations:	Brentwood, Tennessee; San Carlos, California; and Troy, Michigan
Date Founded:	1969
Description of Business:	A leading membership services company providing 40 million consumers with access to a variety of services including home shopping, travel, insurance, auto, dining, and discount coupon programs.
# Employees Current:	9,981
% Female Employees:	not available
# Employees Projected 9/30/96:	not available
Revenues 1995*:	$1,261,700,000
Gross Profit Margin (GPM) 1995:	73.1%
SGA Expenses/Revenues 1995:	45.6%
% Sales Increase 1992 to 1995:	+170.8%
% Change GPM 1992 to 1995:	(.5%)
% Change SGA Expenses/Revenues 1992 to 1995:	(22.7%)
Total Debt/Net Worth:	28.9%
Net Profits Before Taxes 1995*:	$239,000,000
Net Profits Before Taxes/Revenues:	18.9%
Market Value/1995 Revenues*:	4.8x
Traded On:	NYSE (CU)
Opportunity Company Addresses:	In numbers there is strength, and Americans like to join associations and groups because membership has its privileges.
Elegance of Company's Solution:	Relatively few companies have seized the need of people to join associations as well and as thoroughly as has CUC.

*Annualized.

17 European countries. The retailers display ETS logos and flags, which promote the opportunity for tax-free shopping and identify the stores using the ETS system for VAT refunds.

When a traveler eligible for a VAT refund makes a purchase, his or her payment includes VAT. At an ETS-affiliated retailer, the traveler receives at the time of purchase an ETS Tax-free Shopping Cheque for the amount of the refund, which is the VAT on the sales amount less the ETS service charge. The salesperson then informs the traveler how to cash the cheque. On the traveler's departure from the country with the goods, the Tax-free Shopping Cheque is stamped by Customs, certifying the purchase as export goods. The traveler then goes to the nearby ETS refund point and cashes the cheque.

Advance Ross's success is dependent on the volume of tourism and tourist shopping in the European countries in which it operates. Tourism is one of the world's largest industries and has been a growth sector since the Second World War. From 1984 through 1994, world tourism arrivals grew at a compound annual rate of 5.1 percent and, according to the World Tourism Association, international tourist receipts grew at a compound rate of 11.4 percent.

The positive trend in world tourism is expected to continue. Improved and more accessible communications, increased standards of living for many groups of people around the world, and greater interest in ever-expanding travel opportunities should bring even more business to the travel and tourism industry. There are about 95 million European-country arrivals a year by tourists eligible for VAT refunds. Slightly less than half are from countries outside Europe.

Shopping is a leading part of travelers' activities. The average tourist spends between 10 and 30 percent of his or her expenditures in a country in local shops or department stores. The shopping volume on which tourists are eligible to reclaim their VAT in the European markets in which ETS operates was estimated by ETS to be around $6.9 billion in 1994. The shopping volume on which eligible tourists reclaim their VAT in these markets was estimated to be approximately $3.9 billion. The retail sales on which ETS refunded VAT was about $1.7 billion of this amount.

Think about the possibilities of CUC offering membership to 95 million tourists, whose buying patterns it will know quite a lot about from its new ETS operation. At a p/e ratio of 51.0x, CUC could be a stock on its way to a near-term double.

CYBERCASH, INC.

Whenever you swipe your credit card through a magnetic stripe reader, you're using a product developed by Verifone, Inc., a company founded by Bill Melton. Well, he's back, and this time with a payment system for the Internet. Melton calls his new company CyberCash, and he's got a jump start on most of the banking community whose managers were asleep at their tellers' cages.

CyberCash was founded in 1994 to enable electronic commerce by providing a safe, convenient, and immediate payment system on the Internet. The CyberCash payment system facilitates the purchase of goods and services on the Internet by providing a secure environment for transactions between customers, merchants, and their banks, as well as between individuals.

In the CyberCash system, consumers receive client software free of charge that directly communicates with CyberCash servers, which in turn are linked to the banks' own private networks. CyberCash's initial services enable safe credit-card transactions. This service was followed by safe debit-card and electronic-cash services. For these services, consumers are charged small transaction fees, comparable to the price of a postage stamp.

In addition to its benefits to consumers, the CyberCash system provides to the Internet an effective and efficient sales channel for merchants and banks: The guarantee of safe credit- and debit-card transactions significantly reduces the risk of fraud normally associated with these types of transactions. For merchants specifically, safe credit- and debit-card transactions have the potential to reduce the high cost of credit card transactions via telephone or mail. The bankcard associations consider these Card Not Present transactions riskier and more expensive and consequently charge merchants a higher processing fee.

In addition to lower risk, banks that offer the CyberCash system to merchants and consumers have the added opportunity of maintaining and strengthening these relationships—an attractive prospect in an era in which customer interaction with banks is being replaced by contacts with a variety of other competing financial and nonfinancial institutions.

Perhaps the most exciting aspect of the CyberCash system is in the area of electronic cash. The CyberCash system enables financial transactions with the advantages of both checks and hard currency and the disadvantages of neither. Like checks, this hybrid can be used at a distance, but like cash and unlike checks, its validity can be verified

CYBERCASH, INC.

Chief Executive Officer:	William P. Melton
Principal Location:	555 Twin Dolphin Dr. Redwood City, CA 94065
Telephone:	415-413-0110
Fax:	415-594-0899
E-mail:	magdalen@cybercash.com
Web site:	http://www.cybercash.com
Satellite Locations:	none
Date Founded:	1994
Description of Business:	Enables electronic commerce by providing a safe, convenient payment system on the Internet.
# Employees Current:	60
% Female Employees:	50%
# Employees Projected 9/30/96:	90
Revenues 1995*:	not available
Gross Profit Margin (GPM):	The company is privately held and is not required to publish its financial statements.
SGA Expenses/Revenues:	not available
% Sales Increase 1992 to 1995:	not available
% Change GPM 1992 to 1995:	not available
% Change SGA Expenses/Revenues 1992 to 1995:	not available
Total Debt/Net Worth:	not available
Net Profits Before Taxes 1995*:	not available
Net Profits Before Taxes/Revenues:	not available
Market Value/1995 Revenues*:	not available
Opportunity Company Addresses:	What good is a market if you can't buy or sell something in it?
Elegance of Company's Solution:	CyberCash offers a payment system to Internet merchants and shoppers.

*Annualized.

instantaneously. In other words, the hybrid offers the convenience of checks with the reliability of cash. CyberCash further enhances this hybrid by making it usable across the Internet.

Cambridge, Massachusetts-based Forrester Research recently predicted that online transactions will represent $6.9 billion out of $2.1 trillion in overall retail spending by 2000. According to the recent nationwide consumer survey by American Banker and the Gallup Organization, 12 percent of personal computer owners have already conducted some kind of electronic commerce.

These and other surveys indicate that the "cybercommerce" market may be poised for faster-than-expected growth.

Meanwhile, "Banks are more sophisticated about this than people think," says Seamus McMahon, a managing vice president at First Manhattan Consulting. McMahon said bankers view potential sales over the Internet as an extension of their wire-transfer business, as "just another network they have to stay in control of."*
Richard Comandich, a senior vice president at U.S. Bancorp, said it plans to sign an agreement with CyberCash soon and work with merchants on a pilot in the next couple of months. Comandich said his confidence was enhanced by the fact that CyberCash was founded and led by William Melton

Representatives of Mellon Bank, First USA, Compass Bank, U.S. Bancorp, First Union Corp., and National Bank of the Redwoods also plan similar, limited testing of the CyberCash System. The banks could have had the whole enchilada; now they will have to watch a few coins from a few trillion transactions once again drop into Bill Melton's toll collection box.

* "Big Banks and Card Processors to Test CyberCash System for Sales on Internet," Karen Epper, *American Banker*, November 2, 1995.

CYCARE SYSTEMS, INC.

A few years ago there were 7,000 hospitals in the country. Today there are 5,500. Soon there will be 3,500. Never having had the need to learn how to manage their businesses, hospital administrators are failing miserably during the squeeze on their cash flow. They are losing patients to large outpatient physician groups. But physicians are fairly lame in the management department as well. Enter CyCare.

CyCare Systems provides information systems, related support services, and electronic data interchange (EDI) services to physicians, medical group practices, academic practice centers, and integrated delivery networks. CyCare's services and systems are based primarily on integrated-proprietary applications software developed or acquired by the company to improve the productivity and profitability of its customers. Applications include appointment scheduling, patient- and member-registration information, billing and accounts receivable, electronic claims processing, utilization reporting, medical records abstracting, patient care, and patient accounting. In addition, CyCare markets certain financial applications software developed by others.

In November 1993, the company sold its Practice Management business unit to Medaphis Corporation for $24.1 million in cash. The sale of the business unit resulted from CyCare's decision to focus its efforts on those products and services perceived to be the most attractive to the health-care marketplace. Thus, it doesn't show the dramatic sales improvement of most other Quantum Companies.

The excitement at CyCare is the large size of the market that it is addressing, its deep commitment to R&D—the source of most of the company's product innovation, and what appears to be a focused management. The stock market quadrupled CyCare's stock price in 1995, demonstrating that it is paying attention to an elegant company.

Here are three recent product roll-outs to the company's physician base:

CyCare System 3000™ for group practices of 10 or more physicians was introduced after investing more than 40,000 research and development hours to perfect it. A powerful, flexible UNIX-based system, it combines mainstream productivity tools like word processing, electronic mail, and financial spreadsheets with cutting-edge management systems, including patient care, prepaid-managed care, and financial and administrative functions.

CYCARE SYSTEMS, INC.

Chief Executive Officer:	Jim H. Houtz
Principal Location:	7001 North Scottsdale Rd. Scottsdale, AZ 85253-3644
Telephone:	602-596-4300
Fax:	602-596-4483
E-mail:	mschoanu@cycare.com
Web site:	http://www.cycare.com
Satellite Locations:	Dubuque, Iowa; San Diego, California; Marietta, Georgia; Bloomington, Minnesota; Bedminster, New Jersey; Dallas, Texas
Date Founded:	1981
Description of Business:	A leading provider of computer-based information systems and support to medical practices and physician groups.
# Employees Current:	503
% Female Employees:	60.0%
# Employees Projected 9/30/96:	563
Revenues 1995*:	$59,887,000
Gross Profit Margin (GPM):	55.8%
SGA Expenses/Revenues:	34.2%
% Sales Increase 1992 to 1995:	+(79.2%)*
% Change GPM 1992 to 1995:	(.9%)
% Change SGA Expenses/Revenues 1992 to 1995:	+6.5%
Total Debt/Net Worth:	46.1%
Net Profits Before Taxes 1995*:	$4,239,000
Net Profits Before Taxes/Revenues:	7.1%
Market Value/1995 Revenues*:	2.8x
Traded On:	NYSE (CYS)
Opportunity Company Addresses:	The HMO environment is driving patients out of hospitals and into outpatient care, but physicians are not staffed or equipped to handle the load.
Elegance of Company's Solution:	Sophisticated networked information-management tools to assist the outpatient physician.

*Annualized.

By year-end 1994, CyCare had signed 28 contracts to install this product in group practices and several of the most progressive Medical Services Organizations (MSOs) in the nation. CS3000 will complement the company's existing 20 percent market share in group practices with 25 or more physicians.

In February 1994, CyCare introduced SpectraMED™, a Microsoft Windows™-based billing and patient information program for the under-10 physician group. This product exceeded initial sales expectations by 30 percent after selling more than 300 systems by year-end. SpectraMED uses text-based medical records with import/export capabilities, has full video and audio support, and built-in electronic claims processing.

CyData is the leading physician electronic claims clearinghouse. At year-end 1995 CyData was processing more than seven million transactions a month, including claims, remittances, and statements, to achieve a 29 percent increase in revenue.

All of these services enable physicians to practice medicine, build their patient base, and improve their profitability. If CyCare can keep this group of customers happy, it will thrive for years.

DATASTREAM SYSTEMS, INC.

A 1993 benchmarking study published by A. T. Kearney, Inc., indicates that maintenance costs range from approximately 1 percent to as much as 10 percent or more of an organization's sales, depending on the industry. Datastream believes its systems can reduce these costs by 10 to 20 percent. The company estimates that a $1 billion market exists for computerized maintenance management systems (CMMS) software. A recent study prepared for Datastream by Market Insight indicates that only approximately 15 percent of corporate and governmental users surveyed utilize CMMS software to track maintenance functions and that nearly 60 percent of these users still perform such tasks manually. These figures reflect the substantial potential for future growth in the use of CMMS.

The market for CMMS software is relatively fragmented, with an estimated 200 vendors competing for market share. In addition, as an alternative to purchasing CMMS, some companies utilize indirect methods of tracking and monitoring plant, equipment, and supplies such as spreadsheets and word processors, contract maintenance, and in-house computer systems. According to the Market Insight study, these indirect methods represent approximately 13 percent of the market; however, they are not nearly as effective as application-specific computerized systems from either a preventive maintenance or cost-reduction standpoint, and the trend in the industry is toward purchasing third-party maintenance software rather than developing such products internally.

Datastream's objective is to leverage its leadership position in the CMMS market by providing feature-rich software solutions to the maintenance and repair industry and by being a value-price leader in each segment of the market in which it competes.

The foundation of the company's past success has been the innovative quality of its product offerings and the value its products provide to its customers. For example, its lead product, MP2 for Windows (*Plant Engineering* magazine's 1994 software "Product of the Year") includes audit trail, warranty tracking, and statistical predictive maintenance (SPM) features that are not commonly available in competitive products. In 1994 the company introduced the MP2 for Windows "Bundle," which packages an array of standard and most commonly requested optional features, for less than the aggregate price

DATASTREAM SYSTEMS, INC.

Chief Executive Officer:	Larry G. Blackwell
Principal Location:	1200 Woodruff Rd. Greenville, SC 29607
Telephone:	803-297-6775
Fax:	803-627-7227
E-mail:	not available
Web site:	http://www.dstn.com
Satellite Locations:	United Kingdom
Date Founded:	1986
Description of Business:	Leading provider of computerized maintenance management systems.
# Employees Current:	187
% Female Employees:	50.0%
# Employees Projected 9/30/96:	not available
Revenues 1995*:	$14,230,000
Gross Profit Margin (GPM):	72.1%
SGA Expenses/Revenues:	39.2%
% Sales Increase 1992 to 1995:	+346.7%
% Change GPM 1992 to 1995:	+8.3%
% Change SGA Expenses/Revenues 1992 to 1995:	(18.0%)
Total Debt/Net Worth:	30.0%
Net Profits Before Taxes 1995*:	$3,953,000
Net Profit Before Taxes/Revenues:	27.8%
Market Value/ Revenues*:	5.0x
Traded On:	NASDAQ (DSTM)
Opportunity Company Addresses:	A breakdown of a piece of equipment in the heart of a manufacturing line cripples the producer.
Elegance of Company's Solution:	How much would a producer pay to guarantee that a production line never or rarely broke down? Datastream delivers online, continuous maintenance at an affordable price.

*Annualized.

of the individual options. Management believes that the "Bundle" provides value to the customer and increases the company's average sales per transaction.

Unlike many software companies, Datastream provides free upgrades of its products to customers that subscribe to annual maintenance and support contracts.

Given the large and relatively untapped nature of Datastream's potential market, the company seeks to gain market share through its telesales efforts. The relatively inexpensive nature of its systems (which sell for an average of $3,860, about the cost of a high-end personal computer) makes Datastream's telesales approach a cost-effective means of accessing its target market and achieving gains in market share. The company uses its initial sale as a platform from which to sell the customer (or affiliates of the customer) additional products and services. The company is continuing to aggressively add telesales personnel and increase the scope of its telesales efforts.

The company released a client/server version of MP2 for Windows in the fourth quarter of 1995. Management believes that many of their customers and prospects will adopt a client/server computing architecture in the foreseeable future. The client/server model is recognized as an effective and cost-efficient approach for allowing multiple users to access, utilize, and share large databases. A typical client/server system features software operating on "client" computers—high performance desktop personal computers using a Windows graphical user interface that controls all inquiry and command functions—connected through a local area network with database server computers that organize and manage the resident relational database and manage network functions, such as data storage, printing, communications, data security, and data integrity.

The lower cost of increasingly powerful personal computers has made it possible for smaller organizations to adopt a client/server approach to managing their CMMS tasks. Many other factors favor the adoption of client/server solutions, including improvements in operating systems and software environments, the adoption of easy-to-use graphical interfaces supported by Microsoft Windows, and the broader availability of connectivity software that links personal computer "clients" with mainframes and minicomputers to protect an organization's often costly investment in existing host systems. Finally, a PC network client/server system can be deployed on an enterprise-wide basis, on multiple networks, for customers that perform maintenance and repair operations at multiple locations.

Datastream has beautiful ratios: a rising GPM, a declining SGA Expenses/Revenues ratio, and it collects its accounts receivables in less than 45 days. A real "90s company," Datastream began as a division of Wisconsin Power & Light. Oh, how these behemoths let multimillion dollar gems drift away! What gifts they bestow on public investors! Let us say, "Thank you and amen!"

DATA TRANSMISSION NETWORK CORP.

I t may be apocryphal, but it is a glorious story about the creation of one of the wealthiest families of all time. The French Rothschild family set up a courier system to report to it when Bonaparte lost or won the war against Russia. As the first bank to receive the news of his defeat, the Rothschilds discreetly sold francs and bought other currencies and made a fortune.

Information is leverage. And leverage creates economic opportunities. In Ecclesiastes it is proclaimed: "I returned and saw under the sun that the race is not to the swift, nor the battle to the strong . . . but time and chance happeneth to them all." More chances come to the one with the best information and the time to execute a buy or sell order.

In Omaha, Nebraska, there is a very much overlooked gem of a company—Data Transmission Network Corp. (DTN)—that provides highly critical information at affordable prices to traders in niche markets. The niche markets that it servers are finance, commodities, auto dealers, petroleum refiners, golf course operators, used farm-equipment dealers, and produce farmers. The information service that DTN sells to the petroleum industry is point-to-point. For instance, a refiner can send a jobber an invoice, then notify the jobber when the funds have been transferred to his bank account. For the auto dealer market, DTN permits subscribers to instantly check out a vehicle's title history or a buyer's credit history.

In 1994, DTN added DTN PROduce, a service targeted at fruit and vegetable growers and brokers, and DTN FirstRate, which provides access to daily mortgage rates. In 1995, the company added DTN Weather Center—a service aimed at golf courses and other weather sensitive businesses, put two live units in the Chicago Mercantile Exchange, and added hourly two-minute CNN radio news summaries, which users can download on demand.

DTN uses two primary information delivery technologies: FM radio side-band channel and small-dish KU-band satellite. Some DTN services can be delivered via large-dish, C-band satellite, or cable TV. The DTN receiver captures information around the clock and converts the data into video text ready for viewing at the subscriber's convenience.

Prior to 1992, the DTN receiver supported only a monochrome video monitor. In 1992, the company introduced the new Advanced Communications Engine (ACE) receiver, enhancing its ability to provide information and communication services with high-resolution color

DATA TRANSMISSION NETWORK CORP.

Chief Executive Officer:	Roger R. Brodersen
Principal Location:	9110 West Dodge Rd. Omaha, NE 68114
Telephone:	402-390-2328
Fax:	402-390-7188
E-mail:	support@dtn.com
Web site:	http://www.dtn.com
Satellite Locations:	none
Date Founded:	1984
Description of Business:	Satellite delivery of time-sensitive information to 90,000 subscribers in several niche markets.
# Employees Current:	728
% Female Employees:	35%
# Employees Projected 9/30/96:	853
Revenues 1995*:	$52,521,000
Gross Profit Margin (GPM):	not available
SGA Expenses/Revenues:	56.6%
% Sales Increase 1992 to 1995:	+195.9%
% Change GPM 1992 to 1995:	not available
% Change SGA Expenses/Revenues 1992 to 1995:	+2.5%
Total Debt/Net Worth:	399.9%
Net Profits Before Taxes 1995*:	$16,426,000
Net Profits Before Taxes/Revenues:	31.3%
Market Value/1995 Revenues*:	1.2x
Traded On:	NASDAQ (DTLN)
Opportunity Company Addresses:	Time-sensitive information such as weather, mortgage rates, and financial data could make a significant business difference to the earliest recipient.
Elegance of Company's Solution:	The company gathers and transmits critical information at a cost of six cents a day.

*Annualized.

pictures, graphics, and text as well as sound. The ACE receiver has an internal hard drive and phone modem and can use a keyboard or mouse.

The company's revenues exceed $50 million per year, most of that coming from subscriptions, and a small amount from advertising and selling communications services to others. Sales are growing at approximately 50 percent per year. Cash flow as a percentage of revenues is 31.3 percent, a ratio that most CEOs would give their eyeteeth to have. The company's CEO, Roger Brodersen, is seeking niche markets whose members can benefit from rapid two-way communications. There are many Rothschildian opportunities in the present age of information but none more inexpensively priced than Data Transmission Network. You can buy its stock at 1.2x revenue or a little more than 4.0x cash flow. That price is down Warren Buffett's buying level.

DIAMOND MULTIMEDIA SYSTEMS, INC.

Is Bill Schroeder, CEO of Diamond Multimedia Services, the reincarnation of Harold Geneen of the computer industry? The man is acquiring dominant market share in the modem market after establishing a bulkhead in the multimedia market. One is a transactions business; the other is enabling technologies. What does Schroeder see?

Multimedia products such as audio, video, telephone, fax transmissions to remote laptops, graphics, and radio broadcasts can be bundled into PCs or modems. The modem is, after all, a small computer that modulates then demodulates analog signals into digital signals and back to analog. Why not add other functions to the modem and locate new markets for Diamond's tools? That appears to be the game plan. A risky move, but the modem market is fractionalized with no single dominant company. The former leader, Hayes Microcomputer Products, is in Chapter 11 and perhaps will be acquired by Diamond—on the heels of its acquisition of Supra Corp., the fifth-largest player. Quantum Company, US Robotics Corp., is five times larger than Diamond and its modems are number one among Internet service providers. Schroeder has US Robotics in his cross hairs.

The growth of the modem market is outpacing the growth of the PC market. According to International Data Corp., modem unit shipments grew from 6 million in 1993 to 10.2 million in 1994, or 71 percent. Shipments are expected to grow 43 percent and 30 percent respectively in 1995 and 1996.

Modem shipment growth is chiefly attributable to growth of home offices, online services, and the Internet. Modem penetration in home-worker households increased from 46 percent in 1993 to 52 percent in 1994. The online services and Internet service providers are beginning to offer modems to their subscribers, which adds another distribution channel for modems, which are typically bought at retail computer stores and via direct mail.

But modems are one part of a dynamic story. Multimedia products continue to be the straw that stirs the drink. In a *Computer Reseller News* poll, Diamond captured first place for the video graphics board market. Digital video acceleration allows the PC user to run full-screen video without sacrificing picture quality. The resellers who cast their votes cited Diamond's depth in technology and product innovation and applauded its customer service as well.

DIAMOND MULTIMEDIA SYSTEMS, INC.

Chief Executive Officer:	William J. Schroeder
Principal Location:	2880 Junction Ave. San Jose, CA 95134-1922
Telephone:	408-325-7000
FAX:	408-325-7070
E-mail:	alanb@diamondmm.com
Web site:	http://www.diamondmm.com
Satellite Locations:	Slough, Berkshire, United Kingdom; Munich, Germany; Tokyo, Japan
Date Founded:	1994
Description of Business:	Develops, manufactures, and supports multimedia products such as graphics accelerator cards and modems.
# Employees Current:	383
% Female Employees:	33%
# Employees Projected 9/30/96:	483
Revenues* 1995:	$278,586,000
Gross Profit Margin (GPM):	26.4%
SGA Expenses/Revenues:	9.9%
% Sales Increase 1992 to 1995:	+374%
% Change GPM 1992 to 1995:	(.3)%
% Change SGA Expenses/Revenues 1992 to 1995:	+17.9%
Total Debt/Net Worth:	70.4%
Net Profits Before Taxes 1995*:	$24,593,000
Net Profits Before Taxes/Revenues:	8.8%
Market Value/1995 Revenues*:	3.6x
Traded On:	NASDAQ (DIMD)
Opportunity Company Addresses:	Multimedia products—audio, telephone, fax, video, graphics—are becoming essential components among PC users.
Elegance of Company's Solution:	Diamond integrates its multimedia products with many OEM-PC manufacturers.

*Annualized.

Another leg of the rapidly growing Diamond stool is Bill Schroeder and his management team. They have built Diamond's market value to more than $1 billion in a little more than two years. GPM is holding fairly steady in the 26 percent to 27 percent range, and the SGA Expenses/Revenues ratio is less than 10 percent. Diamond has a highly valued stock, which as the reknowned builder of ITT taught us 25 years ago, is the currency of choice among aggressive acquirers.

DSP TECHNOLOGY INC.

The downsizing of the defense industry left a lot of casualties in its wake, but not this piquant little company. It did a lateral arabesque into the automotive market and has thrived mightily. DSP repositioned itself as a supplier of high-speed data-acquisition and control systems that help the automotive industry develop cleaner, safer, more fuel-efficient vehicles. DSP accomplished this transition while retaining key personnel, enhancing core technologies, and increasing profitability.

DSP manufactures and markets CAMAC- and VME-based data-acquisition and control products in the form of integrated systems, modules, and software depending on the customers' needs. These products are sold to both the transportation and advanced research markets. The company also manufactures, markets, and services a series of shock resistant on-board data acquisition systems (ODAS III) sold to the automotive market.

Customers may purchase a configured integrated system from the company or select various modules to create or configure their own systems. The price depends upon the module configurations and options.

DSP designs and manufactures several integrated systems (typically consisting of modules, enclosures, software, and other manufacturers' hardware) for various types of customer applications:

RedLine Advanced Combustion Analysis System (RedLine ACAP). RedLine ACAP is a CAMAC-based system used for applications involving power-train development. The system measures both combustion and/or spark events in real-time. The systems range in price from about $30,000 for a base system to over $150,000 for a system with spark-analysis capabilities.

IMPAX Data Acquisition Systems (IMPAX). IMPAX is a CAMAC-based system typically used in collecting and processing data from full-scale vehicle crash tests, sled simulators, and component test stands. In addition, they have been used for investigating lift-off dynamics for TITAN IV launch vehicles. Systems prices range from about $150,000 to $800,000 depending on the configuration.

On-Board Data Acquisition Systems (ODAS III). ODAS III is a family of state-of-the-art, multichannel, intelligent, on-board data-acquisition systems designed to meet the harsh environmental requirements of in-vehicle barrier-crash tests and impact-sled tests. ODAS III meets the

DSP TECHNOLOGY INC.

Chief Executive Officer:	F. Gil Troutman
Principal Location:	48500 Kato Rd. Fremont, CA 94538-7385
Telephone:	510-657-7555
Fax:	510-657-7576
E-mail:	not available
Web site:	not available
Satellite Locations:	Ann Arbor, Michigan; Walton-on-Thames, United Kingdom
Date Founded:	1984
Description of Business:	Leading manufacturer of computer-automated measurement and instrumentation products used in vehicle manufacturing and advanced research.
# Employees Current:	100
% Female Employees:	not available
# Employees Projected 9/30/96:	not available
Revenues 1995*:	$14,169,000
Gross Profit Margin (GPM):	61.4%
SGA Expenses/Revenues:	34.7%
% Sales Increase 1992 to 1995:	+128.3%
% Change GPM 1992 to 1995:	+2.3%
% Change SGA Expenses/Revenues 1992 to 1995:	(35.9%)
Total Debt/Net Worth:	37.1%
Net Profits Before Taxes 1995*:	$1,770,000
Net Profits Before Taxes/Revenues:	12.5%
Market Value/1995 Revenues*:	1.0x
Traded On:	NASDAQ (DSPT)
Opportunity Company Addresses:	The U.S. automotive industry needs to remain competitive in its drive-train and crashworthiness specifications.
Elegance of Company's Solution:	DSP Technology is one of Detroit's top high-tech problem solvers.

*Annualized.

Society of Automotive Engineers' SAE/ISO J211 standard specifications for impact testing. The systems range in price from $21,000 to $72,000 depending primarily on the number of data acquisition channels required.

SigLab Signal Acquisition Products (SigLab). SigLab high-performance signal-acquisition products are subsystems for personal computers and workstations in the electromechanical device analysis market, which DSP commenced selling in July 1994. SigLab products provide a cost-effective, portable technology for measurement applications like computer hard-disk head-positioning or acoustic noise-suppression systems in automobiles.

DSP keeps a finger in the advanced research world by manufacturing data acquisition and other products for the national and private laboratory markets. Its customers include Sandia Labs, Stanford Linear Accelerator, NASA, and others.

The company has excellent operating ratios and they are trending in the right directions. As a bootstrapped high-tech company, DSP lacks the support of the Silicon Valley *zaibatsu* and their validation. Consequently, DSP's common stock is inexpensive and its market value to revenues ratio is a mere 1.0x.

EDMARK CORPORATION

Edmark is a leading developer and publisher of high-quality, award-winning educational software for children. The company is recognized for its distinctive approach to creating educational products—combining solid educational methodology with rich multimedia technology to develop products that inspire creativity, develop thinking skills, and actively engage children in the learning process.

Founded in 1970 as a developer of print materials for schools, in its early years the company focused on the special education market. In 1985, it began developing Apple II software programs for special education students and shortly thereafter expanded into the preschool market. In 1992, the company launched a new generation of multimedia educational software products for young children and expanded into the consumer and K-8 educational markets.

Edmark now offers thirteen multimedia titles designed for children ages 2 to 14. Its products are designed to invite children to play. While they interact with charming characters and engaging sound, music, and graphics, children explore, discover, create, and take charge of their own learning. The products are designed with educationally rich environments and employ children to pursue their curiosity through investigation, experimentation, role-playing, and construction of ideas and projects.

Edmark's products have won more than 65 important industry awards since it entered the multimedia software arena. Edmark's goal is to develop engaging, high-quality, and educationally sound products. "Products that help children learn how to learn and that encourage them to recognize and believe in the power of their own minds—that is what we strive to achieve most of all," says Donna Stanger, Edmark Vice President of Product Development.

The educational software market is one of the fastest-growing software categories. Fueled by the "echo of the baby boom" and the penetration of computers into households with young children, this category grew by 88 percent in 1994, to $552 million, according to the Software Publisher's Association. Home PC ownership is on the rise; according to Link Resources in 1994, 42 percent of American households with children owned a home computer and Link forecasts the penetration rate will rise to 55 percent by 1998. Midway through 1995, more PCs were being sold into the home market than TV sets. Market

EDMARK CORPORATION

Chief Executive Officer:	Sally G. Narodick
Principal Location:	6727 185th Ave. NE Redmond, WA 98052
Telephone:	206-556-8400
Fax:	206-556-8998
E-mail:	DianeC@edmark.com
Web site:	http://www.edmark.com
Satellite Locations:	none
Date Founded:	1970
Description of Business:	Leading developer and publisher of high-quality, award-winning educational software for children.
# Employees Current:	170
% Female Employees:	42%
# Employees Projected 9/30/96:	225
Revenues 1995*:	$22,719,000
Gross Profit Margin (GPM):	70.2%
SGA Expenses/Revenues:	59.8%
% Sales Increase 1992 to 1995:	+228.9%
% Change GPM 1992 to 1995:	+26.5%
% Change SGA Expenses/Revenues 1992 to 1995:	(32.2%)
Total Debt/Net Worth:	22.0%
Net Profits Before Taxes 1995*:	$2,187,000
Net Profits Before Taxes/Revenues:	13.7%
Market Value/1995 Revenues*:	13.4x
Traded On:	NASDAQ (EDMK)
Opportunity Company Addresses:	The desire and perceived need by many parents to supplement their children's education at home.
Elegance of Company's Solution:	Educational software for home PCs.

*Annualized.

growth such as that should keep Edmark's stock at 13.4x revenues for many years, even though it's in the "hits" business, where a string of bad-selling products could cripple earnings.

But mark ye well the management skills of Edmark's CEO, Sally G. Narodick. She has lifted GPM 26.5 percent over the last four years to a handsome 70.2 percent, while slashing the SGA Expenses/Revenues ratio by 32.2 percent to a high, but not unacceptable 59.8 percent. Edmark owes very little debt and is earning a highly respectable 13.7 percent on revenues. We all know CEOs in established industries who would give away their favorite sand wedge for these numbers. And Edmark dwells in an industry that is in formation where the demand curve is unformed. Keep your eye on Edmark to acquire related companies with established distribution channels.

EMPLOYEE SOLUTIONS, INC.

The employee-leasing industry is a subset of facilities management but excrutiatingly more difficult to operate, because the assets managed are people rather than computers. There are very few barriers to entry and accordingly the business has attracted more than 1,500 competitors. Employee Solutions is one of the largest, and is growing through acquisitions, by becoming the exit strategy of choice for many smaller mom-and-pop competitors.

As an employee-leasing company, Employee Solutions is the employer responsible for paying employees' salaries and payroll taxes and providing agreed-upon employee benefits. The company also performs administrative, personnel, and human resources–related functions to the extent required by individual client contracts. Employee leasing reduces the administrative responsibilities resulting from the employee-employer relationship, thereby increasing the time available for the employer to operate its business. Some customers claim a 36 percent reduction in overhead when they turn over their people responsibilities.

An advantage of employee leasing may be economies of scale. Since Employee Solutions has a large number of employees on its payroll, exposure relating to workers' compensation insurance, health insurance, and unemployment insurance may be spread over numerous employees, thereby potentially reducing the company's rates below those which might otherwise be available to smaller companies. Moreover, as the number of company employees increases, payroll and benefits administration are spread over a larger base, thereby providing potential additional cost savings.

Employee Solutions determines its fees for services rendered by adding a profit margin to the client's estimated payroll, including workers' compensation insurance costs, federal and state unemployment taxes, FICA, check processing, and costs of funds and benefits. The company enters into a standard form of subscriber agreement with its clients, which is cancelable upon 30 days' written notice of termination by either party and also may be canceled without notice by Employee Solutions under certain circumstances.

Each state has enacted a statutory workers' compensation system under which an employer is required to provide its employees with medical care and other specified benefits for injuries or illnesses incurred within the course and scope of employment. Under workers'

EMPLOYEE SOLUTIONS, INC.

Chief Executive Officer:	Marvin D. Brody
Principal Location:	2029 E. Camelback Rd. Phoenix, AZ 85016
Telephone:	602-955-5556
Fax:	602-955-3311
E-mail:	not available
Web site:	not available
Satellite Locations:	Atlanta, Georgia; Irvine, California; Grand Rapids, Michigan; Chicago, Illinois
Date Founded:	1991
Description of Business:	An employee-leasing company providing solutions to small- and mid-sized companies.
# Employees Current:	43
% Female Employees:	36%
# Employees Projected 9/30/96:	71
Revenues 1995*:	$99,150,000
Gross Profit Margin (GPM):	6.5%
SGA Expenses/Revenues:	4.1%
% Sales Increase 1992 to 1995:	+204.1%
% Change GPM 1992 to 1995:	+44.2%
% Change SGA Expenses/Revenues 1993 to 1995:	+36.7%
Total Debt/Net Worth:	73.5%
Net Profits Before Taxes 1995*:	$1,300,000
Net Profits Before Taxes/Revenues:	1.3%
Market Value/1995 Revenues*:	1.2x
Traded On:	NASDAQ (ESOL)
Opportunity Company Addresses:	Some companies are unable to deal with the suppurating problems of workers' compensation and health insurance, three layers of taxation, and summonses from terminated employees.
Elegance of Company's Solution:	Employee-leasing companies are the Prozac of American industry: They eliminate its greatest stresses.

*Annualized.

compensation laws, employees receive treatment for injuries and illnesses without regard to fault or negligence. Barring matters of conduct such as gross negligence for the death of an employee, employers generally are immune to costly lawsuits and unlimited jury verdicts, as workers' compensation is the employee's sole remedy or source of recovery. The benefits and duration of benefits are set by statute and vary among the states. Employee Solutions provides workers' compensation coverage for most of its leased employees, though some client companies maintain such coverage separately.

In fact, the company is the first employee-leasing company to offer workers' compensation insurance. This new cash-flow channel bears watching, as many service providers have waded into a passel of alligators when they chose to offer products. The company's policies are underwritten by American International Group, an insurance carrier rated A+ by A.M. Best.

While Employee Solutions traditionally has specialized in providing services to smaller employers, it recently began expanding its focus to include employers with larger numbers of employees. It has improved its GPM by more than 44 percent over the last three years and its Operating Ratio by 2.3 percent. The company has the troubling habit of capitalizing its acquisition costs and of using the legal services of one of its directors to close its acquisitions. Hopefully, the director is deducting his director fees from the legal fees he charges the company to demonstrate an attempt at objectivity. But aside from this conflict of interest, Employee Solutions is growing like a rocket and is an interesting, relatively undervalued company.

EZ COMMUNICATIONS, INC.

The calluses of a life of regulation have blunted the imaginations of many radio station owners. They are not able to see opportunities right under their noses, because regulation does not reward creativity. It applauds conformity. Thus, when a chain of radio stations pulls out of the pack and becomes aggressively entrepreneurial, the event is Ecclesiastical. Judge Oliver Wendell Holmes, nearing death, gave his only radio broadcast in 1931 at age 90. He said, "The canter that brings you to a standstill need not be only coming to rest. It cannot be, while you still live. For to live is to function." Most radio station owners believe that what they are doing, even though it is cantering and not racing, is all they can do. Alan Box and his management team at EZ Communications believe that they can do more.

The company recently raised $150 million in debt. Notwithstanding that the bonds were rated B-2, or nearly a junk rating, EZ sees opportunities to acquire more radio stations in the recently liberalized atmosphere at the Federal Communications Commission (FCC). When added to existing debt, the company's total funded debt increased to approximately $265 million, or 6.3 times stockholders' equity. That level of borrowing is not done lightly, but the acquisition of more radio stations is not all EZ has on its drawing board.

EZ recently embarked on an exciting and innovative project to investigate the broadcasting of digital data embedded in the FM signal to newly designed receivers placed in personal computers. EZ recruited Michael Rau, a 13-year veteran and senior vice president for science and technology of the National Association of Broadcasters, to head up this newly created subsidiary, which also has as its mission to explore and exploit emerging electronic communications and broadcasting technology. Company management believes that AM digital broadcasting will open the possibility for new levels of success for its AM stations and that the FM "side-band" could be used as the preferred channel for the distribution of information to numerous locations at once (hence the notion of integrating receivers in personal computers and "smart-phones"). As part of this commitment, EZ entered into a strategic alliance with Xing Technology Corp., a Quantum Company, to sell Xing's StreamWorks servers-plus-software to radio stations to enable them to send their broadcasts to millions of PC users over the Internet. As a testament to its drive to remain in the forefront of technology and the

EZ COMMUNICATIONS, INC.

Chief Executive Officer:	Alan Box
Principal Location:	10800 Main St. Fairfax, VA 22030-8003
Telephone:	703-591-1000
Fax:	703-934-1200
E-mail:	not available
Web site:	not available
Satellite Locations:	Charlotte, North Carolina; St. Louis, Missouri; New Orleans, Louisiana; Pittsburgh and Philadelphia, Pennsylvania; Sacramento, California; and Seattle, Washington
Date Founded:	1965
Description of Business:	An owner-operator of radio stations, this company has seized the opportunity to broadcast over the Internet.
# Employees Current:	700
% Female Employees:	not available
# Employees Projected 9/30/96:	not available
Revenues 1995*:	$86,634,000
Gross Profit Margin (GPM):	70.0%
SGA Expenses/Revenues:	4.3%
% Sales Increase 1992 to 1995:	+159.6%
% Change GPM 1992 to 1995:	(8.6%)
% Change SGA Expenses/Revenues 1992 to 1995:	(8.5%)
Total Debt/Net Worth:	290.2%
Net Profits Before Taxes 1995*:	$22,332,000
Net Profits Before Taxes/Revenues:	25.8%
Market Value/1995 Revenues*:	1.7x
Traded On:	NASDAQ (EZCIA)
Opportunity Company Addresses:	A chain of radio stations is a highway whose owner collects tolls. To recognize a second toll-collecting opportunity on the same highway and to seize the opportunity is smart management.
Elegance of Company's Solution:	EZ Communications may become the first chain of radio stations to broadcast its signals over the Internet.

*Annualized.

new possibilities that technology brings, EZ's top-rated country station in Seattle, KMPS-FM, became the first commercial country station to have an interactive World Wide Web site on the Internet. How many times in the life of a business does an opportunity of such magnitude present itself? Once? Twice? Why have so few radio station owners failed to see a second cash flow channel to run on top of the first at a tiny capital cost? It is amazing that only EZ is running to the Internet at Olympic speed while its competitors are coming to a standstill.

The stock market applauds EZ's aggressive style by giving it a P/E ratio of 47.0x. Its cash flow of $22.3 million will have to nearly double over the next two years to service its debts. That should not be difficult with strategically selected acquisitions and the growth of the Internet, EZ's bankers agree.

FEATHERLITE MFG. INC.

T he state of Iowa has produced many exciting entrepreneurial companies over the years from Iowa Beef Packers to Winnebago, but none more interesting than this manufacturer of trailers for horse owners, sports enthusiasts, and livestock owners. With many of us able to live on farms and ranches and fax, e-mail, or Internet our work to a remote office, this company will thrive. Its trailers are so popular that backlog consistently runs about one third of sales. And the customer base is very broad, to wit:

**Trailer Sales by
Product Type—1994**

Horse	36.6%
Livestock	26.2%
Car and race car	18.2%
Commercial and semi	16.0%
Utility and recreational	3.0%

Its rapid sales growth—more than 50 percent per year—is due to market expansion and the shift from steel to aluminum trailers in a highly fragmented industry. Featherlite is the official trailer of NASCAR racing teams, Indy Car, and the All American Quarter Horse Congress. Since management acquired its predecessor operation, the company has evolved from a manufacturer of primarily horse and livestock trailers with sales of $21 million in 1989 to a diversified manufacturer of numerous types of standard and custom aluminum trailers with about $67 million in annualized sales in 1995.

A 1994 IPO has poised Featherlite for significant revenue and earnings growth. With $10.4 million in net proceeds generated from the offering, Featherlite is doubling the capacity of its manufacturing facilities. This expansion is expected to support 100 percent growth in sales and could double Featherlite's dealer network from 190 to 400 during the next five years.

Management has established very high brand-name recognition in an industry of more than 500 competitors. It has achieved this with a broad dealer network and multiple marketing channels. It can produce up to 400 different models. Featherlite seems to abide by the age-old axiom, "When you sell to the masses, you live with the classes."

FEATHERLITE MFG. INC.

Chief Executive Officer:	Conrad D. Clement
Principal Location:	Highways 63 & 9
	Cresco, IA 52136
Telephone:	319-547-6000
Fax:	319-547-6100
E-mail:	not available
Web site:	not available
Satellite Locations:	Nashua, Iowa
Date Founded:	1989
Description of Business:	The leading manufacturer and marketer of specialty aluminum trailers.
# Employees Current:	950
% Female Employees:	not available
# Employees Projected 9/30/96:	950
Revenues 1995*:	$67,383,000
Gross Profit Margin (GPM):	19.0%
SGA Expenses/Revenues:	13.6%
% Sales Increase 1992 to 1995:	+229.2%
% Change GPM 1992 to 1995:	(.4%)
% Change SGA Expenses/Revenues 1992 to 1995:	(17.6%)
Total Debt/Net Worth:	97.9%
Net Profits Before Taxes 1995*:	$4,479,000
Net Profits Before Taxes/Revenues:	6.6%
Market Value/1995 Revenues*:	1.4x
Traded On:	NASDAQ (FTHR)
Opportunity Company Addresses:	With the increase in homeowner businesses in remote locations, the need to transport cars, boats, horses, and commercial goods expands.
Elegance of Company's Solution:	Featherlite is the leading manufacturer of trailers for hobbyists, horse owners, and sports enthusiasts.

*Annualized.

As country living becomes attractive to more workers, there will be more horses, sports cars, and boats being hauled around. Many Featherlites will do the hauling.

CEO Conrad D. Clement is putting some damn good numbers up on the leader board as well. GPM is holding at about 19 percent over the last four years. He has made deep cuts in overhead: Featherlite SGA Expenses/Revenues ratio has fallen 17.6 percent since 1992. Sales are growing with less sales effort—always a good sign. It means the brand name is beginning to catch hold. Net profits are 6.6 percent of sales, and you can be sure this smart bunch of Iowans are going to bring that figure up over 10 percent or be hauled off in one of their trailers, but not for lack of trying.

FTP SOFTWARE, INC.

The initials stand for "file transfer protocol." The stock symbol, FTPS, stands for a market value of $510 million in December 1995, a ratio of 4.9x times annualized revenues. And the business stands for the savvy to repackage something that is free and sell $100 million of it per year at a gross profit margin of 86.5 percent. FTP has copied the commerce cleaning house formula—repackaging free information for fun and profit.

It all began in 1986 when four graduates of the Massachusetts Institute of Technology decided to improve on the public communications standard for accessing the Internet: Transmission Control Protocol/Internet Protocol or TCP/IP (it defines how different personal computers, running incompatible operating systems, can communicate with one another and share information over the Internet).

The IP part of the standard came into being in the late 1960s on a predecessor to the Internet used by academics and the military. IP allows electronic mail composed on, say, a Digital Equipment PDP-11 to be read by a recipient connected to an IBM mainframe. TCP handled the transport of such information. Together, the two protocols mediate such network services as e-mail, the transfer of files, and remote log-on capabilities.

TCP/IP had to be rewritten and customized for each proprietary operating system. Its early history saw it applied only rarely outside its base in the military and research communities. The first version aimed at the masses--for IBM's PC operating system, MS-DOS—was written at MIT in the mid-1980s as part of an experiment to determine if PCs could participate in a network dominated by mainframes and minicomputers.

That version, known as PC/IP, was placed in the public domain, but the undergraduates who wrote it smelled profits.

FTP's software modifies the public communications standard and makes it run faster and crash-free. Customer service and support was a must. This business strategy was developed by FedEx to take the worry out of sending time-sensitive packages. FedEx competes with a well-entrenched public service as well.

But after three years of scrambling, FTP just wasn't going anywhere. One of its employees, Penny Leavy, called her father, David H. Zirkle, recently retired CEO of Racal Corp., an electronics conglomerate, and asked him to come by and dispense some advice. He did and he stayed. Three years later, David H. Zirkle is running one of the most outstanding

FTP SOFTWARE, INC.

Chief Executive Officer:	David H. Zirkle
Principal Location:	100 Brickstone Sq. North Andover, MA 01810
Telephone:	508-685-4000
Fax:	508-659-6557
E-mail:	jld@ftp.com
Web site:	http://www.ftp.com
Date Founded:	1986
Satellite Locations:	Washington, D.C.; Santa Clara, California; Munich, Germany; Paris, France; Bracknell, United Kingdom
Description of Business:	Designs, develops, markets, and supports internetworking software products that enable PC users to access heterogeneous resources across private networks and the Internet.
# Employees Current:	474
% Female Employees:	not available
# Employees Projected 9/30/96:	not available
Revenues 1995*:	$118,688,000
Gross Profit Margin (GPM):	86.8%
SGA Expenses/Revenues:	20.7%
% Sales Increase 1992 to 1995:	+360.0%
% Change GPM 1992 to 1995:	+.5%
% Change SGA Expenses/Revenues 1992 to 1995:	+18.3%
Total Debt/Net Worth:	14.6%
Net Profits Before Taxes 1995*:	$46,882,000
Net Profits Before Taxes/Revenues:	39.5%
Market Value/1995 Revenues*:	4.9X
Traded On:	NASDAQ (FTPS)
Opportunity Company Addresses:	As the Internet spread from universities and think tanks to commercial users, the need arose for faster, error-free access to it.
Elegance of Company's Solution:	The company's founders, with uncommon prescience, saw a future need and rewrote public domain software to enable a PC on any operating system to access the Internet.

*Annualized.

Internet-related software companies in the world. Sales outside the United States accounted for 44 percent of total sales in 1994, up from 33 percent in 1992.

Zirkle has grown GPM over the last four years to 86.8 percent while holding SGA Expenses/Revenues under 21 percent. With these extraordinary Operating Ratios, is there any wonder that FTP earns 39.5 percent on revenues? If there's a worry for FTP it is a need for more products. But Zirkle is on top of that.

The company's strategy has been to license and acquire other Internet-related software products to push through its channel while broadening and developing existing and new marketing channels. With the proceeds of two public offerings swelling its coffers to $92 million at the end of 1994, FTP went on a buying spree. It acquired technology licensed from Spyglass, Inc., to adapt the Mosaic browser into its product lines. It acquired technology licensed from Unipalm, Ltd., to bring advanced messaging applications to the Internet. FTP acquired Keyword Office Technologies in February 1995, developer of protocol-independent document interchange and viewing technology software. Seeking more protocol-independent and universally needed software products and tools, FTP formed a New Ventures Business Unit to acquire and invest in new Internet solutions.

FTP is a story of chasing curves. As the Internet users' curve grows, more TCP/IP software and other FTP software sales will be made into it. But as that curve begins to level off, FTP's growth will have to be found in newer and more utilitous applications.

FUTURE LABS, INC.

Future Labs, Inc., was founded in 1989 and began operations in 1992 to design, develop, produce, and market TALKShow™, an innovative software application for interactive, person-to-person and multiparty electronic conferencing targeted for business and engineering applications. TALKShow™ is a multipoint document-conferencing software product that allows individuals in different locations to exchange and annotate graphics-based information, including documents, spreadsheets, photographs, and drawings on their PCs. A telephone conference call is needed for the audio link. The company's mission is to become the leading producer of document-conferencing software and to offer cost-effective software solutions that allow multiple users to conveniently collaborate via remote electronic meetings, especially through the Internet.

The company sells TALKShow™ under license agreements to OEM customers, who bundle it into their software or PCs, on a direct basis to large corporations with multiple offices, and to resellers and VARs for resale to retailers, distributors, and end-users. The company's OEM customers include Connectix, Corel, IBM, InSoft, Samsung, among others. Its end-users include numerous engineering firms, Hewlett-Packard, Molex, Nike, Novell, Oracle, and a considerable number of universities. TALKShow™ has a suggested retail price of $199 per license.

The use of large conference-room systems and audio-conferencing services indicate the existing demand to communicate over distances in real-time without meeting in person. TALKShow™ makes this possible at the next level of convenience and cost effectiveness. Currently available systems providing graphics and document capability require dedicated conference room facilities and expensive equipment set-ups. These systems cater to the needs of the large and preplanned group meetings; but, they are not readily available for *ad hoc* conferences among users who wish to remain at their desks or for the salesperson in his or her hotel room operating with a laptop. To access TALKShow™, the user needs only an IBM (or Apple) compatible 386/486 portable or desktop PC with 4MB memory, Windows 3.1 or higher, DOS 3.3 or higher. Communications links include Internet access or direct connections via standard modems, LAN/WAN networks, or ISDN.

Airlines beware. Collaborative software such as TALKshow™ means far fewer flights by engineers to get together and design new equipment. Future labs is marketing TALKshow™ aggressively in the Pacific Rim where travel is a nightmare, time consuming, and expensive.

FUTURE LABS, INC.

Chief Executive Officer:	John H. C. Chua
Principal Location:	5150-E21 El Camino Real Los Altos, CA 94022
Telephone:	415-254-9000
Fax:	415-254-9010
E-mail:	jchua@futurelabs.com
Web site:	http://www.futurelabs.com
Satellite Locations:	none
Date Founded:	1989
Description of Business:	Leading developer of software that permits up to 18 people to simultaneously collaborate on a blueprint or a document.
# Employees Current:	15
% Female Employees:	15%
# Employees Projected 9/30/96:	30
Revenues 1995*:	$2,500,000
Gross Profit Margin (GPM):	The company is privately held and is not required to publish its financial statements.
SGA Expenses/Revenues:	not available
% Sales Increase 1992 to 1995:	not available
% Change GPM 1992 to 1995:	not available
% Change SGA Expenses/Revenues 1992 to 1995:	not available
Total Debt/Net Worth:	not available
Net Profits Before Taxes 1995*:	not available
Net Profits Before Taxes/Revenues:	not available
Market Value/1995 Revenues*:	not available
Opportunity Company Addresses:	Your company needs to design a new piece of equipment and the engineers are on critical assignments at locations around the world.
Elegance of Company's Solution:	Rather than postpone the job or fly engineers to one location, they can collaborate on the design from wherever they are using Future Labs software in their laptop.

*Annualized.

GARTNER GROUP, INC.

The information technology purchasing decision within small, medium, and large organizations has become highly complex, replacing the capital equipment purchasing decisions of the past. The difference is that information technology and movement have a far greater impact on the cash flow of an enterprise than capital equipment ever had. Information is brains. Capital equipment is muscle and bones.

Gartner Group is the leading independent provider of research and analysis of the computer, communications, and information technology industries for users and vendors of such products. Its key business is to help clients build, buy, manage, and use computers and software to optimize their time, money, and resources and to do their business better. And this year its advice is producing revenues of more than $200 million.

Think of the corporation that relies on a mainframe and thousands of dumb terminals, with thousands of people loyal to it. Then along comes client/servers, remote computing, and the Internet. The spread of changes is enough to scare the socks off executives. What do they do? Go with the new? But which components of the new do they buy? It's time to call in Gartner.

So important has Gartner Group become to the Age of Information that one-fifth of its customers are the vendors whose equipment or software the company recommends or discourages the use of.

The most intriguing characteristics of Gartner Group are its clean financial statements and unusually high profit margins. The company earned 17.6 percent (annualized) on revenues in 1995. Its SGA Expenses/Revenues ratio has fallen 20.4 percent over the last four years. GPM could do with a little growth. Its receivable days have improved from 128 four years ago to 118 in 1995. The company is sitting on $83 million in cash and marketable securities. With such a stalwart financial statement, Gartner's customers should perhaps pay for one day of information technology consulting and a second day for management.

There are multiple marketing channels that Gartner could sell its library of accumulated knowledge into and incur a fractional cost of goods sold. The seminar business is one that Gartner is currently unfolding. Publishing—print and online—is another. Expensive industry studies is a third. Gartner Group could become a billion dollar business in five years with $350 million of cash flow.

GARTNER GROUP, INC.

Chief Executive Officer:	Manuel E. Fernandez
Principal Location:	56 Top Gallant Rd. Stanford, CT 06904-2212
Telephone:	203-964-0096
Fax:	203-324-7901
E-mail:	not available
Web site:	not available
Satellite Locations:	37 offices in 30 foreign countries
Date Founded:	1979
Description of Business:	The leading independent provider of research and analysis on information technology.
# Employees Current:	not available
% Female Employees:	not available
# Employees Projected 9/30/96:	not available
Revenues 1995*:	$202,269,000
Gross Profit Margin (GPM):	63.8%
SGA Expenses/Revenues:	42.6%
% Sales Increase 1992 to 1995:	+201.6
% Change GPM 1992 to 1995:	(3.3%)
% Change SGA Expenses/Revenues 1992 to 1995:	(20.4%)
Total Debt/Net Worth:	66.3%
Net Profits Before Taxes 1995*:	$35,680,000
Net Profits Before Taxes/Revenues:	17.6%
Market Value/1995 Revenues*:	4.3X
Traded On:	NASDAQ (GART)
Opportunity Company Addresses:	Years ago a company might have had five or six information-technology vendors to choose from. Today there are hundreds, maybe thousands. Choosing is confusing.
Elegance of Company's Solution:	Gartner Group solves problems, answers questions, and sheds light on one of the most confusing markets on the planet.

*Annualized.

GEOWORKS, INC.

Notwithstanding that one of GeoWorks' venture capital funds, Chancellor Capital Management, Inc., recently sold its entire holdings of this development-stage company, GeoWorks is a strong contender in the race to make computers smaller and more mobile and to make cellular phones act more like computers. No easy task this, but CEO Gordon E. Mayer thinks his team can do it. Mayer was being incubated at the esteemed venture capital fund of Merrill, Pickard, Anderson & Eyre when they plugged him into their portfolio company, GeoWorks, in 1993, which had been founded by Brian P. Dougherty, the founder of the highly successful Imagic Corp., an entertainment software company. Mayer had been CEO of Infochip, Inc., a data compression firm.

GeoWorks has Microsoft on its mind. When its targeted consumer computer device (CCD) is a reality, it is GeoWorks' goal to license the operating system to all CCD manufacturers.

GeoWorks develops and markets operating-system and application software for the emerging CCD market. CCDs include a diverse range of compact, affordable computing devices such as electronic organizers (sometimes called personal digital assistants), smart phones, mobile companions, and dedicated word processors. GeoWorks expects that the CCD market will resemble the highly segmented, price-sensitive consumer-electronics market. It believes that its GEOS system software, currently in its fifth generation, offers the functionality and efficiency that will enable hardware manufacturers to provide the features and pricing structure necessary for successful consumer computing devices.

GeoWorks' objective is to establish its GEOS system software as a leading operating system for the CCD market. In pursuit of this objective, GeoWorks intends to focus on the mobile segment of the CCD market in the near term, to continue to enhance the GEOS system software, and to expand its relationships with existing licensees, as well as establish additional relationships in the future. The company's GEOS system software is currently licensed on an OEM basis by Brother International, Canon Business Machines, Hewlett-Packard, Nokia, and Toshiba Corporation for inclusion by such parties in current or future CCDs. In addition, Hewlett-Packard, Nokia, Novell, and Toshiba Corporation have made significant equity investments in GeoWorks.

As the installed base of GEOS-based devices grows, the company intends to broaden its sources of revenue by developing and marketing

GEOWORKS, INC.

Chief Executive Officer:	Gordon E. Mayer
Principal Location:	960 Atlantic Ave. Alameda, CA 94501
Telephone:	510-814-1660
Fax:	510-814-4250
E-mail:	karen@geoworks.com
Web site:	http://www.geoworks.com
Satellite Locations:	none
Date Founded:	1983
Description of Business:	Develops and markets operating systems and applications software for the emerging consumer-computing device market.
# Employees Current:	125
% Female Employees:	28%
# Employees Projected 9/30/96:	not available
Revenues 1996*:	$4,503,000
Gross Profit Margin (GPM):	99.0%
SGA Expenses/Revenues:	208.7%
% Sales Increase 1993 to 1996:	(14.2%)
% Change GPM 1993 to 1996:	+2.0%
% Change SGA Expenses/Revenues 1993 to 1996:	+29.6%
Total Debt/Net Worth:	21.4%
Net Profits Before Taxes 1995*:	$10,407,000
Net Profits Before Taxes/Revenues:	deficit
Market Value/1995 Revenues*:	35.7x
Traded On:	NASDAQ (GWRX)
Opportunity Company Addresses:	All of us from time to time complain that our PCs are too klugey, too slow, and not sufficiently portable.
Elegance of Company's Solution:	GeoWorks is developing a solution to that problem with its consumer-computing device—a mobile phone and electronic organizer rolled into one.

*Annualized.

aftermarket application software, delivering upgrades to the GEOS system software and associated object libraries, sharing in the revenues of communication services providers, and distributing its own and third-party software. The anticipated diversity of products and users in the CCD market will create opportunities to market a variety of communications, connectivity, information publishing, entertainment, and productivity applications for GEOS-based devices. In addition, GeoWorks plans to develop and facilitate technology that will provide CCD users with access to the rapidly growing stream of electronic content and communications on the Web.

Imagine dialing into the Web or reading your e-mail from your smart cellular phone. The prospects of doing that from a car, in an airport, or at a sales presentation are mouth-watering. Can it happen? The private investors in GeoWorks have bet $20.2 million and the public, approximately $62 million on GeoWorks.

GeoWorks is not the only company working on the de facto CCD operating system. Industry sources indicate Microsoft's pending mobile computing-operating system may ship by mid-1996. In addition, the possibility that Microsoft might introduce an operating system for one or more CCDs—whether anticipated, announced, or actually shipping—may have the effect of causing hardware vendors to delay committing to another operating system.

General Magic has also received significant media attention for its Magic Cap operating system and its Telescript communications protocol. General Magic's OEM customers have shipped two CCD products, the Sony MagicLink and the Motorola Envoy. These products, which contain features similar to those found in GEOS, are generally considered to be competitive CCDs with those released by GeoWorks' OEM customers. Apple Computer intended to release an upgrade to its Newton operating system in late 1995, which was expected to include improved handwriting recognition and other capabilities and so increase its competitive strength in the market.

Although one of its investors has taken its chips off the table, Toshiba has recently made a significant investment. Toshiba and the other strategic partners are not passive investors. Some of them have board seats and cooperate with company systems engineers.

GeoWorks is a company to follow closely. If we are known by our friends, GeoWorks has some high-powered electronics industry giants who brought it to the dance and stick pretty close to it.

GLOBAL VILLAGE COMMUNICATIONS, INC.

Communications is one of the fastest-growing areas in personal computing today. Take, for instance, the rise of the fax. The facsimile has gained enormous popularity as a primary method of instantaneous communication. One recent estimate showed that one out of every three long-distance international business calls is a fax transmission. By 1995, according to BIS Strategic Decisions, the number of fax transmissions sent by computer will equal that of fax transmissions sent by traditional fax machines.

Global Village's systems approach to communications enables people to effortlessly send faxes directly from their computer without having to do much more than click a single button. More and more people are seeing the benefit of this approach. In fact, BIS Strategic Decisions has estimated that in 1994 alone, 14 billion pages were faxed directly from computers. They project that the figure will rise to well over 100 billion by the year 1997. In 1994, sales of personal-computer fax devices eclipsed stand-alone fax machine sales.

Mobile computing and telecommuting are two other important trends. Portable and notebook computer sales are rising, accounting for the largest share of the growth in the personal computer industry. Executives, students, managers, and professionals now have the freedom to work the way they want, where they want, whenever they want. And as a result, the number of people who telecommute in the United States grew by more than one million in 1995. Historically, the challenge for these users has been to find a way to stay connected to the office, classroom, or library—without having to be there. Global Village makes it possible for users to access information and to stay in touch by using fax and remote-access technology.

The Internet is also driving modem sales and Global Village is benefiting from this new market. According to a recently published Nielsen Media Research survey conducted for Commerce Net, 24 million people in North America 16 years of age or older are frequent users of the Internet. The bulk of them (70 percent) use it at work rather than at home or at school. As the chart on page 168 shows they are using it for a number of reasons.

The report also says that 37 million people have access to the Internet through an online service such as America Online. Access to the features of the Internet requires a modem.

GLOBAL VILLAGE COMMUNICATIONS, INC.

Chief Executive Officer:	Neil Selvin
Principal Location:	1144 East Arques Sunnyvale, CA 94086
Telephone:	408-523-1000
Fax:	408-523-2404
E-mail:	mary_cravalho@globalvillage.com
Web site:	not available
Satellite Locations:	none
Date Founded:	1989
Description of Business:	Leading manufacturer of modems and related communications software for the Apple Macintosh family of personal computers.
# Employees Current:	300
% Female Employees:	not available
# Employees Projected 9/30/96:	not available
Revenues 1995*:	$92,000,000
Gross Profit Margin (GPM):	45.1%
SGA Expenses/Revenues:	20.1%
% Sales Increase 1992 to 1995:	+2,186.3%
% Change GPM 1992 to 1995:	+37.5%
% Change SGA Expenses/Revenues 1992 to 1995:	(43.2%)
Total Debt/Net Worth:	25.1%
Net Profits Before Taxes 1995*:	$13,616,000
Net Profits Before Taxes/Revenues:	14.8%
Market Value/1995 Revenues*:	1.9x
Traded On:	NASDAQ (GVIL)
Opportunity Company Addresses:	There is a growing need to simplify access to the Internet and to integrate the functions of the telephone, fax, and PC.
Elegance of Company's Solution:	Global Village has taken the lead in developing easy-to-use networking products.

*Annualized.

It is one thing to address a major opportunity. It is another thing to make one of the most elegant solutions to sell into that nearly vertical hypotenuse of a demand curve. But it is quite another thing to do the above and maintain outstanding operating ratios and tight controls. Global Village's GPM is rising continuously while its SGA Expenses/Revenues ratio works its way downward. This ratio has fallen 42.5 percent over four years. Neil Selvin, Global Village's CEO, never saw an overhead item that he liked. Global Village has ample cash on hand with which to acquire multimedia companies, if it cannot develop what they have in beta but lacks the funds to market.

CYBER CENSUS

Web access	5.0 million
E-mail	4.5 million
Noninteractive chat	2.5 million
Downloading software	2.1 million
Remote computer use	2.1 million
Interactive discussion	1.5 million
Real-time audio or video	1.5 million

Source: *The New York Times*, October 30, 1995.

IDT CORP.

Howard Jonas won an inventor's prize while a sophomore at Bronx High School of Science. Also while in high school he ran a hot dog stand outside a Bronx methadone clinic and launched an advertising agency. To pay for his Harvard education, Jonas ran a mail-order firm from his dormitory room, selling the likes of bonsai trees and Venus flytraps from ads placed in *TV Guide*. Jonas accumulated a net worth of $75,000 and upon graduation he bought a trade journal, *Auto and Flat Glass*. Over the next ten years, Jonas built a successful publishing business comprising trade directories, which he ran out of a converted Bronx funeral home.

Jonas then tried to branch into trade journal publishing in Israel, but when he saw his monthly telephone bill, he put on his inventor's hat and with $300 of off-the-shelf components, constructed a little device that automatically dialed his Israeli salesman back when he called. This knocked 75 percent off the phone call. Thinking that other international businesses could use the savings, Jonas began hiring agents to sell the service worldwide.

Orders soon flooded IDT Corp. and Jonas raised $1.4 million in venture capital to meet demand. In 1992 when IDT began to cut into AT&T's revenues, the telecommunications giant sued: The most profitable segment of AT&T's business is international calls, a market that AT&T dominates with a $7-billion market share. AT&T lost the suit.

In 1995, Jonas implemented another handful of off-the-shelf components and developed a system that turns a personal computer into a voice-based telephone by digitizing speech and transmitting it to U.S. telephone networks via the Internet. The service costs about six cents a minute and will undercut British Telcom and other foreign and domestic long-distance carriers by about 50 cents a minute.

With IDT's service, users can connect a PC anywhere in the world to a telephone in the United States. The PC needs voice/IP software (in this case provided as part of IDT's subscription), a microphone and a sound card. Also needed to complete calls is a compression/decompression algorithm located at IDT's switches in the United States. The algorithm allows carriers to dial-up at their desktops, where the signal is translated into analog and routed onto the public network.

IDT is using its value-added Internet service to enhance its international dial-up access in Asia. The company already offers dial-up

IDT CORP.

Chief Executive Officer:	Howard Jonas
Principal Location:	294 State St.
	Hackensack, NJ 07601
Telephone:	201-928-1000
Fax:	201-928-1057
E-mail:	jp@tribeco.ios.com
Web site:	http://www.idt.net
Satellite Locations:	None
Date Founded:	1990
Description of Business:	Offers international telephone service for the price of a local phone call to anyone in the United States who has an Internet hookup.
# Employees Current:	350
% Female Employees:	50.0%
# Employees Projected 9/30/96:	500
Revenues 1995*:	$100 million (est.)
Gross Profit Margin (GPM):	The company is privately held and not required to publish its financial statements. SGA Expenses/Revenues: not available
% Sales Increase 1992 to 1995:	not available
% Change GPM 1992 to 1995:	not available
% Change SGA Expenses/Revenues 1992 to 1995:	not available
Total Debt/Net Worth:	not available
Net Profits Before Taxes 1995*:	not available
Net Profits Before Taxes/Revenues:	not available
Market Value/1995 Revenues*:	Mario Gabelli invested six figures for 1 percent ownership in 1994.
Opportunity Company Addresses:	People around the world pay huge sums each month to their long-distance carriers to telephone or fax their friends, relatives, and business associates in the United States.
Elegance of Company's Solution:	IDT has slashed 30 percent or more off the costs of international calls, and the cuts will be deeper with IDT's Internet connections.

*Annualized.

services in France, Italy, and South Korea and has 272 U.S. points of presence (POPs) built around its own nodes and local alliances.

According to Jonas, IDT expects competition to be the national telephone companies of foreign countries where the Internet is underdeveloped. Phone companies there will not be offering voice over the Internet.*

IDT has tested the technology between London and New Jersey and said it costs six cents a minute for the company to transport a call over the Internet. When you consider the various factors that led to the break-up of AT&T into smaller, more responsive business units, add IDT's low-cost international phone call rates via the Internet to your list.

The Regional Bell Operating Companies (RBOCs) are waiting patiently for a handful of Internet service providers (ISPs) to become sufficiently robust and large to acquire. Then they will lower the price of Internet Access to a commodity level. Those ISPs with value-added services, such as IDT, will survive the RBOC onslaught. In fact, IDT may become larger than some of the RBOCs someday and force a handful of them to merge in order to survive the IDT onslaught.

---

* Source: "IDT joins IP Rush with PC-to-Phone Service", *Telecom 95 Daily*, Richard Castillo, October 6, 1995.

INCONTROL, INC.

Implantable devices are widely used for the treatment of cardiac disorder, such as pacemakers for bradycardia and implantable cardiac defibrillators for rapid ventricular disorders. Pacemakers shock the ventricles, the lower pumping chambers of the heart, back into efficient rhythms when faulty rhythms develop. These devices have become increasingly accepted as a result of continuous product upgrades, which improve ease of implementation, programmability, memory, and device life. There were more than 370,000 pacemakers and approximately 21,500 implantable cardiac defibrillators implanted worldwide in 1994.

Atrial fibrillation is a frequent and costly health-care problem representing the most common arrhythmia resulting in hospital admission. Although medical therapy is the standard for atrial fibrillation, the safety and efficacy of controlling atrial fibrillation with antiarrhythmic drugs recently has been questioned. As a result, nonpharmacologic therapy for atrial fibrillation has been investigated. With the success of the implantable defibrillator for refractory ventricular arrhythmias, implantable devices capable of recognizing and terminating atrial fibrillation are now being developed.

InControl is very near to developing an implantable atrial defibrillator device, the Metrix System, which will identify a rapidly beating atria and convert it to sinus rhythm via a low-energy shock. With the backing of Mayfield and Medical Innovations funds and a $30 million U.S. and $15 million public offering, InControl is betting $68 million that it can bring Metrix to market.

InControl's Metrix System is composed of four components, including:

- The Metrix 3000 implantable device, which will identify and convert irregularly beating atria to sinus rhythm. The device has electrogram storage, biphasic waveform, back-up pacing, and R-R interval safety timing.
- The Perimeter transvenous three-lead system, which will connect the implantable device to the heart. The Perimeter leads will transmit electrical signals from the heart to the Metrix 3000 implantable device for analysis to determine regularity of beat. (The company recently settled a U.S. Patent Office interference proceeding with Medtronic relating to a Medtronic shock-vector patent. Small royalty payments will be made to Medtronic, and InControl will have rights to the patent on a worldwide, nonexclusive basis.)

INCONTROL, INC.

Chief Executive Officer:	Kurt C. Wheeler
Principal Location:	6675 185th Ave. NE Redmond, WA 98052
Telephone:	206-861-9800
Fax:	206-861-9301
E-mail:	jodi@incontrol.com
Web site:	not available
Satellite Locations:	none
Date Founded:	1990
Description of Business:	Leader in developing new therapies for atrial fibrillation.
# Employees Current:	133
% Female Employees:	38%
# Employees Projected 9/30/96:	160
Revenues 1995*:	-0-
Gross Profit Margin (GPM):	not available
SGA Expenses/Revenues:	not available
% Sales Increase 1992 to 1995:	development stage
% Change GPM 1992 to 1995:	not available
% Change SGA Expenses/Revenues 1992 to 1995:	not available
Total Debt/Net Worth:	21.1%
Net Profits Before Taxes 1995*:	($22,870,000)
Net Profits Before Taxes/Revenues:	deficit
Market Value/1995 Revenues*:	$182,715,000
Traded On:	NASDAQ (INCL)
Opportunity Company Addresses:	Atrial fibrillation, a result of a malfunctioning of the heart's electrical system, can lead to stroke and congestive heart failure. It afflicts more than 2 million Americans.
Elegance of Company's Solution:	An implantable defibrillator that administers a brief electrical shock to the heart to convert an irregular or rapid heart beat back into sinus rhythm.

*Annualized.

- The Defibrillation System Analyzer, which will enable the physician to determine proper lead placement and test device settings before implementation.
- The InControl Programmer, which will allow the physician to monitor and adjust the device both prior to and after implantation.

The device will be implanted beneath the skin near the collarbone (like a pacemaker) and will administer shocks of up to 3 joules. A very low-energy warning signal will be emitted by the device to let the patient know that a shock is imminent. The device weighs approximately 76 grams and is similar in size to recent-generation dual-chamber pacemakers and half the size of most recent-generation implantable cardiac defibrillators. Device life, which is highly dependent on battery life and will vary depending on frequency of shocks delivered, should be four years from the date of initial implantation.

The market size is estimated at 2 million people in the United States and Europe and 160,000 new cases per year. C. J. Lawrence estimates the market size in dollars to be $1.3 billion to $2.1 billion per year.

INFORMATION STORAGE DEVICES, INC.

By using a single chip developed by Information Storage Devices (ISD), audio messages can be recorded, stored, and played back on pagers, security alarm systems, cellular phones, credit-card-size pocket recorders, telephone-answering machines, and a variety of toys, interactive books, and compact learning aids. Voices are reproduced in their natural state. The company's customers are a who's who of consumer electronics and communications products manufacturers, including Casio, Polaroid, AT&T, Philips, Sanyo, Sony, Tandy, and Motorola.

Although rich in applications—recordable greeting cards, recordable picture frames, and point of sale displays are among the more interesting ones—ISD is a highly focused company and very serious about maintaining technology leadership. In 1995, the company acquired EUROM Flashware Solutions, Ltd., a start-up developer of voice-recording chip technology for $10.4 million in cash. The acquisition will result in an $8.5 million write-off and may create a loss for the year. Timing is everything, they say, and before the stock market could absorb the frisson of the write-off against proforma net profits for 1995 of $3.9 million, some insiders and employees sold 2,400,000 of their shares to the public. Not a "quantum" thing to do ordinarily.

Not to worry; ISD is an extremely tightly run ship. When in doubt about a possible management bailout, I always check GPM, SGA Expenses/Revenues, and accounts receivable turnover. ISD's GPM is a robust 36.4 percent and growing, which means, *inter alia*, that the company is raising prices or lowering production costs.

ISD's operating expenses as a percentage of sales has been declining over time. The product is selling by word-of-mouth, in many cases, rather than relying on wasteful advertising and scatter-shot outbound selling. And, notwithstanding ISD's rapid growth and strong cash position, its accounts receivables were being collected more rapidly in 1995 (51 days) than in 1993 (59 days).

One overhanging problem is concerning: ISD subcontracts its manufacturing to Samsung and Sanyo. They in turn rely on the flash chip technology of Atmel, a Quantum Company, which is terribly unhappy with ISD and claims it is the co-owner of the company's chip-based products. Atmel is seeking a license fee. The courtroom has entered the boardroom at ISD.

INFORMATION STORAGE DEVICES, INC.

Chief Executive Officer:	David Angel
Principal Location:	2045 Hamilton Ave. San Jose, CA 95125
Telephone:	408-369-2400
Fax:	408-369-2422
E-mail:	not available
Web site:	not available
Satellite Locations:	Sarasota, Florida; Austin, Texas
Date Founded:	1987
Description of Business:	Designs, develops, and markets integrated circuits for voice recording and playback using the company's proprietary high-density storage technology.
# Employees Current:	108
% Female Employees:	42%
# Employees Projected 9/30/96:	170
Revenues 1995*:	$49,629,000
Gross Profit Margin (GPM):	36.4%
SGA Expenses/Revenues:	14.1%
% Sales Increase 1992 to 1995:	+848.6%
% Change GPM 1992 to 1995:	+37.9%
% Change SGA Expenses/Revenues 1992 to 1995:	(68.9%)
Total Debt/Net Worth:	16.6%
Net Profits Before Taxes 1995:	$3,908,000
Net Profits Before Taxes/Revenues:	7.8%
Market Value/1995 Revenues*:	4.1x
Traded On:	NASDAQ (ISDI)
Opportunity Company Addresses:	There are disadvantages in recording and playing back voice on magnetic tape, including wear and tear of parts, large size, and power usage.
Elegance of Company's Solution:	A chip that records, stores, and plays back voice messages.

*Annualized.

ISD's customer base is deep and broad, but its profit margins could not endure, for long, a substantial per device payment to Atmel. Hence, the EUROM acquisition: a defensive step the company had to take to replace its technology base. Management and insiders seem to be at least half-convinced: Their ownership declined from 32.6 percent to 16.0 percent in 1995. The stock market is more sanguine about ISD's prospects.

INSO CORPORATION

The brilliance and grace of Jerome S. Rubin has mentored this creative little software toolmaker. Rubin founded Lexus, the legal documents search firm, and thereby accelerated the research process in the legal profession and probably saved the world economy $1 trillion or more.

Someone should promote Rubin for Secretary of the Treasury, for now he is behind INSO Corporation, whose software can translate foreign language documents in seconds—another couple of billion dollars will be saved because this remarkable entrepreneur.

Responsive to its customers, INSO studies their needs and optimizes the design and content of its products to satisfy both OEM and end users. The company enables its OEM customers to implement INSO products in ways that add maximum value to their applications. As a result, INSO's customers rely upon the functionality, compactness, speed, and extensive platform coverage that characterize the company's products. INSO's unique development team, consisting of computational linguists, language-focused software engineers, and information-based developers, has enabled INSO's powerful technology to reach users through eighteen languages worldwide.

INSO's products are incorporated into hundreds of applications marketed by 350 OEM customers. Examples of INSO's OEM implementations include Microsoft's *Word and Office*; Lotus's *AmiPro, 1-2-3, Notes,* and *SmartSuite*; Sharp's *Wizard*; office automation software systems marketed by Digital and Siemens; and dedicated word processors sold by Brother and Panasonic. Other OEM customers include Artisoft, Apple, Banyan Systems, Broderbund, Caere, Claris, Corel, Casio, CompuServe, Dataware, Da Vinci, Fulcrum Technologies, MINDSCAPE, Novell Applications Group, Parsons Technology, Scholastic, and Verity. INSO's 120 corporate customers include Cigna, Boeing, Motorola, Bank of America, Merck, TVA, Bell South, Southern Company Services, and Flour Daniel, Inc.

Alas, toolmakers shrink their market with every sale they make. Growth must come from diversification or there will be no growth at all a few years hence. INSO recognizes that. Information Management Tools, INSO's newest product line, enables users to locate, access, and retrieve information faster and more easily than previously possible. The first product in this line, *IntelliScope*, is a multilingual tool that greatly enhances the power and precision of information retrieval systems by

INSO CORPORATION

Chief Executive Officer:	Steven R. Vana-Paxhia
Principal Location:	31 St. James Ave. Boston, MA 02116
Telephone:	617-753-6500
Fax:	617-753-6666
E-mail:	nkosar@inso.com
Web site:	http://www.inso.com
Satellite Locations:	none
Date Founded:	1982
Description of Business:	Leading provider of multilingual software products for proofing, electronic reference, and information management.
# Employees Current:	132
% Female Employees:	45%
# Employees Projected 9/30/96:	not available
Revenues 1995*:	$30,998,000
Gross Profit Margin (GPM):	87.3%
SGA Expenses/Revenues:	31.3%
% Sales Increase 1992 to 1995:	+326.7%
% Change GPM 1992 to 1995:	+5.6%
% Change SGA Expenses/Revenues 1992 to 1995:	(14.7%)
Total Debt/Net Worth:	48.5%
Net Profits Before Taxes 1995*:	$11,588,000**
Net Profit Before Taxes/Revenues:	37.4%
Market Value/1995 Revenues*:	6.6x
Traded On:	NASDAQ (INSO)
Opportunity Company Addresses:	The need of software firms to market their products multilingually.
Elegance of Company's Solution:	An efficient tool that connects English to other languages and vice versa in milliseconds.

*Annualized
**Adjusted for write-off incurred as a result of acquisition.

adding sophisticated linguistic features. *IntelliScope* ultimately gives users a more exact way to access and manage the vast amounts of information now available on their desktops. Already adopted by several leading applications vendors, *IntelliScope* helps people and organizations get more value out of their information resources. *Quick View Plus*, INSO's file viewing technology, allows the user to instantly view, search, copy, and print virtually any file with its full formatting intact.

The *Reference Works* product line has expanded to include electronic versions of the best known almanacs, dictionaries, encyclopedias, thesauruses, and professional references. These high-quality reference works, which are well-structured, highly compressed, and fully indexed databases, include the *International Electronic Thesaurus* line, the *American Heritage* dictionaries, *The Columbia Encyclopedia*, and more. The company made two acquisitions recently to enhance its position in advance file-viewing technologies: Systems Compatibility Corp., Chicago, Illinois, and ImageMark Software Labs, Kansas City, Missouri. These acquisitions underscore INSO's dedication to building a strong new product line in file viewing of any kind of document in any format.

CEO Steven R. Vana-Paxhia runs a tight ship. With sales growing at a rate of 90 percent per year, GPM has risen by 5.6 percent since 1992—a nontrivial accomplishment for a company whose GPM is well above 80 percent. SGA Expenses/Revenues has declined 14.7 percent since 1992, which says a lot about word-of-mouth marketing. INSO earns a whopping 37.4 percent on revenues, after adjusting for a write-off attributable to an acquisition. A rising GPM, a declining SGA Expenses/Revenues ratio, a strong cash flow, and Jerry Rubin's track record place INSO in our top drawer of favorites.

INTERDIGITAL COMMUNICATIONS CORP.

One of the largest opportunities in the telecommunications industry is to provide phones and phone systems to consumers and industry in the emerging democracies. Beginning with very little in the way of a copper-wire-installed base, it appears that wireless will be the preferred telecommunications system in Eastern Europe and China. InterDigital is filling the need.

The company began operations in 1972 and until 1987 was primarily engaged in research and development activities related to its TDMA wireless digital communications technology. In 1986, it introduced the UltraPhone system, a fixed-digital wireless loop telephone system employing its patented TDMA technology, which it began installing in 1987. The company's operations from 1987 through 1992 were characterized by increasing revenues accompanied by substantial operating losses. During this period, significant costs were incurred related to the commercialization and continued development of the UltraPhone system, development of production sources and capacity, and the implementation of a broad-based sales and marketing effort designed to promote regulatory and market acceptance of the UltraPhone system. During 1993 and 1994, UltraPhone revenues were significantly lower than in 1992: Losses increased significantly as a result of the decline in UltraPhone revenues and other increases in costs—such as the increased investment in B-CDMA research and development, engineering of product redesigns and enhancements, the increase in litigation costs, and the expense associated with enforcement of its intellectual property rights.

In 1994, InterDigital began to realize positive results from its efforts to capitalize on the revenue potential of its TDMA and CDMA patent portfolio. It recognized $28.7 million of licensing revenue from Matsushita, Sanyo, Mitsubishi, Hitachi, NEC, and others. During the first half of 1995, it grew its revenue base considerably achieving $62.1 million of licensing revenue and generated $40.7 million of net income.

The company's primary product is the UltraPhone, a radio telephone system providing wireless communications. InterDigital has sold more than 210 UltraPhone systems worldwide for more than $120 million. It reaches foreign markets through marketing alliances with telecommunications giants such as Siemens, P.T. Amalgram (the Indonesian telephone company), Telefonos de Mexico, and others. Siemens agreed

INTERDIGITAL COMMUNICATIONS CORP.

Chief Executive Officer:	William J. Burns
Principal Location:	2200 Renaissance Blvd. King of Prussia, PA 19406
Telephone:	610-878-7800
Fax:	610-878-6801
E-mail:	not available
Web site	http://www.interdigital.com
Satellite Locations:	Great Neck, New York
Date Founded:	1972
Description of Business:	Develops and markets advanced digital wireless using proprietary technologies.
# Employees Current:	166
% Female Employees:	32%
# Employees Projected 9/30/96:	215
Revenues 1995*:	$117,495,000
Gross Profit Margin (GPM):	72.5%
SGA Expenses/Revenues:	24.5%
% Sales Increase 1992 to 1995:	+295.9%
% Change GPM 1992 to 1995:	+172.6%
% Change SGA Expenses/Revenues 1992 to 1995:	(10.0%)
Total Debt/Net Worth:	24.5%
Net Profits Before Taxes 1995*:	$40,920,000
Net Profits Before Taxes/Revenues:	34.8%
Market Value/1995 Revenues*:	3.0x
Traded On:	ASE (IDC)
Opportunity Company Addresses:	When a person experiences democracy and the free-enterprise system for the first time, he or she wants a phone.
Elegance of Company's Solution:	Most emerging democracies do not have copper cable, thus their phone systems are wireless. The company fills this demand curve.

*Annualized.

to pay InterDigital $20 million in 1995-96 and provide technical assistance to enhance the company's research and development activity.

InterDigital does more than license to foreign telecom giants. It also sells wireless phone systems in rural America, but these sales are not growing very rapidly. It acquired **SCS Mobilecom** a few years ago to give it a beachhead in **CDMA** communications, the competing satellite broadcast system. To hedge against relying on the support of others, InterDigital maintains an UltraPhone test and assembly shop at its Pennsylvania headquarters.

This 24-year-old company has out-innovated the giants of its industry, then turned around and granted them the rights to sell its phones in their markets. Has it shrunk its overall market in so doing? Perhaps, but it has an active **R&D** activity and the currency to make a few key acquisitions of needed technology. Plus, there are billions of people who still want phone service.

A review of InterDigital's operating statement makes for pleasant reading. The company's sales are galloping at 60 percent per year. GPM is rising in huge jumps. Overhead has fallen 10 percent over the last four years. The company's operating ratio is 34.8 percent. The stock market values InterDigital at about 8.5x cash flow. This company's stock is poised for a stunning leap.

INTERIM SERVICES, INC.

The commercial temporary help industry has grown rapidly over the last ten years. According to the 1995 Staffing Industry Research Guide, industry revenues increased from approximately $5.7 billion in 1983 to approximately $18.8 billion in 1994, an average annual growth rate of 13.8 percent.

The use of temporary personnel has become widely accepted as a valuable tool for managing personnel costs and for meeting specialized or fluctuating employment requirements. According to the National Association of Temporary Services, studies show that more than 90 percent of all businesses use temporary help services. Vacations, illness, resignations, seasonal increases in work volume, marketing promotions, and month-end requirements have historically created demand for temporary help. More recently, the growing cost and difficulty of hiring, laying off, and terminating full-time workers has also encouraged a greater use of temporary workers.

Effective use of temporary workers enables businesses to staff their organizations with a core level of full-time personnel and to augment their full-time workforce as needed with temporary help. A business pays only for the actual hours worked by the temporary personnel and may terminate their service upon completion of the assignment without the adverse effects of layoffs. The inconvenience and expense of hiring additional full-time employees for assignments of limited duration is therefore avoided.

Organizations have also begun using flexible staffing to reduce administrative overhead by outsourcing operations that are not part of their core business functions. By utilizing temporary employees, businesses are able to avoid the management and administrative costs incurred if full-time personnel are employed. An ancillary benefit, particularly for smaller businesses, is that such use shifts employment costs and risks (e.g., workers' compensation, unemployment insurance) to the temporary service companies, which can spread the costs and risks over a larger pool of employees.

Home care is one of the fastest-growing sectors of the health-care industry. According to the National Association for Home Care, home-care personnel service revenues grew at a compound annual rate of 10 percent between 1986 and 1993, the latest date for which such data is available. Contributing to this growth is national pressure on reducing health-care costs. Studies indicate that health care at home costs 40

INTERIM SERVICES, INC.

Chief Executive Officer:	Raymond Marcy
Principal Location:	2050 Spectrum Blvd. Fort Lauderdale, FL 33309
Telephone:	305-938-7600
Fax:	305-938-7775
E-mail:	not available
Web site:	not available
Satellite Locations:	Offices in 46 states; District of Columbia; Puerto Rico; Canada
Date Founded:	1966
Description of Business:	A national provider of temporary help personnel to businesses, hospitals, and service organizations and for home health care.
# Employees Current:	500
% Female Employees:	66.7%
# Employees Projected 9/30/96:	600
Revenues 1995*:	$669,662,000
Gross Profit Margin (GPM):	29.5%
SGA Expenses/Revenues:	19.1%
% Sales Increase 1992 to 1995:	+156.0
% Change GPM 1992 to 1995:	-0-
% Change SGA Expenses/Revenues 1992 to 1995:	(10.3%)
Total Debt/Net Worth:	54.9%
Net Profits Before Taxes 1995*:	$27,476,000
Net Profits Before Taxes/Revenues:	4.1%
Market Value/1995 Revenues*:	0.6x
Traded On:	NASDAQ (INTM)
Opportunity Company Addresses:	In an increasingly regulated business environment, companies will turn to trained temporary workers rather than hire permanent workers who they must train.
Elegance of Company's Solution:	Interim has found large and growing niche markets in the health-care and professional services fields.

*Annualized.

percent to 70 percent of the cost of institutional care. In addition, industry growth is driven by the aging American population, which is increasing overall demand for health care, and technological advances, which now make it possible to perform many sophisticated medical procedures in the home. Most patients, when given a choice, prefer to be cared for at home.

The demand for temporary institutional staffing depends directly on fluctuations in the number of patients in hospitals and nursing homes and shortages of specific personnel. Over the last few years, hospitals and other health-care facilities have developed expertise in planning their supplemental staffing needs and have therefore decreased reliance on temporary health personnel for routine staffing. Health-care institutions continue to rely on temporary personnel for scarce, hard-to-find specialists, such as physical and respiratory therapists and critical-care nurses.

Interim's management believes that size is a major competitive advantage in the temporary health-care industry. Private insurers use case managers and contract managers who purchase home-care services in volume, while private individuals rely on physicians, HMOs, hospital discharge planners, and insurers for referrals for home-care providers. As national and regional organizations increasingly dominate health-care purchases, the ability to provide home-care services nationally is becoming a competitive advantage. A national distribution network is important to winning business as these organizations prefer to have one or two suppliers who can provide health-care personnel over a broad geographic region.

Interim Services has developed a comprehensive system of assessing, selecting, training, and providing quality assurance for its temporary help operations, based on support materials designed and produced by the company for branch, franchised, and licensed offices. In addition, the company conducts a series of classes for all employees, including training classes for service representatives and managers.

In addition to more than 700 owned and franchised facilities, the company began selling licenses a few years ago, and they have caught on with more entrepreneurial managers. In licensing arrangements, Interim retains the equity in the office, finances accounts receivable, and funds the temporaries. The licensee pays all operating expenses. They split profits 25/75 with Interim keeping 25.

A 1991 spin-off out of H & R Block, which also owns CompuServe, Interim is a consistently profitable, rapidly growing temporary help firm. Its sales are growing at the rate of 40 percent per year while GPM is holding steady at 29.5 percent. Raymond Marcy, the company's CEO, has slashed SGA Expenses/Revenues by 10.3 percent over the last four years. Net profits in 1995 are running at a rate of 4.1 percent of revenues. The stock market, however, appears unimpressed, valuing the company at 60 percent of revenues. Interim is worth a good bunch more than that.

JACK HENRY & ASSOCIATES, INC.

This rapidly emerging company, located in the center of the country, in Monett, Missouri, provides integrated computer systems for in-house data processing to banks and other financial institutions. Jack Henry has developed several banking applications for software systems that it markets, along with the computer hardware, to financial institutions throughout the United States and overseas. Jack Henry also performs data conversion, software installation, and software customization for the implementation of its systems and provides continuing customer maintenance/support services after the systems are installed.

The company's primary market consists of the approximately 14,000 commercial banks and other financial institutions in the United States with less than $10 billion in total assets. Community banks and other financial institutions (assets under $250 million) account for approximately 12,500 of that number. The population of community banks decreased by 3 percent in 1993. According to "Automation in Banking 1994," in 1993 small financial institutions spent approximately $3.5 billion on hardware, software, services, and telecommunications. In-house vendors have 49 percent of the commercial banks as customers. Centralized off-site service bureaus provide data processing for 45 percent of those banks, down from two-thirds in the mid '80s. Many organizations provide data processing to banks through a service-bureau approach. Some service bureaus are affiliated with large financial institutions that may have other relationships with potential bank customers, but this is less prevalent than in the past. Typically, a bank that is making a data-processing decision will consider both service bureau and in-house alternatives.

Of the small-to-midsize banks with in-house installations, 42 percent utilize IBM hardware. Unisys Corporation and AT&T/NCR have 28 percent and 19 percent of that market, respectively. All other vendors are well under 10 percent share of the in-house community bank market. In 1993, five of the top ten software providers in this market, ranked by number of installed customers, utilized IBM hardware. According to that survey, Jack Henry had the most installed customers (approximately 911) of the IBM providers. Two other software providers had larger customer bases than Jack Henry, but both of them enjoyed a more exclusive and less competitive relationship with their hardware supplier. Although the top ten software providers accounted for about 88 percent

JACK HENRY & ASSOCIATES, INC.

Chief Executive Officer:	Jerry D. Hall
Principal Location:	663 Highway 60 Monett, MO 65708
Telephone:	417-235-6652
Fax:	417-235-8406
E-mail:	not available
Web site:	not available
Satellite Locations:	none
Date Founded:	1976
Description of Business:	Provides in-house data processing systems for small banks in the United States and abroad.
# Employees Current:	333
% Female Employees:	41.4%
# Employees Projected 9/30/96:	not available
Revenues 1996*:	$57,739,000
Gross Profit Margin (GPM):	49.5%
SGA Expenses/Revenues:	22.7%
% Sales Increase 1993 to 1996:	+177.2%
% Change GPM 1993 to 1996:	+15.2%
% Change SGA Expenses/Revenues 1993 to 1996:	+13.0%
Total Debt/Net Worth:	99.2%
Net Profits Before Taxes 1996*:	$11,404,000
Net Profits Before Taxes/Revenues:	19.7%
Market Value/1996 Revenues*:	4.8x
Traded On:	NASDAQ (JKHY)
Opportunity Company Addresses:	The Internet, the fax, and Federal Express make living in remote places and transmitting one's work to the office a reality.
Elegance of Company's Solution:	Banks in these happy Internet communities will continue to thrive and need sophisticated data processing systems.

*Annualized.

of in-house systems installed, the study identified 20 other software vendors in this arena. That number has been declining in recent years.

Jack Henry's business and operations include three major categories: software and installation, maintenance/support, and hardware. Software includes the development and licensing of applications software systems and the conversion, installation, and customization services required for the customer's installation of the systems. Maintenance/support consists of the ongoing services to assist the customer in operating the systems and to modify and update the software to meet changes in banking. Hardware relates to the sale (often referred to as remarketing) of both the computer equipment and the equipment maintenance on which the Jack Henry software systems operate. The following table illustrates the significance of each of these three areas, expressed as a percentage of total revenues:

Year Ended June 30

	1995	1994	1993	1992
Software and Installation	27%	34%	29%	32%
Maintenance/Support	34%	18%	18%	20%
Hardware	39%	48%	53%	48%
Total Revenues	100%	100%	100%	100%

A key ratio to follow in the financial statements of companies such as Jack Henry is service and maintenance revenue as a percentage of total revenue. If it grows faster than new software and new hardware sales then we would know that the company is upgrading its old customers to newer, faster systems. There are excellent profits in the service, maintenance, and support business. Jack Henry is growing aggressively, extending itself into the Pacific Rim with a new sales office in Kuala Lumpur and in other foreign markets.

As the banking industry consolidates due to fewer distribution companies to lend to and competition from commercial paper, community banks are prospering because distributed computing allows people to live and work where they choose. More than likely, they choose small communities. As ISDN becomes more prevalent, community banks will become more in demand.

Why this beautiful company pays a dividend to its stockholders is beside me. It makes the statement that stockholders may be able to achieve higher ROI than the company can. But that is unlikely, unless management sees a flatter horizon in the future than do industry analysts and futurists.

KRONOS INC.

*S*oftware jocks, when they start their own businesses and get a product out into a market niche, frequently license everybody and his brother to market it. These OEM deals, as they are known, bring in some up-front cash but frequently sacrifice at least five years of building brand recognition through establishing one's own sales and marketing systems. Like the Sinatra song, Kronos did it the hard way; it built a large sales, marketing, and service team and it is blanketing its markets like the blizzard of 1996 covered New England.

Richard J Dumler, a partner in Lambda Funds Management Co., Kronos's long-suffering, brilliant investor, is finally reaping the rewards of its investment after a more than 12-year lock-up. The company's market today is worth $250 million and rising.

Another lesson for software entrepreneurs is to sell a system with a service contract. It opens up another cash flow channel, is generally profitable, and puts an intelligent person in a customer's shop looking for new business. Kronos's service income represents one-fourth of total revenues. If that ratio shoots up, it could mean that product sales are slipping.

With 60,000 customers, Kronos management may be seeing a saturation point. Thus it is making acquisitions slowly and carefully to bring some new products onto the menu. In March 1994, the company acquired ShopTrac Data Collection Systems, a private manufacturing software company based in Calabasas, California. ShopTrac provides manufacturers with off-the-shelf, configurable applications such as work-in-process, labor and quality management. The acquisition has enabled Kronos to combine the ShopTrac suite of manufacturing management applications with Kronos's data collection products for a comprehensive shop-floor manufacturing system.

Kronos manufactures its own terminals that collect and verify data and communicate this data to a computer for use with Kronos's application software. Kronos's terminals incorporate firmware, which allows them to be configured for different data collection applications. The company offers a variety of terminals designed to meet specific customer price/performance requirements. Terminal choices include wall-mounted, desk-mounted, and hand-held devices that are available in various sizes and models, some of which are designated to operate in harsh environments. Most terminals can be configured to use a wide array of data entry methods, including bar code wands, badge and time

KRONOS INC.

Chief Executive Officer:	Mark S. Ain
Principal Location:	400 Fifth Ave. Waltham, MA 02154
Telephone:	617-890-3232
Fax:	617-890-8768
E-mail:	main@internet.kronos.com
Web site:	http://www.kronos.com
Satellite Locations:	none
Date Founded:	1977
Description of Business:	Designs, develops, markets, and services time and attendance and related software to measure labor's costs in industry in an integrated manner.
# Employees Current:	1,062
% Female Employees:	34%
# Employees Projected 9/30/96:	not available
Revenues 1995*:	$116,070,000
Gross Profit Margin (GPM):	59.1%
SGA Expenses/Revenues:	42.2%
% Sales Increase 1992 to 1995:	+194.5%
% Change GPM 1992 to 1995:	(.8%)
% Change SGA Expenses/Revenues 1992 to 1995:	(.7%)
Total Debt/Net Worth:	40.0%
Net Profits Before Taxes 1995*:	$11,459,000
Net Profits Before Taxes/Revenues:	9.9%
Market Value/1995 Revenues*:	2.2x
Traded On:	NASDAQ (KRON)
Opportunity Company Addresses:	The need to know when workers are getting to work and what they are doing while at work is a means to better manage manufacturing costs.
Elegance of Company's Solution:	The company has survived in a once-crowded market to become the dominant time-and-attendance software and systems companies.

*Annualized.

card readers, laser and charge-coupled device scanners, and alpha and numeric keypads. The company's terminals provide it with an important advantage over its competition.

In May and June 1995, Kronos purchased all of the territories covered by Giscal de Mexico S. A. de C. V., a dealer headquartered in Mexico City, all of the territories covered by The Lanyard, a dealer of the company headquartered in Austin, Texas, and all of the territories covered by Action Business Systems, Inc., another of the company's dealers headquartered in Richmond, Virginia. As a result of these acquisitions, Kronos has established new direct sales and support offices in the three states and has established a subsidiary to perform sales and support in Mexico. The combined cost of these acquisitions of approximately $1 million largely relates to intangible assets that are being amortized on the straight-line method over a period of eight years. Thus earnings may be a little softer than expected while Kronos lays more pipe through acquisitions.

LEGATO SYSTEMS, INC.

The ease of use and low cost of personal computers and workstations, along with the development of personal-productivity software and advances in network connectivity, relational-database software, and application-development tools, together with a growing number of off-the-shelf applications, are fueling a transition to distributed-network computing. In recent years, the number of desktop computers employed in a typical network has increased, making today's networks much larger and more complex than earlier networks. These networks often consist of multiple servers (application servers, file servers, database servers, and communications servers) manufactured by a number of vendors and dozens, hundreds, or even thousands of desktop clients running a number of different operating systems. In addition, there has been a proliferation of personal productivity applications that permit individual users to create and store files on the desktop client. The distributed nature of these networks, along with the increased use of computers throughout organizations, has resulted in an increase in the amount and dispersion of critical data across the clients and servers on these networks. These factors, coupled with decreasing costs of physical storage, are resulting in significant increases in the volume of data on networks. Today, network administrators are increasingly required to manage heterogeneous network environments consisting of clients and servers located at many different locations across an organization, as well as to manage widely distributed stored data.

Storage management has, therefore, become a critical component of the overall management of the network. The goal of storage management in a distributed environment is to permit network administrators to efficiently and cost-effectively protect, manage, and access network data and to allow end users to easily access storage-management functions. This requires, first and foremost, a storage-management system that can quickly and efficiently back up large volumes of data resident on a variety of clients and servers running different operating environments, as well as data generated by a wide range of applications. At the same time, the system must be manageable through a variety of interfaces familiar to network administrators, and the user interface employed must be sufficiently intuitive so that end users can access managed data without requiring intervention by the network administrator.

One of the most critical ways Legato accommodates an increasing number of clients while retaining high performance is by implementing

LEGATO SYSTEMS, INC.

Chief Executive Officer:	Louis C. Cole
Principal Location:	3145 Porter Dr. Palo Alto, CA 94304
Telephone	415-812-6000
Fax:	415-812-6032
E-mail	lcole@legato.com
Web site:	not available
Satellite Locations:	Lowell, Massachusetts; El Segundo, California; Chicago, Illinois; Amsterdam, the Netherlands; Berkshire, United Kingdom; Munich, Germany; Mosman, Australia
Date Founded:	1988
Description of Business:	Develops, markets, and supports network storage management software products for heterogeneous client/server computing environments.
# Employees Current:	170
% Female Employees:	25%
# Employees Projected 9/30/96:	255
Revenues* 1995:	$18,856,000
Gross Profit Margin (GPM):	88.8%
SGA Expenses/Revenues:	55.7%
% Sales Increase 1992 to 1995:	+328.0%
% Change GPM 1992 to 1995:	+29.8%
% Change SGA Expenses/Revenues 1992 to 1995:	(27.3%)
Total Debt/Net Worth:	13.7%
Net Profits Before Taxes '95*:	$3,111,000
Net Profit Before Taxes/Revenues:	16.5%
Market Value 9/95/* '95 Revenues:	8.9x
Traded On:	NASDAQ (LGTO)
Opportunity Company Addresses:	A proliferation of networks, servers, and PCs and productivity applications has created heterogeneous network environments requiring storage management.
Elegance of Company's Solution:	A heterogeneous storage management system that permits network administrators to efficiently protect, manage, and access network data.

*Annualized.

parallel-data transfers from the clients to the storage-management server in the same way that adding more tellers to serve customers allows a bank to process more transactions in the same amount of time. When an additional client's data is managed, it may be scheduled for processing by the storage management server at the same time as the data from other clients. Thus, one slow client need not slow down the entire storage management process.

Legato achieves this parallelism by writing multiple-client data streams to the tape simultaneously. This allows the full bandwidth of the tape drive to be used since the data from many clients can be delivered to the tape drive in the same amount of time as the data from one client. As a result, one high-capacity tape drive can be shared effectively by more than one client on the network, and therefore, it may not be necessary to purchase several tape drives to accomplish data protection in the required amount of time.

An increasingly important function of the storage-management database to some end users is to facilitate the management of data according to its criticality. As an example, a set of quarterly reports may be grouped together and filed away. This "archive" data may not need to be accessed on a regular basis but be retrievable for a period of years because of certain regulatory requirements. When archived data is needed, it must be explicitly retrieved, typically from off-site storage. It is also possible to archive data in such a way that it appears to be online, when in reality it is stored elsewhere. This process is referred to as hierarchical storage management. The indexing technology embedded within Legato's product, called NetWorker, is designed to support the management of protected, archived, and hierarchically managed data. NetWorker clients are capable of generating data for data-protection purposes, and on certain UNIX platforms, for archival purposes. Client software that implements data archival on other UNIX platforms, and hierarchical storage management on certain platforms, is under development.

Legato is a small company—only $19 million in 1995 revenues, but as the sportscasters say, ". . . with its whole future in front of it." It has a GPM of 88.8 percent, up nearly 30 percent from 1992. Its SGA Expenses/Revenues ratio in 1995 is 55.7 percent, *down* from 76.8 percent in 1992. This means that word-of-mouth is beginning to sell the product. Legato competes with two other Quantum Companies, Cheyenne Software and Platinum Technology among others, both of which are larger. But its management team, drawn from Novell, Informix, Banyan, and Verifone, are in their 40s and 50s, experienced, industry-hardened, and prime for the big score.

LEXI INTERNATIONAL, INC.

A Mercedes-Benz dealer in Los Angeles contacted Robin Richards, the founder and CEO of Lexi International, a few years ago with a problem: Customers who were buying cars from the dealer would return for their first service requirement but after that would go elsewhere for service and, ultimately, to buy their next car. Millions of dollars were being lost as follow-up revenues went down the street. Lexi took on the assignment and analysis of the paradigm, which led to a questionnaire used by a portion of Lexi's 1,200 telemarketing personnel. Within a month three-fourths of the dealers' customers were contacted and interviewed for 30 minutes, and their responses were put through the Lexi brain trusts, human and electronic. The problem was identified: The purchase of a Mercedes-Benz from Lexi was wife-influenced. Even though the husband frequently made the purchase and did the driving, wives were bringing the cars in for their first service calls. The company's mechanics were changing the radio dial to Spanish music stations about 50 percent of the time and forgetting to turn it back. The wives apparently didn't like this and showed their displeasure by going to another dealer for service. When the dealer read the report, he corrected the problem and rehired Lexi for a prospecting assignment.

In the field of prospecting for new car purchasers, Lexi is able to demonstrate a conversion rate (i.e., sales closed divided by leads generated) higher than any competitor or form of media. It costs the automobile dealer industry approximately $650 per car in advertising dollars for every new car sold. Lexi has been able to cut that cost to about $350 to $450. In fact, if a new car dealer that sells 10,000 cars a year canceled all media ads, aggregating $6,500,000, and put $3,500,000 into telemarketing-based prospecting, Lexi claims it would earn $3,000,000 more. What is more, sales would increase by 20 percent—from a close ratio of one in five to two in five. That is because a prospect qualified by a one-on-one conversation is a better lead than one who walks in on his or her own after seeing or hearing an ad. J. D. Powers may be the best-known name in consumer purchasing habits, but Lexi is the company the car makers rely on for really hard, current data.

With a solid background in the automobile industry, Lexi took its knowledge base into other markets: long-distance telephone; waste management where it expanded the customer base of Browning-Ferris, Inc.; cellular phone sales for Pac Tel; PC sales for Tandy Corp.; and more.

LEXI INTERNATIONAL, INC.

Chief Executive Officer:	Robin D. Richards
Principal Location:	1645 N. Vine St.
	Los Angeles, CA 90028
Telephone:	213-467-3334
Fax:	213-856-9733
E-mail:	not available
Web site:	not available
Satellite Locations:	none
Date Founded:	1987
Description of Business:	A provider of outbound tele-marketing services to large corporations and associations.
# Employees Current:	1,200
% Female Employees:	72.5%
# Employees Projected 9/30/96:	1,700
Revenues 1995*:	$70 million (estimated)
Gross Profit Margin (GPM):	The company is privately held and is not required to publish its financial statement.
SGA Expenses/Revenues:	not available
% Sales Increase 1992 to 1995:	not available
% Change GPM 1992 to 1995:	not available
% Change SGA Expenses/Revenues 1992 to 1995:	not available
Total Debt/Net Worth:	not available
Net Profits Before Taxes 1995*:	not available
Net Profits Before Taxes/Revenues:	not available
Market Value/1995 Revenues*:	not available
Opportunity Company Addresses:	Qualified leads. Few words in consumer or small-business marketing have as much value. Finding them at the lowest cost is quite another matter.
Elegance of Company's Solution:	Lexi International is among the leaders in finding prospective customers for the insurance, automobile, waste management, long-distance carrier, personal computers, and credit card industries.

*Annualized.

The advantages of database telemarketing to generate prospects as well as customers over more conventional forms of advertising and marketing are becoming appreciated by a growing number of businesses— and not only because of the continuous increases in postal rates. Not only does it generate higher response rates versus direct mail, but the results are known far more rapidly, validity testing can be achieved with smaller samples, and there is less waste in telemarketing.

The Internet is Lexi's next challenge. Richards believes that commercial transactions on the Web will soon represent one third of all commerce in the United States and in developed countries. With a paid-for telecommunications system and client/server computer base with 1,200 telemarketer terminals linked to a server, Lexi is in a position to take in any data from any source, slice it, dice it, and print out reports within 30 minutes. "Our installed base of database-management-skilled people and software makes us a natural to advise advertisers on the Internet or on the new cable-based Internet channels like @Home (a Quantum Company) or the Microsoft-Xing Technology-NBC channel," Richards says. Thus, when Paul Grand, the founder of NetCount (a Quantum Company) went looking for a database manager to partner with his new Internet market research firm, he selected Lexi. "We talked with A. C. Nielsen and Lexi, but Robin persuaded us that Lexi would hustle for us because they are smaller and hungrier, so we linked up with them," said Grand.

The Internet and cable-based Internet services are interactive, and those of us who will be ordering a third of our goods and services through the Internet will gain more information about the product in a shorter period of time than if we drove to a store and spoke with a sales person. That's the plus. The negative, or at least its perception, is that we may give up, unwittingly, too much personal information, wittingly or otherwise, to the Internet database managers and their clients. Clearly, a comfortable medium will have to be found.

In the meantime, Lexi is growing so fast that the building it rents at the corner of Hollywood and Vine streets is in a constant state of renovation. Lexi recently expanded into check processing and preparation to make better use of its computers. Richards explains this peripheral diversification thus: "A paycheck is the result of data collection. We collect, slice, and dice data as well as anyone in the country and better than most. The diversification puts us into a related and profitable service business." Lexi will doubtless make an interesting public company someday but a tough one to categorize.

LOGIC DEVICES, INC.

ollowing the companies on which Burton Kanter takes a board seat is pretty healthy for the pocketbook. (HealthCare Compare Corp., the Chicago-based utilization review company, is a particular favorite of mine.) When I saw Kanter on the Logic Devices board, I followed the trail of this brilliant lawyer-turned-venture capitalist. Voila! Another winner.

Logic Devices, in conjunction with Pinnacle Systems, pooled their expertise at the systems and DSP chip levels to develop a high-performance 3-D workstation for the desktop that sells for under $10,000. The system, dubbed Alladin, was introduced to the video industry at the spring 1994 National Association of Broadcasters (NAB) convention in Las Vegas. During the ensuing months market response has confirmed the industry's need for a user-friendly digital video enhancement (DVE) desktop workstation, offering both high performance and reasonable cost.

Alladin combines powerful new video-imaging DSP chips and hardware innovations with the latest in DVE multimedia software, operating in a Windows-driven environment. By breaking the $10,000 price barrier, the expectation is that Alladin will greatly expand the market for DVEs in the mid '90s—just as the microprocessor and laser printer made desktop publishing affordable a decade ago.

Alladin bridges the gap between linear and nonlinear video-production systems. Nonlinear editing is rapidly gaining acceptance as a powerful new approach to video production. Alladin users can look forward to an easy migration path from linear to nonlinear, allowing full-quality output on a desktop system—much like the laser printer did for desktop publishing. Compared with conventional designs offering comparable performance, the Alladin system achieves a remarkable 60 percent reduction in cost and a 65 percent reduction in component parts.

One of the investing rules of thumb I follow is to track those companies that inculcate the "Rule of the 60s": to bring new products to the market that are 60 percent more efficient, 60 percent more powerful, and 60 percent less expensive than existing models.

"Two years ago, less than a half-dozen feature films employed the use of computer graphics; this year maybe a half-dozen won't use any sort of digital enhancements."* Silicon is overtaking Hollywood. Digital video

---

* Snider, Burr, "The Toy Story Story," *Wired*, December 1995, p. 147.

LOGIC DEVICES, INC.

Chief Executive Officer:	William J. Volz
Principal Location:	628 E. Evelyn Ave. Sunnyvale, CA 94086
Telephone:	408-737-3300
Fax:	408-733-7690
E-mail:	not available
Web site:	not available
Satellite Locations:	none
Date Founded:	1983
Description of Business:	Develops and markets high-performance integrated circuits for applications that require very high operating speeds and low operating power.
# Employees Current:	50
% Female Employees:	40%
# Employees Projected 9/30/96:	50
Revenues 1995*:	$14,997,000
Gross Profit Margin (GPM):	43.4%
SGA Expenses/Revenues:	30.2%
% Sales Increase 1992 to 1995:	+122.5%
% Change GPM 1992 to 1995:	+7.6%
% Change SGA Expenses/Revenues 1992 to 1995:	+14.4%
Total Debt/Net Worth:	54.4%
Net Profits Before Taxes '95*:	$1,584,000
Net Profits Before Taxes/Revenues:	10.6%
Market Value/1995 Revenues*:	not available
Traded On:	NASDAQ (LOGC)
Opportunity Company Addresses:	Video professionals have an insatiable appetite for ever more innovative real-time digital video effects.
Elegance of Company's Solution:	Logic Devices produces video imaging DSP integrated circuits that bring 3-D video to the desktop PC.

*Annualized.

enhancement systems at under $10,000 give the smallest, youngest independent producer the graphics capability of Viacom. Thank you, Logic Devices.

Moreover, William J. Volz, Logic Device's CEO, runs a pretty tight ship. Logic Device's GPM has increased over the last four years by 7.6 percent. Couple that with sales increases of 122.5 percent and a debt-to-worth ratio of 54.4 percent, and you really come to the conclusion that at a price of 6¼, this stock has plenty of upside.

LUMISYS INC.

The use of medical film images to diagnose and treat diseases and injuries has been an important medical tool since the invention of X-ray technology and the emergence of radiology as a medical specialty. Today radiologists review and interpret images from a variety of imaging modalities, including X-rays, CT, MRI, ultrasound, and nuclear medicine. These modalities are used in a range of different applications requiring specialized equipment to produce images on film or video displays. Medical imaging has reduced the need for exploratory surgical procedures and has enabled clinicians to make faster and more precise diagnoses and prescribe more targeted courses of treatment. Medical imaging is used in all stages of the patient management cycle, from screening to diagnosis, treatment, and posttreatment assessment. According to the American College of Radiology, in 1994 over 179 million radiographic and fluoroscopic studies were performed in the United States, resulting in an estimated 537 million sheets of film. In 1992, approximately 19 million CT scans (from approximately 6,500 CT scanners), approximately 8 million MRI scans (from approximately 3,100 MRI systems), approximately 10 million nuclear medicine examinations (from approximately 9,600 gamma cameras), and approximately 48 million diagnostic ultrasound scans (from approximately 74,000 ultrasound scanners) were performed in the United States. According to an industry source, approximately one billion dollars of medical film was consumed in the United States in 1992.

The health-care industry in the United States continues to change dramatically in response to the escalating costs associated with medical products and services. An increased emphasis on lowering costs and optimizing resources has encouraged it to evolve toward managed regional health-care systems. These changes are having a profound impact on the practice of radiology. In the past radiologists were located in a medical facility close to the patient where they performed examinations and interacted face-to-face with the local clinician and the patient. As reimbursement for radiological interpretations has declined, radiologists are under pressure to increase the number of interpretations and compete for business over much larger geographic areas. In addition, with the development of advanced medical imaging technologies, radiologists have been able to sub-specialize, becoming, for example, neuroradiologists, mammographers, orthopedic radiologists, angiographers, or pediatric radiologists. These two trends—the evolu-

LUMISYS INC.

Chief Executive Officer:	Stephen J. Weiss
Principal Location:	238 Santa Ana Ct. Sunnyvale, CA 94086
Telephone:	408-733-6565
Fax:	408-733-6567
E-mail:	lumisys.com
Web site:	not available
Satellite Locations:	Chelmsford, Massachusetts
Date Founded:	1987
Description of Business:	Designs, manufactures, and markets a family of precision digitizers that convert medical images on film or video into digital format.
# Employees Current:	81
% Female Employees:	not available
# Employees Projected 9/30/96:	not available
Revenues 1995*:	$14,721,000
Gross Profit Margin (GPM):	53.7%
SGA Expenses/Revenues:	16.0%
% Sales Increase 1992 to 1995:	+228.7%
% Change GPM 1992 to 1995:	(1.8%)
% Change SGA Expenses/Revenues 1992 to 1995:	(34.4%)
Total Debt/Net Worth:	52.8%
Net Profits Before Taxes 1995*:	$2,684,000**
Net Profits Before Taxes/Revenues:	18.2%
Market Value/1995 Revenues*:	3.9x
Traded On:	NASDAQ (LUMI)
Opportunity Company Addresses:	The need to lower the costs of health-care delivery, particularly in the radiology lab.
Elegance of Company's Solution:	Lumisys delivers medical images to the point of care faster and at a lower cost than by conventional means.

*Annualized.
**After adding back $1,442,000 of acquisition costs.

tion toward managed regional health-care systems and increasing radiologist specialization—have resulted in a need to develop equipment and systems capable of transmitting medical images rapidly to and from remote locations.

Concurrent with these changes in radiology, the computing and telecommunication industries have experienced rapid growth and technological advancements. Put it all together and the result is accelerated acceptance of teleradiology, the practice of radiology from remote locations. In teleradiology, medical images at the point-of-care are digitized and transmitted to central locations for interpretation, bringing the patient's information to the radiologist faster and at significantly lower cost.

Lumisys designs, manufactures, and markets a family of precision digitizers that convert medical images on film or video into digital format. Once in digital form, the medical images can be stored, transmitted, viewed, enhanced, manipulated, and printed at any PC or workstation within a medical network. The company currently offers a comprehensive family of products for digitizing medical film images under the Lumiscan label and video images under the Imascan label. These digitizers process images from all commercially available medical-imaging modalities, including X-ray, computer tomography (CT), magnetic resonance imaging (MRI), ultrasound, and nuclear medicine. The company is the leading supplier of laser-based film digitizers, with sales of over 1,400 Lumiscan units since its first product was introduced in 1990. It also offers high-quality, board-level digitization and compression products for the capture of video images, which have applications in medical imaging as well as in scientific and industrial inspection, broadcast video, and multimedia imaging.

The slight degradation in Lumisys's GPM from 54.7 percent in 1992 to 53.7 percent in 1995 and its slower turning accounts receivables—38 days in 1993, 49 days in 1994, and 53 days in 1995—almost disqualify the company from inclusion in *Quantum Companies II*. Couple that with the high percentage of selling stockholders at the IPO, and you've got to be cautious with an investment in Lumisys. But its SGA Expenses/ Revenues ratio improved by 34.4 percent from 1992 to 1995, which suggests that the products almost sell themselves. Combined with the company's strong sales increases, these positive factors override the blinking yellow lights.

MACROMEDIA, INC.

There is dog-eat-dog competition in the authoring software market. Macromedia competes with Adobe Systems, Autodesk, Corel (a Quantum Company), Gold Disk, Microsoft, Strata, and other companies for a dominant position in this $1 billion market. Macromedia may not be the fastest-growing company in this market, but it is certainly one of the most profitable ones. Its net profit margin was 18.1 percent in 1995, greater than the 13.6 percent margin it enjoyed in 1994, which exceeded the 10.2 percent margin of 1993. Its gross profit margin climbed two percentage points from 1992 to 1995 annualized while its ratio of SGA Expenses/Revenues declined from 49.9 percent in 1992 to 39.6 percent in 1995. In a nutshell, the company's production costs are around 18 cents out of every dollar and its overhead and marketing costs, about 40 cents.

Macromedia is able to use its very high priced stock to acquire hot little software firms, and indeed it has been doing just that with purchases of MacroMind, Paracomp, Authorware, Altsys, the Richardson, Texas developer of FreeHand, and Fontographer. Freehand was a languishing product until Macromedia's management team breathed new life into it in early 1995.

Macromedia's objective is to continue to market above and beyond its competitors. This means continuing to offer a large number of user's conferences (the Macromedia User's Conference is the largest developer's conference in the world with 5,000 attendees) and support groups, as well as continuing to acquire companies that can help them round out their Digital Design Studio. Furthermore, Macromedia has initiated an aggressive marketing program by ending run-time licensing on titles made with their tools and instead asking all developers to include the "Made with Macromedia" logo on all packages, which allows the company to make millions of additional "impressions" per year.

Macromedia is also attempting to broaden its international exposure since its core revenue from outside North America represented only 32 percent of total revenues in 1995. It should have a good deal of incremental opportunity internationally in the next several years. This percentage should double by the end of the decade.

Multimedia-PC penetration in the home continues to grow. Consumer-oriented PCs accounted for nearly 30 percent of U.S. PC-unit shipments in 1994 but outsold television sets for the first half of 1995. The growth

MACROMEDIA, INC.

Chief Executive Officer:	John C. (Bud) Colligan
Principal Location:	600 Townsend St. San Francisco, CA 94103-4945
Telephone:	415-252-2000
Fax:	415-626-0554
E-mail:	bcolligan@macromedia.com
Web site:	http://www.macromedia.com
Satellite Locations:	Richardson, Texas; Berkshire, United Kingdom; Tokyo, Japan; Victoria, Australia.
Date Founded:	1988
Description of Business:	Designs, develps, markets, and supports authoring and production software used to create interactive multimedia applications—2-D and 3-D graphics animation, sound, and digital video—for corporate training, sales kiosks, entertainment, and multimedia presentations.
# Employees Current:	380
% Female Employees:	45%
# Employees Projected 9/30/96:	600
Revenues 1995*:	$65,702,000
Gross Profit Margin (GPM):	81.6%
SGA Expenses/Revenues:	39.6%
% Sales Increase 1992 to 1995:	+108.8%
% Change GPM 1992 to 1995:	+2.5%
% Change SGA Expenses/Revenues 1992 to 1995:	(20.6)%
Total Debt/Net Worth:	28.4%
Net Profits Before Taxes* 1995:	$11,912,000
Net Profits Before Taxes/Revenues:	18.1%
Market Value/1995 Revenues*:	16.3x
Traded On:	NASDAQ (MACR)
Opportunity Company Addresses:	The toolmakers in the emerging multimedia markets—PC, CD-ROM developers, WWW developers, online service developers, and 2-D and 3-D artists—need the current equivalent of hammers, chisels, and carving knives.
Elegance of Company's Solution:	Its authoring tools make Macromedia the Black & Decker of the multimedia markets.

*Annualized.

rate for PC sales to consumers will continue to grow faster than expected, and those PCs typically have CD-ROMs attached.

In the privacy of one's home, every PC user is a graphic designer. But there are multichannels of opportunity that Macromedia is addressing. They are the following:

Authoring Tools (Director and Authorware)

- PC CD-ROM developers—estimated at more than 300,000 and growing.
- Web-site developers—growing from 1 million today to 20 million in 1999.
- Enhanced audio CDs—the audio recording market (measured in hundreds of thousands) and virtually untapped today.
- Online service developers—fewer than 100,000 today, but with introduction of MSN should increase dramatically.
- Interactive training.
- Kiosks
- Interactive advertising (Internet, online and CD-ROM).

2-D Drawing (Freehand)

- More than 3.5 million users, or a market of more than $400 million.
- CorelDRAW has more than 2.6 million customers and Macromedia will offer a competitive upgrade to these users for less than it costs to upgrade to a new version of CorelDRAW from an existing CorelDRAW product.
- Freehand is available on both Macintosh and Windows (3.1, 95 and NT) versus CorelDRAW on Windows only.

3-D Modeling, Rendering and Animation (Extreme 3-D)

- 3-D will be as pervasive as 2-D—$400+ million estimated market.
- Extreme 3-D available on both Macintosh and Windows (3.1, 95 and NT) versus Autodesk, which is available on Windows NT only.*

Macromedia's total market opportunity exceeds $1 billion. A multiproduct company that sells through multichannels and can acquire any company with a p/e ratio below 100.0x without suffering dilution is very well poised for the next decade.

---

* Source: Mary Meeker, Gillian Munson of Morgan Stanley & Co.

MAPINFO CORPORATION

George Orwell would love MapInfo. The company gathers millions of pieces of geographic micro data in computers and merges files of neighborhood information with area codes and zip codes, all of it publicly available, and then sells or licenses its databases to mutual funds and high-priced consumer products companies to enhance their sales-prospecting abilities. When a telemarketer calls you and knows your name and various facts, such as the existence of a tennis court in your back yard, the telemarketer probably got her data from MapInfo. She knows your buying power and the range in which your household income falls. More than 100,000 people currently use MapInfo's software, which can now be moved in micro seconds from servers to laptops to inform road salespeople about commercial prospects in their market segments.

In today's business environment, organizations are under constant competitive pressure to improve their products and services, reduce costs, and improve operating efficiency. In response to this pressure, many organizations are seeking to reengineer their decision-making and operational processes at all levels so that they can react more quickly and effectively to competitors and changing market conditions. As part of this business-process reengineering, organizations are seeking new ways to manage, analyze, and use the vast amount of internal and external data available to them.

The need to improve corporate decision making and enhance operating efficiency has contributed to the growing acceptance of client/server computing and the increased use of relational databases and graphical-user interfaces. In client/server computing environments, common servers provide shared access to data and applications, while client computers, such as PCs and workstations, provide the user-interface and local-processing functions. Client/server systems can improve information sharing by making corporate data and applications accessible on the desktop. Critical accounting, manufacturing, sales, marketing, and other data, which have historically been locked in legacy systems on an organization's mainframe computer, are becoming accessible to users not only through relational databases residing on servers dispersed throughout the organization but also through local databases and spreadsheets located on the desktop. Graphical user

MAPINFO CORPORATION

Chief Executive Officer:	Brian D. Owen
Principal Location:	One Global View Troy, NY 12180
Telephone:	518-285-6000
Fax:	518-285-6060
E-mail:	not available
Web site:	not available
Satellite Locations:	Bracknell, United Kingdom; Waterbury, Connecticut; San Mateo, California; Bethesda, Maryland; Dallas, Texas; and Schaumburg, Illinois
Date Founded:	1986
Description of Business:	Develops, markets, licenses, and supports desktop mapping software and geographic and demographic information products.
# Employees Current:	268
% Female Employees:	38%
# Employees Projected 9/30/96:	378
Revenues* 1995:	$38,008,000
Gross Profit Margin (GPM):	80.3%
SGA Expenses/Revenues:	52.6%
% Sales Increase 1992 to 1995:	+359.1%
% Change GPM 1992 to 1995:	+8.2%
% Change SGA Expenses/Revenues 1992 to 1995:	+2.9%
Total Debt/Net Worth:	16.3%
Net Profits Before Taxes 1995*:	$5,036,000
Net Profits Before Taxes/Revenues:	13.2%
Market Value/1995 Revenues*:	7.1x
Traded On:	NASDAQ (MapInfo)
Opportunity Company Addresses:	Eighty percent of all corporate data has some geographic content such as zip codes or area codes.
Elegance of Company's Solution:	Desktop mapping software enables business users to correlate, visualize, and analyze that data.

*Annualized.

interfaces (GUIs), which are intuitive and easy-to-use, help make both data and applications more accessible to computer users throughout an enterprise.

MapInfo has developed desktop mapping software that can assist businesses in improving decision making and operating efficiency through geographic visualization and analysis of data. The company's products enable users to capture, manage, and use data in a meaningful way and thus improve organizational responsiveness and flexibility. The software enables users to access multiple libraries of data presented in on-screen maps of areas ranging in size from countries to cities, neighborhoods within cities, streets, and factory floor plans. Extensive bodies of census figures, market survey results, and other demographic data can also be overlaid on geographic areas.

MapInfo spends more than $4 million per year on new product development and new ways to deliver its product. The Internet should triple MapInfo's sales within three years because of its ease of use and inexpensiveness. Very small companies can gain the same advantages of larger competitors. The company's GPM is increasing year-to-year, which means the data is becoming increasingly valuable to its users.

MAXIS, INC.

One of the joys of playing Monopoly is that we suspend reality for an hour and pretend that we are real estate tycoons. Replicating that feeling in front of a personal computer is an awesome task, but it is done exquisitely well by Maxis, Inc.

Widget Workshop, the company's first title in its Software Toys for Kids, designed for children ages 8 and up, puts kids into a computerized laboratory where they can experiment with hundreds of realistic objects. SimTown, the second release, allows kids to manage their own neighborhood complete with individual houses, streets, parks, stores, pizza parlors, video arcades, and movie theaters. Zaark and the Night Team: The Quest for Patterns, the third release, sends kids on four missions to explore how patterns exist everywhere in the world around us.

SimTower turns players into instant real estate tycoons as they attempt to construct a soaring skyscraper tower. Klik & Play is a revolutionary new concept—an instant game creator. In minutes, users can design and produce their own computer games in a variety of genres—arcade, strategy, logic games, and more.

Taking advantage of CD-ROM storage technology, the SimCity 2000 CD Collection contains the ultimate compilation of SimCity products on one disk: SimCity 2000, Sim City 2000 Urban Renewal Kit, SimCity 2000 Scenarios Volume 1, and bonus cities and scenarios. The Urban Renewal Kit gives players the power to create different and unique cityscapes using all new graphics and easy-to-use editing tools. SimCity 2000 Scenarios Volume I lets players wrestle with different cities on the brink of destruction.

Maxis is rapidly growing and its GPM is improving, while its SGA Expenses/Revenues ratio is declining, a sure sign that word-of-mouth selling is clicking in. The product line is beginning to sell itself, sort of like when kids saw *Star Wars* more than once. Moreover, the company is managed with tight controls. Accounts receivable days on hand improved from 60 to 55 from 1994 to 1995. Inventory days on hand improved from 43 to 10 between 1994 and 1995. Most producers would give their eye teeth to have to carry only 10 days of inventory. Maxis not only makes terrific products—this is an elegantly run company.

MAXIS, INC.

Chief Executive Officer:	Jeffrey B. Braun
Principal Location:	2121 N. California Blvd. Walnut Creek, CA 94596-3572
Telephone:	510-933-5630
Fax:	510-927-3736
E-mail:	support@maxis.com
Web site:	http://www.maxis.com
Satellite Locations:	Salt Lake City, Utah; San Mateo, California; and London, United Kingdom
Date Founded:	1987
Description of Business:	Leading provider of challenging and entertaining personal computer software.
# Employees Current:	152
% Female Employees:	not available
# Employees Projected 9/30/96:	not available
Revenues 1995*:	$47,636,000
Gross Profit Margin (GPM):	70.0%
SGA Expenses/Revenues:	34.7%
% Sales Increase 1993 to 1996:	343.6%
% Change GPM 1993 to 1996:	+13.6%
% Change SGA Expenses/Revenues 1993 to 1996:	(8.4%)
Total Debt/Net Worth:	15.4%
Net Profits Before Taxes 1995*:	$7,019,000
Net Profits Before Taxes/Revenues:	14.7%
Market Value/1995 Revenues*:	6.6x
Traded On:	NASDAQ (MXIS)
Opportunity Company Addresses:	The home-computer user is buying increasingly sophisticated PCs with high-resolution monitors, graphics boards, and CD-ROM drives and is demanding increasingly sophisticated software.
Elegance of Company's Solution:	The company has responded with challenging and exciting entertainment, learning, and personal-creativity software.

*Annualized.

MEDPARTNERS, INC.

MedPartners, Inc., develops integrated health-care-delivery networks in selected geographic areas through affiliation with locally prominent physician practices. The company targets highly productive physicians with significant shares of their markets and reputations among patients, payors, and peers for providing quality medical care, and then acquires the operating assets of these practices and contracts with the physicians for the provision of all medical care—in exchange for a fixed percentage of practice revenues. The company's profitability depends upon enhancing operating efficiency, expanding health-care services, increasing market share, and assisting affiliated physicians in managing the delivery of medical care. MedPartners believes that affiliation with the company is attractive to physicians because it offers them the opportunity to maintain current physician income levels and gain access to capital, management expertise, sophisticated information systems, and managed-care contracts. Since its inception in January 1993, the company has affiliated with 34 physician groups representing 190 physicians in 12 geographic markets.

The Health Care Financing Administration forecasts that 1994 national spending on physician services approximated $200 billion, with an additional $61 billion directly under physician control. Concerns over the accelerating cost of health care have resulted in the increasing prominence of managed care. Traditional physician practices are at a disadvantage in a managed-care environment because they typically have high operating costs, little purchasing power with suppliers, and must spread overhead over a relatively small revenue base. In addition, physician practices often have insufficient capital to purchase new technologies and lack the sophisticated systems necessary to contract effectively with managed-care entities. As a result, physicians are increasingly abandoning traditional practices in favor of larger organizations, such MedPartners.

The key elements of MedPartner's strategy are (1) the integration of geographically proximate practices into coordinated networks in order to deliver comprehensive patient care; (2) targeting of high-quality, productive physicians who are committed to expanding their practices and providing cost-effective care; (3) utilization of sophisticated information systems to control quality and cost; (4) achieving economies

MEDPARTNERS, INC.

Chief Executive Officer:	Larry R. House
Principal Location:	3000 Galleria Tower Birmingham, AL 35244
Telephone:	205-733-8996
Fax:	205-987-4044
E-mail:	not available
Web site:	not available
Satellite Locations:	Boca Raton, Florida
Date Founded:	1993
Description of Business:	Acquires physician practices and manages their operations, which permits them to deliver health care free of the increasing hassles brought on by HMOs, malpractice litigation, and accumulating paperwork.
# Employees Current:	1,175
% Female Employees:	not available
# Employees Projected 9/30/96:	not available
Revenues 1995*:	$111,611,000
Profit After Phys. Services (PAPS):	39.1%
SGA Expenses/Revenues:	2.6%
% Sales Increase 1992 to 1995:	+407.5%
% Change PAPS 1994 to 1995:	+3.4%
% Change SGA Expenses/Revenues 1994 to 1995:	5.6%
Total Debt/Net Worth:	35.1%
Net Profits Before Taxes '95*:	$1,252,000
Net Profits Before Taxes/Revenues:	1.1%
Market Value/1995 Revenues*:	3.4x
Traded On:	NASDAQ (MPTR)
Opportunity Company Addresses:	Physicians who want to practice medicine free of most administrative hassles require a reliable management company under whose umbrella they can operate.
Elegance of Company's Solution:	The company acquires the assets of physician practices and puts the physicians under contract.

*Annualized.

of scale in purchasing supplies, equipment, and services; and (5) focusing on managed-care contracting opportunities.

MedPartners develops multispecialty physician networks, or "cells," that are designed to meet the specific medical needs of a targeted geographic market, utilizing stringent criteria in identifying physicians for participation in a MedPartners network. The company believes that information technology is critical to the growth of integrated health-care-delivery systems and that the availability of detailed clinical data is fundamental to quality control and cost containment. As a result the company has developed sophisticated management information systems that collect and analyze clinical and administrative data to allow it to effectively control overhead expenses, maximize reimbursement, and provide effective utilization management.

The economies of scale inherent in a network allow MedPartners to reduce operating costs by negotiating national or regional purchasing contracts for supplies, equipment, and services and by centralizing billing, collections, management, payroll, and accounting services of the affiliated practices. In addition, the network configuration gives the company the leverage to negotiate rates and contract terms with HMOs and other payors favorable to those rates and terms physician groups have historically been able to obtain independently.

The complexities of the managed-care environment create a significant administrative burden for physicians. The growth of capitated reimbursement presents the challenge of projecting costs of care based upon patient populations, physician-treatment patterns, and the specific requirements of managed-care contracts. MedPartners utilizes its information systems to improve productivity, manage complex reimbursement methodologies, measure patient satisfaction and outcomes of care, and integrate information from multiple sources. Its primary focus has initially been the southeastern United States, with physician networks currently under development in Alabama, Florida, Georgia, South Carolina, North Carolina, Tennessee, Texas, and Virginia, but it believes its business model is replicable and will allow it to compete nationwide.

MERCURY INTERACTIVE CORP.

Companies from airlines to stock brokerage firms have replaced mainframe computers and dumb terminals with client/server systems. (Think of the users as "clients" working from individual terminals; from these terminals, they can access or send information to the central processor, the "server." Any client can access the server at any time, and many clients can access the same data point within the server simultaneously.) With this convenience, however, comes the potential for problems. This is because Graphical User Interface (GUI, pronounced "gooey"), which permits the user to input a command by pointing and clicking, is becoming ubiquitous. Mercury's products test Windows-based applications that run on IBM and UNIX platforms. Mercury packages formulate test scripts with countless combinations of input-output commands.

A second member of the Mercury family of products is a stress tester, which simulates many workers working on the system simultaneously and determines the system's breaking point.

As is the case with many small software companies, Mercury, in its formative years, licensed a handful of established software firms—Oracle, Compuware, Andersen Consulting, and Sybase among them—to private-label its systems. Sales to them now account for about 20 percent of sales. Mainstream industrial companies account for the bulk of sales; they pay up for the safety they receive. GPM has increased from 83.7 percent in 1992 to 89.1 percent in 1995, which indicates no price erosion and a reduced reliance on OEM licenses.

Aryeh Finegold founded Mercury. Only 48 years old, he also founded and built Daisy Systems Corp., and did a repair and turnaround on Ready Systems Corp. before founding Mercury. Finegold has built Mercury without conventional venture capital, relying on Israeli investors and R&D grants from the Israeli government.

Eventually companies such as Mercury saturate their markets and are either acquired or buy compatible software companies. With a p/e ratio of more than 150.0x, no company can acquire Mercury and look at its stockholders with a straight face. So Mercury will do some acquiring. In May 1995, it bought Blue Lagoon Software for $2.3 million and took a $2.2 million charge against earnings. This acquisition held down 1995 earnings and according to its August 1995 prospectus, the Israeli government is concerned about future R&D efforts in Israel, as Blue Lagoon will become a U.S. product-development center.

MERCURY INTERACTIVE CORP.

Chief Executive Officer:	Aryeh Finegold
Principal Location:	470 Potrero Ave. Sunnyvale, CA 94086
Telephone:	408-523-9900
Fax:	408-523-9911
E-mail:	jillr@merc-int.com
Web site:	not available
Satellite Locations:	8 sales locations in the United States; 1 in Canada; 3 in Europe; an R&D facility in Israel
Date Founded:	1989
Description of Business:	Develops, markets, and supports software solutions that automate and manage testing and quality assurance for developers of client/server software and systems.
# Employees Current:	100
% Female Employees:	15%
# Employees Projected 9/30/96:	180
Revenues 1995*:	$30,600,000
Gross Profit Margin (GPM):	89.1%
SGA Expenses/Revenues:	59.4%
% Sales Increase 1992 to 1995:	+606.4%
% Change GPM 1992 to 1995:	+6.5%
% Change SGA Expenses/Revenues 1992 to 1995:	(51.6%)
Total Debt/Net Worth:	24.0%
Net Profits Before Taxes 1995*:	$3,172,000
Net Profits Before Taxes/Revenues:	10.4%
Market Value/1995 Revenues*:	12.0x
Traded On:	NASDAQ (MERC)
Opportunity Company Addresses:	Software bugs—the glitches and malfunctions that plague every software program under development—go undetected until late in the development process, when it is more expensive and time-consuming to get rid of them.
Elegance of the Company's Solution:	Software products that enable the testing of client/server software, which enable quick and easy testing throughout the development process.

*Annualized.

There are 14 sales offices for this small company, and 59.4 percent of sales are spent on selling and administration. That is a high ratio, but Finegold would doubtless call it building for the future. The client/server paradigm is mushrooming throughout the world. And just as most of us keep bandages and cough medicine in our homes, most businesses will need repair kits for their computers.

MERIX CORP.

Merix began in 1959 as the Circuit Board Division of electronics pioneer Tektronix Inc. From the beginning the division was chartered to provide all forms of interconnect technology—initially printed circuit boards, and later backplanes, flexible circuits, and high-performance circuits—for Tektronix's growing family of measurement, video, and computational products.

By the mid-1980s the quality and technological sophistication of the division's products were becoming obvious to the parent company. In 1985 Tektronix, recognizing a potential new profit center, chartered the division to sell to outside customers. Soon the Circuit Board Division had a customer base that included the likes of Pro-log, NCR (now AT&T), IMS (Integrated Measurement Systems), Methus, Rockwell, and IBM.

By the early 1990s it employed more than 600 people and was selling to global companies. Joining with key competing manufacturers, members of its customer base, and Original Equipment Manufacturers (OEMs) and suppliers, the Tektronix Circuit Board Division team—which later became the Merix team—created the October Project in October 1989. The Project's purpose was to move the interconnect industry forward through improved manufacturing techniques, quality enhancement, waste reduction, and cost-cutting methodologies and was sponsored by the IPC (Institute for Interconnecting and Packaging Electronic Circuits).

In 1983 Tektronix moved the division's printed circuit board manufacturing operations to its current site in Forest Grove. The operation includes a 174,000-square-foot manufacturing facility and a 6,300-square-foot water treatment plant, all on a 73-acre industrial park. It was headed by Lawrence C. Neitling.

One final factor was missing. If the Circuit Board Division was to successfully spin off from Tektronix, it would need a CEO with not only extensive senior corporate experience but also a strong reputation in the computer and systems industries.

The answer came in 1992, when Debi Coleman announced she was leaving Apple Computer and Silicon Valley to move to the Pacific Northwest to join her old Apple compatriot, Del Yocam, then the COO of Tektronix. At Apple, Coleman helped introduce both the Macintosh and Laserwriter printer, which shepherded in the age of desktop publishing. Next, she took over Apple's failing Macintosh manufacturing plant in

MERIX CORP.

Chief Executive Officer:	Debi Coleman
Principal Location:	1521 Poplar Lane Forest Grove, OR 97116
Telephone:	503-359-9300
Fax:	503-357-1504
E-mail:	not available
Web site:	not available
Satellite Locations:	none
Date Founded:	1994
Description of Business:	Leading manufacturer of technologically advanced electronic interconnect solutions, including printed circuit boards.
# Employees Current:	910
% Female Employees:	not available
# Employees Projected 9/30/96:	not available
Revenues 1995*:	$106,425,000
Gross Profit Margin (GPM):	28.7%
SGA Expenses/Revenues:	8.3%
% Sales Increase 1992 to 1995:	+151.3%
% Change GPM 1992 to 1995:	+15.3%
% Change SGA Expenses/Revenues 1992 to 1995:	(14.4%)
Total Debt/Net Worth:	30.9%
Net Profits Before Taxes 1995*:	$18,208,000
Net Profits Before Taxes/Revenues:	17.1%
Market Value/1995 Revenues*:	2.2x
Traded On:	NASDAQ (MERX)
Opportunity Company Addresses:	In the rapidly growing computer industry, contract manufacturers that can deliver high-quality components on short notice are in critically short supply.
Elegance of Company's Solution:	In its first year as a stand-alone company, Merix has met and overcome every challenge and won kudos from its customers.

*Annualized.

Fremont, California, and turned it into one of the most admired and emulated factories in the world and, in the process, restored Apple's sagging profits. She then became, at 34, the youngest chief financial officer in the Fortune 100.

With Coleman and Neitling, Tektronix had its management team in place; the skills and experience of the pair fit together neatly. Neitling had been manufacturing manager for Tektronix's $250 million component manufacturing group before joining the division. He was a leading figure in the industry and also enjoyed strong relationships with the division's suppliers. Coleman, conversely, knew (and had the respect of) the people who bought the division's products.

Note the remarkable improvement in profitability of Merix since it has been employee-owned. GPM has jumped 15.3 percent since 1992, the SGA Expenses/Revenues ratio has fallen by 14.4 percent, and the Operating Ratio at 17.1 percent in 1995 is up an eye-popping 44.9 percent. Equity is a stronger glue than Elmer's ever made. The folks at Merix are probably having more fun also.

NETCOM ONLINE COMMUNICATIONS, INC.

There are currently 1,800 Internet service providers in the United States. One hundred years ago there were more than 1,000 telephone companies; now there are fewer than 10 long-distance carriers. The Internet is a mass media similar to the telephone and the printing press, and it too will devolve into a handful of providers. Today there are 1,800 peacocks. Tomorrow there will be 1,790 feather dusters and 10 peacocks. I believe NETCOM will remain among the handsomest of peacocks. But I am one of its subscribers, so perhaps I am partial.

Already there is fierce competition among Internet service providers, as witness NETCOM's gross profit margin erosion. Prices seem stabilized from individuals at $20 per month, but just as cable TV providers encourage subscribers to pay more for additional channels and services (I pay TCI, my cable-TV provider, $49.50 per month on average) the Internet service providers are attempting to provide value-added services.

NETCOM has added 200,000 subscribers since early 1995 and is on its way to 500,000. Its appeal to the user is its price, quality of service, short wait-times, and a multitude of directories such as McKinley, an Internet directory service. When you surf the Web with your Yahoo surfboard, point and click on Legal and soon visit 488 Web sites to find specialized legal services, expert witnesses, and consultants to write and file a complaint for you. Who needs lawyers anymore?

NETCOM recently teamed up with AmeriData (a Quantum Company), a $1 billion provider of PC-based computers and networks that will market NETCOM's service along with its computers. NETCOM has a strategic alliance with Quantum Company Xing Technology Corp. to offer radio and television broadcasts over the Internet using Xing's Streamworks software-plus-server.

Securities analysts at Hambrecht & Quist project NETCOM's revenues to reach $117.8 million in FY1996 and $246 million in FY1997. At a multiple of 10x revenues, relatively low for the industry, NETCOM's stock should triple in two years, giving GeoCapital, its first-round venture capital investor, an 80x return on its money.

Nipping at NETCOM's heels are small but rapidly growing Internet service providers such as BEST Internet, CRL, Digital Express, Earthlink, IDT Corp., Concentric, and Mindspring. Along with established companies such as BBN Planet, PSINet, and UUNet, you're looking at what will probably be the top ten companies in three years.

NETCOME ONLINE COMMUNICATIONS, INC.

Chief Executive Officer:	David W. Garrison
Principal Location:	3031 Tisch Way San Jose, CA 95128
Telephone:	408-983-5950
Fax:	408-556-3155
E-mail:	barrie@netcom.com
Web site:	http://www.netcom.com
Satellite Locations:	Dallas, Texas
Date Founded:	1992
Description of Business:	A leading Internet-service provider to individuals in the United States.
# Employees Current:	not available
% Female Employees:	not available
# Employees Projected 9/30/96:	not available
Revenues 1995*:	37,395,000
Gross Profit Margin (GPM):	30.8%
SGA Expenses/Revenues:	54.0%
% Sales Increase 1993 to 1995:	+1550.4%
% Change GPM 1993 to 1995:	(41.9%)
% Change SGA Expenses/Revenues 1993 to 1995:	35.0%
Total Debt/Net Worth:	16.0%
Net Profits Before Taxes 1995*:	deficit
Net Profits Before Taxes/Revenues:	deficit
Market Value/1995 Revenues*:	16.8x
Traded On:	NASDAQ (NETC)
Opportunity Company Addresses:	The need of individuals to be connected to the Internet and the World Wide Web.
Elegance of Company's Solution:	Ease of access virtually anywhere in the country to dial into the Web.

*Annualized.

NET COUNT, LLC

I t began in an ant farm, but Paul Grand may still become the dominant personality among content providers who broadcast entertainment or publish information on the Web. He formed Digital Planet, Inc., in 1994 to design Web sites for commercial users and gained a dominant market share among the Hollywood studios that want to promote their movies on the Web. Some of these Web sites cost more than $100,000 per movie: "The studios require the use of a lot of graphics, and they are very demanding customers," says Grand. "We earn every penny."

Web-site design is essentially a service business that garners little business after design and installation. "I wanted to have a business with continuous revenue, so my partners and I wrote an algorithm to accurately identify inquiries at the Web site and report to the owner as much demographic information as we could collect." Which is why Grand launched Net Count, Inc., and went looking for a partner that could add value on the demographics measurement side. He interviewed most of the likely suspects in the market-research field before selecting Lexi International, Inc., a Quantum Company that pumped several million dollars into Net Count. The strategic alliance works like this: When a Web site records a session with a prospect, the prospect leaves a "fingerprint." Lexi can run the fingerprint through its census tract and other demographic data and within 20 minutes provide the company that owns the Web site with a number of reports on the gender, age, ethnic background, estimated household income, size of residence, and so forth of the prospects. Let's say the Web site owner is Ford, and Net Count reports to it that 90 percent of the recorded sessions on its Web site are 13-year-old girls. Clearly the Web site is appealing to the wrong market. "It can be changed in a few hours," says Grand. "I can turn my hat around to where it says 'Digital Planet' and make the changes."

But that's not all. Through a joint venture with Xing Technology Corporation, another Quantum Company, Net Count's software is imbedded in Xing's StreamWorks server software and marketed to TV broadcasters. As they broadcast an event, say the Super Bowl, over the Internet, they can record the sessions of the viewers on the first commercial of the game, the second, the third, and so forth. Let's say Pizza Hut bought the first commercial for $250,000 and the sixth commercial for the same amount. Net Count then reports to Pizza Hut 15 minutes after the first commercial runs that 67 percent of its viewers

NET COUNT, LLC

Chief Executive Officer:	Paul Grand
Principal Location:	1645 N. Vine St.
	Los Angeles, CA 90028
Telephone:	213-848-5700
Fax:	213-848-5750
E-mail:	pgrand@netcount.com
Web site:	http://www.netcount.com
Satellite Locations:	Culver City, California
Date Founded:	1994
Description of Business:	The leading market-research firm servicing Web site owners.
# Employees Current:	25
% Female Employees:	not available
# Employees Projected 9/30/96:	not available
Revenues* 1995:	not available
Gross Profit Margin (GPM):	The company is privately held and is not required to publish its financial statements.
SGA Expenses/Revenues:	not available
% Sales Increase 1992 to 1995:	not available
% Change GPM 1992 to 1995:	not available
% Change SGA Expenses/Revenues 1992 to 1995:	not available
Total Debt/Net Worth:	not available
Net Profits Before Taxes* 1995:	not available
Net Profits Before Taxes/Revenues:	not available
Market Value/1995 Revenues*:	not available
Opportunity Company Addresses:	The need to know if an ad will pull or a movie should be released.
Elegance of Company's Solution:	Net Count offers greater predictability and frequency through its software that measures viewer attitude than any other market-research system.

*Annualized.

were Hispanic American—non-pizza-eaters. What does Pizza Hut do? It slips in a Taco Bell commercial for the sixth paid time slot. (Both companies are owned by PepsiCo.)

Or, conversely, the first commercial is viewed by 55 percent males who drive 1-ton flatbed trucks that are three years old or more. What an opportunity for the Ford Truck Division to reach 10 million men! The television station can hold out a late-in-the-game commercial minute and contact Ford, e-mail them the data, and charge $1,500,000 for that minute.

With the coming of the cable modem (Quantum Company Bay Networks is one of the leaders in this field), the servers on the Internet will stream the games and entertainment through the cable system and at that point, Net Count's market will expand to include every cable TV advertiser. Television marketing will never be the same.

Grand got all the bugs out of his software when he relocated Net Count's headquarters into Lexi's offices. When he started his business, he looked for the cheapest rent he could find and took the former offices of Uncle Miltie's Ant Farm in Culver City, California. "The previous tenant sold ant colonies, and when he left, he didn't take all of the ants with him," says Grand. "In the back room, where we wrote some serious code, the computers were crawling with ants."

The techies at Net Count weren't bothered by the ants swarming everywhere. In fact they nicknamed their group "The Ant Farm."

NETSCAPE COMMUNICATIONS CORP.

Most of us carry billfolds that contain our driver's licenses and credit cards along with other personal items. We provide merchants with credit cards or cash or we pay via checks and proffer our driver's licenses when we make purchases. The Netscape Navigator is an electronic-powered billfold carrier that zooms our billfolds through the Web in nanoseconds, enabling us to make purchases and enabling merchants to verify our identity.

That's not enough to make Netscape the first company to achieve a valuation of more than $5 billion in 18 months. Our driver's license contains other information about us as do the other items in our billfolds. Netscape has the ability to capture that information, such as our nine-digit zip code, and within seconds, by running correlations against census tracts and public records, know our buying patterns. You may say that is interesting to advertisers and merchants on the Internet, but what about other markets where non-PC users shop?

The answer is that the Internet is just the beginning. The cable TV industry has come up with a response of its own, using cable modems. Cable TV runs over fiber-optic lines, which carry video and can carry a whole lot more, such as interactive shopping. That function requires a PC, and that gets us back to Netscape, whose electron-powered billfold carrier will soon be operating on cable TV.

Want to vote electronically and privately? The Netscape Navigator will carry your choice. If an advertiser wants to know who will be watching the next Michigan v. Notre Dame game and their buying patterns, it will use the Netscape Navigator.

Netscape has become Microsoft's toughest competitor for the hearts and minds of programmers who seek to make their fortunes by designing new applications for the Web. Netscape has turned its software for browsing the Web into a new platform for developing add-on products. And that platform isn't exclusively tied to the Microsoft operating systems that are standard on most personal computers. Netscape claims that 8,500 companies are using its technology to develop Web sites as well as software programs and services.

Netscape adopted Java, a programming language for interactive Internet programs that relies on a radical change in software design. Instead of playing only programs that reside in a PC, tiny Java programs, called "applets", can be sent over the Internet and run by browser

NETSCAPE COMMUNICATIONS CORP.

Chief Executive Officer:	James L. Barskdale
Principal Location:	501 East Middlefield Rd. Mountain View, CA 94043
Telephone:	415-254-1900
Fax:	415-528-4124
E-mail:	jimb@netscape.com
Web site:	http://www.netscape.com
Satellite Locations:	none
Date Founded:	1994
Description of Business:	Produces the Navigator, the first available client that enables commercial transactions on the Web.
# Employees Current:	550
% Female Employees:	25%
# Employees Projected 9/30/96:	1,000
Revenues (Nine Months):	$37,428,195
Gross Profit Margin (GPM):	87.8%
SGA Expenses/Revenues:	66.0%
% Sales Increase 1992 to 1995:	not available
% Change GPM 1992 to 1995:	not available
% Change SGA Expenses/Revenues 1992 to 1995:	not available
Total Debt/Net Worth:	22.5%
Net Profits Before Taxes (9 Months)*:	($2,937,323)
Net Profits Before Taxes/Revenues:	deficit
Market Value/1995 Revenues*:	114.5x
Traded On:	NASDAQ (NSCP)
Opportunity Company Addresses:	The need to conduct commerce on the Web.
Elegance of Company's Solution:	Think of a billfold powered by electrons containing a buyer's driver's license and credit card moving through and engaging in commerce privately and seamlessly.

*Annualized.

software. That means that users don't need a particular machine or operating system and might even rent code rather than buy application programs.

Microsoft plans to fight back with chunks of software code called OLE controls that can be transferred over the Internet to handle simple tasks. But many observers believe that Netscape's Navigator, carrying Java in its electronic billfold, has jumped out in front of Microsoft.

Netscape is not an accidental venture. It was conceived by James H. Clark, the past chairman of Silicon Graphics, Inc., who mentored the developer of the Navigator, and Marc L. Andreesen, 24, vice president, technology, who coauthored the original Mosaic Web browser when he was at the University of Illinois in the early 1990s. Clark brought in the inimitable venture capital fund Kleiner Perkins Caulfield & Byers, and together they brought in as strategic partners some of the leading content providers in the country: TCI, Times Mirror, Knight-Ridder, The Hearst Corporation, and International Data Group. In doing this, Clark announced to the community of publishers and broadcasters that the water is fine on the Internet; come in for a swim. It took the edge off and validated Netscape as a company content providers could deal with confidently and confidentially. Without its assemblage of strategic partners, Netscape would never have its $5 billion-plus valuation and be the lead horse in the Internet race.

NETWORK EXPRESS, INC.

Think of the communications channels that bring information and entertainment into our homes and businesses as pipe. The wider the pipe, the more information and entertainment can be brought in. Currently, the widest pipe is ISDN (Integrated Services Digital Network). The U.S. local telephone companies will tell you when you call them that they will install ISDN for a couple of hundred dollars and they will do it in a few days. Not true. It will take them more than a month. The demand caught them by surprise. So, it will take probably two months to bring video onto your PC over the Internet. Not so in France or Japan. ISDN is ubiquitous there, and that is where Network Express is cutting its teeth.

The company's core software technology is embodied in an architecture to address the special needs of dial-up ISDN Internetworking involving transparent bandwidth management, security, interoperability, and call management. The principal market for its products to date has been large corporations in Japan where ISDN has been fully deployed for some time. A principal component of Network Express' business strategy, however, is to expand sales in the United States, where the deployment of ISDN has been slow but more recently has begun to increase. The company believes that its experience in meeting the needs of large corporations in Japan gives it a competitive advantage as it is able to offer its customers products of proven functionality and performance. As of March 31, 1995, the company had sold over 3,600 units, 3,300 of which were sold in Japan.

Although other services are technologically feasible, ISDN remains the most widely used global digital service for data, video, and voice. ISDN uses internationally recognized standards for switched services, which were adopted in 1982 by the United Nations Consultative Committee on International Telegraphy and Telephony to transmit data, voices, and images over digital lines. Relative to the prior technology, ISDN is inexpensive and flexible. ISDN was initially slow to develop, however, principally because its implementation required the telephone companies to make major investments in software and hardware in each local office to bring the service to their customers. Until ISDN became widely available, its utility was limited because network managers could not depend on using it in most of their locations. Moreover, the

NETWORK EXPRESS, INC.

Chief Executive Officer:	Richard P. Eidswick
Principal Location:	4251 Plymouth Rd. Ann Arbor, MI 48105
Telephone:	313-761-5005
Fax:	313-995-1114
E-mail:	not available
Web site:	not available
Satellite Locations:	Tokyo, Japan; New York, New York; Iselin, New Jersey; San Ramon, California; London, United Kingdom
Date Founded:	1990
Description of Business:	Designs, manufactures, and markets data communications hardware and software products that provide high-speed LAN switched-access using ISDN.
# Employees Current:	86
% Female Employees:	19%
# Employees Projected 9/30/96:	100
Revenues (Annualized) 1995:	$13,750,000
Gross Profit Margin (GPM):	$44.1%
SGA Expenses/Revenues:	13.6%
% Sales Increase 1992 to 1995:	+979.3%
% Change GPM 1992 to 1995:	+6.3%
% Change SGA Expenses/Revenues 1992 to 1995:	(77.9%)
Total Debt/Net Worth:	6.0%
Net Profits Before Taxes* 1995:	$778,000
Net Profits Before Taxes/Revenues:	5.6%
Market Value/1995 Revenues*:	7.8x
Traded On:	NASDAQ (NETK)
Opportunity Company Addresses:	More companies have LANs, more people want to get onto the Internet from their homes, and both groups are wearing out their modems sending an increased amount of data.
Elegance of Company's Solution:	The bandwidth requirements of emerging applications have created an opportunity to offer equipment plus software to bring ISDN to dial-up networks.

*Annualized.

telephone companies themselves lacked experience in data services and had to train their employees in the service and support of a new class of customer.

The justification for remote ISDN access is based on the ability to deliver intermittent, high-speed access on a cost-effective basis. If bandwidth requirements are modest, an analog modem connection or packet-switched connection may be sufficient. If traffic volume is consistently high, however, a dedicated digital circuit could be cost-effective. In between these two extremes is ISDN, which has a low fixed-monthly cost and a variable usage cost.

Network Express has grown tenfold over the last four years. Its GPM has grown 6.3 percent and its SGA Expenses/Revenues ratio has fallen 77.9 percent, which means that word-of-mouth, the world's most persuasive salesperson, is moving lots of goods for the company. Once ISDN is the pipe of choice in the United States, Network Express will begin to sell its hardware and software into a much larger market.

NETWORK-1 SOFTWARE & TECHNOLOGY, INC.

ecurity problems have been intensifying with the growth of the Internet. In effect, any person with access to the Internet can enter into a private, local area network (LAN) operated by an Internet host by passing through the router that connects that network to the Internet. Firewalls prevent this passage by unauthorized users. Typically, the greater the security needed, the more complex the installation and programming required to configure and maintain the firewall. Therefore, firewalls with high levels of security have not been available to organizations that lack highly technical capabilities in-house or the money to hire skilled systems integrators.

Until now, Robert Russo, an experienced computer industry consultant and marketer, teamed up with William M. Hancock, a renowned computer designer and pioneer of the ISDN protocol as well as author of the RSA encryption algorithm for the new CCITT x.32 network standards, to develop a new and much more user-friendly firewall. They enticed Corey M. Horowitz, head of CMH Capital Management, an early investor in PSInet, which translates into "large capital gain" fund, who provided the venture capital.

According to the book *Firewalls and Internet Security*, by William Cheswick, firewalls are a collection of components placed between two networks that have the following properties:

- all traffic from inside to outside, and vice versa, must pass through the firewall
- only authorized traffic, as defined by the local network security policy, is allowed to pass
- the firewall itself is immune to penetration

Firewalls, after passwords, are the first guard against intrusion. They stop unauthorized users, or hackers, from entering the system at its "front door." Firewalls are typically placed between the organization and the outside world. Many organizations are finding a need for internal firewalls to isolate certain corporate areas for which tighter security is required.

Firewall/Plus, Network-1's initial product, provides a high level of security in an intuitive format; installation and configuration can be done without technical computer expertise. Firewall/Plus accomplishes this due to its unique platform. As an MS-DOS-based firewall,

NETWORK-1 SOFTWARE & TECHNOLOGY, INC.

Chief Executive Officer:	Robert M. Russo
Principal Location:	909 Third Ave. New York, NY 10022
Telephone:	212-293-3082
Fax:	212-293-3090
E-mail:	cmh@interramp.com
Web site:	http://www.interramp.com
Satellite Locations:	none
Date Founded:	1990
Description of Business:	Designs, develops, markets, and services computer network security products.
# Employees Current:	19
% Female Employees:	25%
# Employees Projected 9/30/96:	40
Revenues 1995*:	not available
Gross Profit Margin (GPM):	The company is privately held and is not required to publish its financial statements.
SGA Expenses/Revenues:	not available
% Sales Increase 1992 to 1995:	not available
% Change GPM 1992 to 1995:	not available
% Change SGA Expenses/Revenues 1992 to 1995:	not available
Total Debt/Net Worth:	not available
Net Profits Before Taxes 1995*:	not available
Net Profits Before Taxes/Revenues:	not available
Market Value/1995 Revenues*:	venture capital stage company
Opportunity Company Addresses:	The most secure firewalls have heretofore been available only to organizations with highly technical capabilities.
Elegance of Company's Solution:	Network-1's firewall is simple to use, requiring a mouse and 10 minutes of installation time.

*Annualized.

Firewall/Plus is more secure than UNIX-based firewalls, the operating system on which all other firewalls are based. MS-DOS-based systems are "deaf" and "blind," which prevents attackers from talking to Firewall/Plus. In comparison, UNIX-based systems can "see" and "hear"; a UNIX-savvy attacker who knows Internet protocols can penetrate the system.

Firewall/Plus is the first firewall to support token-ring networks directly. All other commercial firewalls require the use of a router, another piece of equipment, to complete the connection from the firewall to the token ring. The company also plans to introduce a scaled-down version of Firewall/Plus, called Firewall/Plus-LE, designed for small businesses. Firewall/Plus-LE allows for a limited number of simultaneous connections, whereas Firewall/Plus allows for unlimited simultaneous connections.

Firewall/Plus uses a graphical interface and MS-DOS mouse driver that enables the user to point and click through various configurations. Installation can be completed within 10 minutes and users do not need to know sophisticated computer language to modify Firewall/Plus's standard settings to meet their specific needs. (UNIX-based systems take significantly longer to install—several days, in some cases—and modifications require some knowledge of UNIX, an operating system.) Firewall/Plus significantly reduces the time and skill required to install and operate a firewall.

The company's marketing strategy includes cultivating highly visible customers, which it has in General Motors, AT&T, MCI, Kodak, and DEC, and then to sign up the top value-added resellers in the United States and abroad. Network-1's reputation is growing. It has virtually eliminated the network security problem at Kraft/General Foods, which had been plagued by 15 to 20 hacker attacks every day, using AccessPlus, a LAN/WAN security product.

With a distinguished client base and an easy-to-install, very efficient product, Network-1 should be one of the most remarkable companies of the coming decade.

NEUREX CORPORATION

Neurex is addressing an enormous market with a highly focused drug development program and a *Zaibatsu*-like team of corporate sponsors, scientific advisors, and venture capital investors. It has raised more than $66 million in capital in seven-plus years and its burn rate is $7 million a year or $20,000 a day. But the size of the problem—the Big "P"—is the glue that holds the team together.

More than 5 million people suffer from chronic, neuropathic, and acute pain, creating a market of more than $275 million per year that is being targeted by the company's SNX-111 pain program. A second product line seeks therapies for ischemia, or brain damage, as a result of cardiac arrest, head trauma, and stroke. It's in Phase II clinical trials with this product line.

Neurex is in Phase I/II studies for the treatment of cancer/ neuropathic pain with its N-type neuron-specific calcium channel blocker SNX-111. Initial results from these studies indicated that patients who were resistant to morphine therapy obtained symptomatic relief, and this has been maintained in those patients treated in the long-term part of the protocol. Expanded studies are now under way.

Also in April 1994, Neurex signed a collaborative agreement with Medtronic, Inc., for the development of SNX-111 for the treatment of chronic neuropathic pain by direct administration into the spinal space using the Medtronic SynchroMed pump, an implantable, programmable drug delivery system. Under the terms of the collaborative agreement, Neurex will receive up to $16 million in equity and milestone payments to develop SNX-111 with Medtronic. To date, Neurex has received $10 million in equity investment and a convertible loan from Medtronic. This capital injection kept the company afloat in 1995.

As a result of its strong preclinical profile for cerebral ischemia, SNX-111 is also being developed as a treatment for brain damage in the United States for patients undergoing coronary-artery-bypass graft procedures and in Europe for head trauma. Stroke and cardiac arrest are also being considered as additional clinical development targets.

In April 1994, Neurex licensed worldwide rights, excluding Germany, to SmithKline Beecham's CORLOPAM, enhancing the company's acute-care product development portfolio and positioning it as a significant player within this area. CORLOPAM has been targeted for a range of indications, including control of blood pressure following cardiovascular surgery, treatment of malignant/severe hypertension,

NEUREX CORPORATION

Chief Executive Officer:	Howard E. Greene Jr.
Principal Location:	3760 Haven Ave. Menlo Park, CA 94025-1012
Telephone:	415-853-1500
Fax:	415-853-1538
E-mail:	not available
Web site:	not available
Satellite Locations:	none
Date Founded:	1988
Description of Business:	Product-development company focused on acute-care disorders and neurological disorders.
# Employees Current:	57
% Female Employees:	47%
# Employees Projected 9/30/96:	60
Revenues 1995*:	$3,141,000
Gross Profit Margin (GPM):	not available
SGA Expenses/Revenues:	64.9%
% Sales Increase 1992 to 1995:	+51.2%
% Change GPM 1992 to 1995:	not available
% Change SGA Expenses/Revenues 1992 to 1995:	(38.3%)
Total Debt/Net Worth:	182.9%
Net Profits Before Taxes 1995*:	deficit
Net Profits Before Taxes/Revenues:	deficit
Market Value:	$120 million
Traded On:	NASDAQ (NXCO)
Opportunity Company Addresses:	There are more than 200,000 reported neurological disorders, 500,000 victims of head injuries, and 500,000 stroke victims per year in the United States.
Elegance of Company's Solution:	The company is developing solutions to these disorders.

*Annualized.

congestive heart failure, and acute kidney failure, all of which can result in a medical emergency. Neurex is currently in Phase III clinical trials with CORLOPAM in an intravenous form for the treatment of blood pressure control and expects to file a New Drug Application in 1996. Regulatory approval has already been granted in several countries.

Continuing with the company's strategy to further expand and diversify its portfolio of products, Neurex acquired Creagen, Inc., in July 1994. Creagen's lead product, Pro-urokinase, is a thrombolytic agent, which because of its clot-specific properties and safety characteristics, may have a favorable profile in the treatment of Acute Myocardial Infarction (AMI) and stroke, as well as a number of additional indications. An application for marketing approval has been submitted in Europe by Grunenthal GmbH, the Neurex licensee in European countries for this product.

With a market value of $119,800,000, investors are betting big chips that Neurex will become one of the next pharmaceutical start-ups to become a major company.

OCCUSYSTEMS, INC.

Ihe raison d 'etre of some collective-modality companies is to become the exit-of-choice for owners of businesses who seek a capital gain for their years of hard work. For others, it is the effectiveness that can be achieved by combining and turning over the administrative functions to a skilled team of experienced, computer-literate people. The fingertips of venture capital investors glow with the color gold when they spot an opportunity that represents both of these operating modalities. Welsh Carson Anderson & Stowe is the best venture capital fund at capitalizing on them, and health-care delivery is the garden in which they plant and harvest their fruit.

Overlooked for decades as a money sinkhole, occupational medicine (OM) is a relatively small specialty, with just over 2,000 physicians out of approximately 550,000 total patient-care physicians in the United States. Most of the occupational medicine specialists are in small practices of one to four physicians. Approximately 30 percent are board-certified in occupational medicine. Other practicing OM physicians may be board-certified in family practice or internal medicine.

OM focuses on the primary-care treatment of occupational injuries and illnesses. In 1992, almost 6.8 million nonfatal injuries were reported by employers, along with an additional 4,200 work-related fatalities. There is a wide range of injury rates among industries. Manufacturing, construction, mining, agriculture and forestry, and transportation/ shipping companies all have high injury rates. Because a few industries account for a high proportion of the injuries, it has been possible for a medical specialty to develop around the types of injuries treated.

Since OM is mostly a primary-care specialty, few of the injured workers need to be hospitalized, and most injuries are fairly minor— cuts, bruises, broken bones, and soft-tissue injuries from overuse of muscles and joints. The preponderance of injuries can be handled by the primary-care OM physician, who either directly or indirectly through referral controls up to 80 percent of the health care provided in OM. More serious injuries are referred to specialists, with orthopedists and neurologists comprising the bulk of specialty referrals. Physical and occupational therapy are very important, since the injured worker often needs rehabilitation.

OccuSystems' approach to workers' compensation provides significant reductions in total costs for employers. Using its care-management system, OccuSystems follows the patient through the entire health-care

OCCUSYSTEMS, INC.

Chief Executive Officer:	John K. Carlyle
Principal Location:	3010 LBJ Freeway Dallas, TX 75234
Telephone:	214-484-2700
Fax:	214-620-9172
E-mail:	not available
Web site:	not available
Satellite Locations:	Throughout the Southwest and Midwest United States
Date Founded:	1990
Description of Business:	The nation's largest physician-practice management company focusing on occupational health care.
# Employees Current:	2,000
% Female Employees:	not available
# Employees Projected 9/30/96:	not available
Revenues 1995*:	$124,226,000
Gross Profit Margin (GPM):	not available
SGA Expenses/Revenues:	6.0%
% Sales Increase 1992 to 1995:	+831.7%
% Change GPM 1992 to 1995:	not available
% Change SGA Expenses/Revenues 1992 to 1995:	(71.4%)
Total Debt/Net Worth:	32.4%
Net Profits Before Taxes 1995*:	$6,068,000
Net Profits Before Taxes/Revenues:	4.9%
Market Value/1995 Revenues*:	2.2x
Traded On	NASDAQ (OSYS)
Opportunity Company Addresses:	Workers' compensation costs are a significant cost factor in corporate America, representing $63 billion in 1993, of which $38 billion was legal fees and lost wages and $25 billion was health-care costs.
Elegance of Company's Solution:	OccuSystems provides an elegant solution to the problem by lowering the costs through efficient delivery of services and returning the worker to the job more rapidly.

*Annualized.

system and coordinates the employee's return to work. The goal is to minimize total workers' compensation costs, which include variable costs, such as wage replacement, disability, legal, and administration, as well as the nonvariable health-care costs. By avoiding an overly narrow focus on health-care cost containment and by making sure the patient returns to work as quickly as possible, OccuSystems' treatment protocols lower an employer's workers' compensation burden far more significantly than other managed-care programs. Because of this, the company has been able to achieve large gains in market share in its established markets.

OccuSystems has developed proprietary occupational medicine treatment protocols that are a significant barrier to entry. It has accumulated information on the best treatment methods for hundreds of occupational injuries. The protocols are segmented by injury and industry and are unique in the specialty of occupational medicine. The company's database would be very difficult and expensive to replicate.

OccuSystems' practice-management capabilities are among the most sophisticated of all the physician-practice-management companies. By taking an industrial engineering approach to the physician practice, OccuSystems is able to improve physician productivity and generate higher revenues, with margin improvement of more than 15 percent in the years following an affiliation. The company's SGA/Revenues ratio has plunged over the last four years to an eye-popping 6 percent.

OccuSystems has experienced revenue growth of more than 800 percent since 1992. The number of OM practices that it could acquire over the next five years could quadruple its market value.

ORTHOPEDIC TECHNOLOGY, INC.

The company supports the quarterbacks whose blockers are not up to the task. There must be many of them because, ORTH (its NASDAQ symbol) is one of the fastest-growing firms in the field of orthopedic sports-medicine products. The firm's principal products are knee braces, foot and ankle supports, and other devices for the rehabilitation and treatment of musculoskeletal problems or injuries. ORTH has unique and demonstrable economic advantages that set it apart from its competitors. It has established a reputation for quality products with patented proprietary designs. Second, it has set up a system whereby an order for, say, even custom-fitted knee braces can be shipped within 48 hours. Third, in the demanding world of professional sports, its products have been accepted by some of the most acclaimed stars. Among the beneficiaries of its patented knee brace, called the Performer Plus, are NFL quarterbacks John Elway and Randall Cunningham, baseball star George Brett, and Olympic skier Suzy Chaffee. And finally, with more people using seat belts and with more cars equipped with air bags, auto-related deaths decline while debilitating injuries rise.

ORTH has developed new products to take some pressure off knee braces, including CryoLogic, a cold-therapy management system which received FDA's 510K device approval in July 1995. Since the product is often used by patients following knee surgery for short-term relief of pain and swelling, it was a natural adjunct to its knee brace business. The device enables the patient to obtain portable cold therapy treatment, providing continuous circulation of cold water to the affected area following injury or surgery.

C-Tech is a wrist-support product for the treatment of carpal tunnel syndrome, an ailment becoming more widespread with the growth of the use of keyboards for personal computer equipment. The design allows the device to be placed on the dorsal or palm regions of the hand where it provides comfortable support without the use of straps or attachments that would impair free movement of the hand.

The third new product is Quick Lock, recently added to the post-operative knee brace line. It provides a simple, secure lock to achieve and maintain full extension of the leg. ORTH also introduced Ultra 4, a replacement of its Ultra 3 model in the foot and ankle support category. An improved design provides improved comfort and stability on a lightweight frame that allows proper foot alignment.

ORTHOPEDIC TECHNOLOGY, INC.

Chief Executive Officer:	Calvin G. Andre
Principal Location:	1905 N. MacArthur Dr. Tracy, CA 95376
Telephone:	209-832-5200
Fax:	209-832-8010
E-mail:	not available
Web site:	not available
Satellite Locations:	none
Date Founded:	1973
Description of Business:	Designs, develops, manufactures, and markets patented orthopedic products for the sports medicine market.
# Employees Current:	251
% Female Employees:	55.5%
# Employees Projected 9/30/96:	275
Revenues 1995*:	$17,257,000
Gross Profit Margin (GPM):	51.2%
SGA Expenses/Revenues:	37.0%
% Sales Increase 1992 to 1995:	+145.7%
% Change GPM 1992 to 1995:	+2.0%
% Change SGA Expenses/Revenues 1992 to 1995:	(6.8)%
Total Debt/Net Worth:	16.3%
Net Profits Before Taxes '95*:	$1,947,000
Net Profits Before Taxes/Revenues:	11.3%
Market Value/1995 Revenues*:	1.5x
Traded On:	NASDAQ (ORTH)
Opportunity Company Addresses:	An aging but essentially healthier population and increased injuries (as opposed to deaths) due to seat belt laws, as well as the increased size and speed of athletes in contact sports, creates more demand for knee and other braces.
Elegance of Company's Solution:	The company's knee braces are proprietary and preferred by many othorpods. They can ship any product anywhere in 48 hours.

*Annualized.

With annual sales approaching $20 million, ORTH is an early stage company with a mere 3.4 million shares outstanding and minimal institutional interest, the shares are underfollowed on Wall Street. An IPO in 1993 allowed the company to retire the equity interests of a number of earlier investors and to pay off practically all of its long-term obligations, of which only a minimal amount remains. ORTH is discussing acquisition with DePuy, a diversified producer/marketer of rehabilitation products.

A growing sales and earnings base and limited debt should provide ORTH the resources to pursue acquisitions of complementary product lines in the sports medicine market and thus enjoy greater productivity from its sales force.

OVID TECHNOLOGIES, INC.

As readers of the financial press know, the *Encyclopedia Brittannica* has been losing money for the last three years and its board of directors has hired investment banker Lazard Freres to locate an acquiror. The esteemed encyclopedia producer gainsaid the CD-ROM market and even agreed contractually, when it sold its Compton subsidiary to the Tribune Companies, not to connect its huge print volumes to CD-ROM, relying instead on its sales force who said print would sell. Not! Oh, what a mistake to listen to one's sales force prior to making a decision that could hurt them!

Ovid Technologies and other entrepreneurial companies are obtaining CD-ROM and on-line rights to many popular databases and making large and increasing profits as a result.

The databases offered by Ovid are licensed from various governmental entities, not-for-profit associations, and commercial businesses that compile and abstract information from a variety of sources. Approximately 95 percent of the company's customers subscribe to the Medline database, a bibliography of the world's leading biomedical literature produced by the National Library of Medicine. The National Library of Medicine compiles the databases and licenses third parties, including Ovid, to distribute the database in electronic form. Ovid's licensing agreement with the National Library of Medicine is perpetual, subject to the right of either party to cancel the agreement on 90 days' written notice, and grants Ovid a license to use the databases on a royalty-free basis in the United States and for a small royalty internationally. Other databases that are frequently subscribed to by Ovid's customers are CINAHL, a bibliography of nursing literature produced by CINAHL Information Systems, and PsycLIT, a bibliography of psychological literature produced by the American Psychological Association, a not-for-profit professional society. Most databases are updated either weekly or monthly.

In addition to stand-alone CD-ROMs and local CD-ROM and magnetic networks, as a result of Ovid's acquisition of the BRS Online component of InfoPro Technologies, Inc., in March 1994, the company is now able to offer an extensive collection of bibliographic databases online. In addition, the BRS acquisition enables Ovid to distribute the full text of recently published and archival articles from over 60 leading biomedical and scientific journals and other publications. Ovid is developing software capable of displaying color illustrations, graphics,

OVID TECHNOLOGIES, INC.

Chief Executive Officer:	Mark L. Nelson
Principal Location:	333 Seventh Ave. New York, NY 10001
Telephone:	212-563-3006
Fax:	212-563-3784
E-mail:	not available
Web site:	not available
Satellite Locations:	none
Date Founded:	1989
Description of Business:	Provides electronic information retrieval services to 55 percent of the major medical centers in North America.
# Employees Current:	150
% Female Employees:	40%
# Employees Projected 9/30/96:	160
Revenues 1995*:	$25,934,000
Gross Profit Margin (GPM):	70.2%
SGA Expenses/Revenues:	38.7%
% Sales Increase 1992 to 1995:	+268.1%
% Change GPM 1992 to 1995:	+4.0%
% Change SGA Expenses/Revenues 1992 to 1995:	(20.8%)
Total Debt/Net Worth:	85.8%
Net Profits Before Taxes '95*:	$2,700,000
Net Profits Before Taxes/Revenues:	10.4%
Market Value/1995 Revenues*:	3.3x
Traded On:	NASDAQ (OVID)
Opportunity Company Addresses:	Physicians and medical researchers rely on information retrieval processes to locate publications applicable to their patient-care practices and research processes. But the volume of information is much too vast and unwieldy to identify pertinent information quickly.
Elegance of Company's Solution:	The company offers its subscribers a comprehensive collection of databases licensed from third parties.

*Annualized.

and tables as contained in the original print format of these articles. These bibliographic and full-text databases are accessed online via commercial telecommunications networks or the Internet. The full-text database can be searched either through an automatic link feature after searching and identifying articles in Medline or by a free text search of the database itself. Ovid enhances the utility of the database through extensive preloading editorial work that standardizes the organization of the articles and normalizes the use of symbols, abbreviations, and other scientific representations.

Ovid's revenues are derived from database subscriptions, which include CD-ROM subscriptions and online access and usage fees, proprietary software licenses, software and hardware maintenance agreements, and hardware sales. Revenues comprise both recurring revenues from the company's installed customer base and from first-time sales. Several revenue trends have emerged as their domestic and worldwide sales have grown. Recurring revenues, comprising annual renewals of CD-ROM and network database subscriptions, and mandatory software maintenance for all network customers, have become an increasingly larger component of Ovid's traditional revenues, growing from 28 percent of total revenues in 1992 to 37 percent of total revenues in 1994. Revenues from hardware sales have decreased significantly from 37 percent of total revenues in 1992 to 3 percent in 1994, as customers' needs for turnkey network solutions have decreased. Revenues from operations outside of the United States have increased from 13 percent of total revenues in 1992 to 19 percent in 1994, with the addition of international sales personnel and the use of third-party distributors.

Ovid's revenues are growing swiftly with concomitant improvements in GPM and SGA Expenses/Revenues. But, accounts receivable days on hand got out of hand in 1995, growing to more than 100 days. Scientists and universities are knows as "slow pays," but Ovid has clever enough managers to get the company's subscribers to pay faster. Perhaps posting the recent articles about management's faux pas at *Encyclopedia Brittannica* in select locations throughout Ovid's office would be an incentive.

PACIFIC PIONEER CORP.

W omen entrepreneurs are the silent strength underpinning the vibrant U.S. economy. They are starting more companies than their male counterparts and women tend to hire more women than men. Among Quantum Companies, the percentage of women to total employees is around 50 percent—much higher than for the economy as a whole—because Quantum Companies tend to be problem solvers in the information and health care fields, markets in which women have fewer barriers to entry and upward mobility.

The businesses they launch are typically those in which the customer provides the capital by paying up-front for a subscription, a franchise, or a license. Insurance is open sesame to any entrepreneur. It is gender neutral. A gap was spotted about ten years ago in the area of property and casualty insurance for oriental business owners. Here's the story of how one tenacious woman entrepreneur spotted the need and filled it. Lin Lan began her company more out of need than by design. "For many years I was an obedient housewife," Lan explains. "Every morning I would wake up and turn on the shower for my husband. Then I would put out his suit, shirt, socks, underwear, tie, and shoes. I would even light his cigarette, and I don't even smoke.

"Then I would make his and the children's breakfast and send them off to work and school. That was my life. I always knew there was more. But to go out and get it, I had to leave my husband."

Needing to support her children, Lan got a job as an insurance rater with Travelers Insurance Company and simultaneously began attending evening classes at the local college. Five years later, she graduated with a Chartered Property and Casualty Underwriter degree.

In 1980, Lan left the comfortable vice president's position at Union Federal Savings & Loan, where she managed the insurance brokerage and insurance loan servicing operation, to form her first company, Unico Insurance Agency.

For the next twelve years, she built up a large agency serving the Asian-American business community in southern California, while also adding a risk management subsidiary. Her route had many serious obstacles. Most people would have given up during the conspiratorial litigation, investigations, and libelous attacks on her character she had to put up with, but Lan hung in and defeated her detractors. Her court-ordered victory over her former partners provided Lan with ample expansion capital.

PACIFIC PIONEER CORP.

Chief Executive Officer:	Lin Wu Lan
Principal Location:	18300 S. Pioneer Blvd. Artesia, CA 90702
Telephone:	310-865-7134
Fax:	310-860-8036
E-mail:	not available
Web site:	not available
Satellite Locations:	Phoenix, Arizona
Date Founded:	1985
Description of Business:	Property and casualty insurer and general agency serving primarily the Asian market.
# Employees Current:	100
% Female Employees:	75.0%
# Employees Projected 9/30/96:	150
Revenues 1995*:	$35,000,000 estimated
Gross Profit Margin (GPM):	The company is privately held and is not required to publish its financial statements.
SGA Expenses/Revenues:	not available
% Sales Increase 1992 to 1995:	+250.0%
% Change GPM 1992 to 1995:	not available
% Change SGA Expenses/Revenues 1992 to 1995:	not available
Total Debt/Net Worth:	not available
Net Profits Before Taxes 1995*:	not available
Net Profits Before Taxes/Revenues:	not available
Market Value/1995 Revenues*:	not available
Opportunity Company Addresses:	Ethnic groups frequently trust their members when it comes to critical products and services such as insurance.
Elegance of Company's Solution:	The company focuses on the casualty risks that could befall Asian-American business owners.

*Annualized.

In 1992, she purchased the California-licensed Enterprise Insurance Company and an Oklahoma-licensed underwriter and merged them with Unico to form Pacific Pioneer Insurance Company. To help raise the $6 million in capital needed to purchase these underwriters, many venture capitalists and private investors were interested in joining hands with Lan. However, Lan decided to invest her own savings and to borrow the balance of the purchase price because she felt that she needed full control of a new company in its early stages to ensure growth in the direction that she chose to follow. She was willing to take on the entire financial risk in order to own 100 percent of the enterprise. "I don't partner very well," Lan admits.

Today, Pacific Pioneer has gross annual premiums of $35 million and the company is growing at a rate of 25 percent per year on internally-generated cash flow plus acquisitions. It is the largest woman-owned insurance carrier in the country. "We have some men working here," Lan says with a smile. "I would be lost without David Einhorn our CFO," she continues. "He tells me how fast we can grow." Pacific Pioneer has a relatively low claims rate, hence its ample cash flow which is used to fuel its growth.

PARKERVISION, INC.

To relieve the pressure on college administrators to hire an instructor for every subject or to downsize classroom size to make the learning experience more interactive, ParkerVision has developed CameraMan, an automated video camera that pans, tilts, and zooms. The base unit utilizes ParkerVision's exclusive autoTRACK technology that tracks by reading an infrared sensor placed on presenters. Zoom and other functions are controlled by a wireless pad held by the instructor. Wireless or lavaliere microphones supply sound.

The Student System allows students to raise their hand "electronically" by pressing a locator button on a microphone or through a voice-activated system. The Response Camera automatically zooms to the individual student, magnifying the images and gestures that may otherwise be lost in typical wide-angle shots. In conjunction with the Response Programmer Keypad, this allows the system to be customized for the best visual image for each student. The Student System also automatically activates video switching and other room functions as a result of the student activating the system.

As a result, every student can hear and talk to each other. The instructor's wireless microphone can override all others. Three students share a microphone, and all voices are muted out as one student speaks. Each classroom has eight 2-feet-high monitors, four over the students' heads for the instructor to see and four above the instructor. Here's the good part: Students at off-campus sites can see the other students and the instructor. Soon, off-campus will be tied in via the Internet or private WAN.

The markets for videoconferencing and distance-education systems are continually evolving due to customer demand to achieve the "just like being there" effective communications. Other companies have commercialized technologies and products that are competitive with certain functions of the CameraMan system. In the distance-education market, manufacturers of manual pan/tilt heads, such as Panasonic, Sony Corporation, Canon USA, Inc., Vicon, Inc., TSM, Inc., Telemetrics, Inc., and Fujinon, compete with ParkerVision's products. Some of these pan/tilt heads have present-location capabilities but offer no tracking capabilities and must be operated either by a camera operator or from a monitor or control pad.

In the videoconferencing market, ParkerVision competes with the CODEC (network transmission) manufacturers, the largest of which are

PARKERVISION, INC.

Chief Executive Officer:	Jeffrey Parker
Principal Location:	8493 Baymeadows Way Jacksonville, FL 32256
Telephone:	904-737-1367
Fax:	904-731-0958
E-mail:	not available
Web site:	not available
Satellite Locations:	none
Date Founded:	1989
Description of Business:	Leading developer of camera systems for the distance learning and other markets.
# Employees Current:	51
% Female Employees:	not available
# Employees Projected 9/30/96:	not available
Revenues 1995*:	$2,092,000
Gross Profit Margin (GPM):	39.8%
SGA Expenses/Revenues:	158.2%
% Sales Increase 1992 to 1995:	+326.4%
% Change GPM 1992 to 1995:	(25.6%)
% Change SGA Expenses/Revenues 1992 to 1995:	(29.1%)
Total Debt/Net Worth:	30.5%
Net Profits Before Taxes 1995*:	deficit
Net Profits Before Taxes/Revenues:	deficit
Market Value/1995 Revenues*:	35.1x
Traded On:	NASDAQ (PRKR)
Opportunity Company Addresses:	Large seminar-style classrooms have more sleeping and inattentive students than those paying attention to the instructors.
Elegance of Company's Solution:	The company's CameraMan System II Instructor/Student Cameras involve every student.

*Annualized.

PictureTel, VTEL, Compression Labs, and Work Station Technologies (a Quantum Company), which offer a main camera with their CODEC, as well as an auxiliary camera for presentation purposes. The company is currently targeting the auxiliary camera market where it competes based on the system capabilities and price. In addition, the successful development of a joint product with VTEL would allow ParkerVision to compete as the main camera in a CODEC-based system.

ParkerVision's CameraMan is less expensive than the CODECs. Moreover, the company can deliver in 3 to 5 weeks, much faster than the larger competitors can.

To get its product to market quickly, the company has sacrificed profit margin, but that should come back once the word spreads, as it is doing from instructor to administrator, that CameraMan is the best thing to hit the education market since Guttenberg.

PEDIATRIC SERVICES OF AMERICA, INC.

oe Sansone, founder and CEO of Pediatric Services of America, started his home-care career as a respiratory therapist. In 1989, while working for Charter Medical Group, he learned that they were going to shut down or spin-off their adult home-care division. Sansone put a second mortgage on his house, raised $75,000, and bought it. He quickly added home child-respiratory services and home medical equipment. Six years later, 69 percent of the company's revenues come from pediatric home health care and 31 percent from adult home-health care. Revenues jumped from $23.2 million in 1992 to approximately $100 million, a quantum leap from the $75,000 salary he gave up at Charter.

The company's services are designed to comprehensively address the full range of home-health-care needs of pediatric patients, particularly medically fragile children dependent on sophisticated nursing care and medical technology. Many pediatric patients suffer from complex medical problems, most of which result from premature births or genetic abnormalities, including bronchopulmonary dysplasia, digestive and absorptive diseases, cystic fibrosis, and neurologically related respiratory problems. Patients suffering from these disorders typically require intensive and specialized treatment over an extended period of time by specially trained professionals in neonatal and pediatric care. Subsequently all of Pediatric Services' nurses have received specialized training in neonatal and pediatric care and generally are required to have had at least one year of prior experience in a neonatal critical-care unit.

In addition to nursing, Pediatric Services also provides technically advanced equipment for use at home, such as ventilators, apnea monitors, aerosol generators, and other specialized medical equipment. The company has also developed case-administration procedures that enable it to efficiently manage all aspects of patient care by coordinating the efforts of third-party payers, physicians, case managers, and referral sources.

Payers and referral sources recognize the specialized needs of medically fragile children and the high cost of rehospitalization associated with inadequate care. One payer, Metropolitan Life, who recently entered into a contract with Pediatric Services as a preferred provider of pediatric home-health-care services in selected geographic

PEDIATRIC SERVICES OF AMERICA, INC.

Chief Executive Officer:	Joseph D. Sansone
Principal Location:	3159 Campus Dr. Norcross, GA 30071
Telephone:	770-441-1580
Fax:	770-729-0316
E-mail:	not available
Web site:	not available
Satellite Locations:	74 branch offices in 19 states
Date Founded:	1989
Description of Business:	Provider of pediatric home care including nursing, respiratory, and infusion therapy, and medical equipment.
# Employees Current:	3,000
% Female Employees:	75%
# Employees Projected 9/30/96:	not available
Revenues 1995*:	$99,861,000
Gross Profit Margin (GPM):	not available
SGA Expenses/Revenues:	7.8%
% Sales Increase 1992 to 1995:	+300.6%
% Change GPM 1992 to 1995:	not available
% Change SGA Expenses/Revenues 1992 to 1995:	(45.1%)
Total Debt/Net Worth:	26.9%
Net Profits Before Taxes '95*:	$4,996,000
Net Profits Before Taxes/Revenues:	5.0x
Market Value/1995 Revenues*:	1.11x
Traded On:	NASDAQ (PSAI)
Opportunity Company Addresses:	Rising costs of hospital care are driving the need for inexpensive, efficient home health care.
Elegance of Company's Solution:	Most in-home health-care companies go after the adult and elderly segment, leaving a small but growing niche in the pediatric sector.

*Annualized.

areas, finds its services to be a high-quality, cost-effective alternative to prolonged hospitalization of such children.

Pediatric Services and a subsidiary of OrNda have formed a joint venture to provide pediatric home-health-care services in conjunction with OrNda's operations in Los Angeles and Orange County, California. This joint venture will enable OrNda to offer highly specialized pediatric home-health-care services to its clients and will provide Pediatric Services with access to a significant base of potential patients. Pediatric Services also has entered into preferred-provider contracts with several local and regional insurance companies and managed-care companies.

The company is growing primarily by acquiring similar operations in a hub-and-spoke pattern that fans out from its headquarters in Georgia. The acquisitions are small, around $10 million or less apiece, but they are occurring at an ever faster pace and are being integrated very smoothly. Note that the ratio of SGA Expenses/Revenues has declined 45.1 percent since 1992. In other words, when Pediatric Services makes an acquisition, virtually all administrative services and personnel are eliminated at the acquiree. This formula has been done brilliantly by other Quantum Companies, such as American Response Corp. and Home Health Care, among others, and by Conseco in the insurance industry. As the company grows, it will become the exit strategy of choice for owners of pediatric home care companies.

With internal growth of 21 percent per annum, Pediatric Services is a well-managed, high-growth company in an important, expanding niche market.

PERCLOSE, INC.

For reasons unknown to the layperson and, if known, probably too baffling to comprehend anyhow, the Libertarian-like Leviathan that swept into Congress in the 1994 elections has been unable to mitigate the crushing barrier to entry known as the Food and Drug Administration or the FDA. "We invest in health-care companies knowing in advance that, for a while at least, we'll be solving medical problems in foreign countries," says Gary P. Stoltz, general partner of Pathfinder Venture Funds, Minneapolis.

Case in point: Perclose, Inc., whose first 2,500 products have been sold and used in Germany, France, Canada, the United Kingdom, the Netherlands, Sweden, and Norway. These countries have FDA-equivalents, but without the high degree of restrictiveness that borders on merry shadenfreude. The FDA is still analyzing tests. A similar thing occurred in 1910: The Wright Brothers were taking orders for aeroplanes in France while the U.S. government was wondering if the darn things would fly.

More than 6 million people in the United States have been diagnosed with coronary artery disease, which is a formation of atherosclerotic plaque that causes blood flow restrictions, or blockages, within the coronary arteries. These blockages can occur anywhere within the complex network of arteries that provide blood to the heart muscle. If left untreated, coronary artery disease can cause severe chest pain and lead to heart attacks. The principal means of treating coronary artery disease include coronary artery bypass grafting (CABG), a highly invasive open surgical procedure, and percutaneous transluminal coronary angioplasty (balloon angioplasty), as well as other new, percutaneous catheter-based procedures such as atherectomy and stenting. Since its clinical introduction in 1978, balloon angioplasty has emerged as the principal, less-invasive alternative to CABG.

Industry sources estimate that during 1994 approximately 850,000 balloon angioplasty, atherectomy, stenting, and intra-aortic balloon pump procedures were performed worldwide, including approximately 525,000 such procedures in the United States. Industry sources estimate that the number of therapeutic and diagnostic catheter-based coronary procedures worldwide increased at an annual rate of 13 percent and 5 percent respectively, from 1990 to 1994.

At the beginning of a balloon angioplasty procedure, the physician initiates anticoagulation drug therapy, which is continued throughout

PERCLOSE, INC.

Chief Executive Officer:	Henry A. Plain Jr.
Principal Location:	199 Jefferson Dr. Menlo Park, CA 94025
Telephone:	415-473-3100
Fax:	415-473-3110
E-mail:	perclose@.com
Web site:	not available
Satellite Locations:	none
Date Founded:	1992
Description of Business:	Produces a family of minimally invasive systems used to close arterial access sites in catheterization procedures.
# Employees Current:	59
% Female Employees:	52%
# Employees Projected 9/30/96:	not available
Revenues 1995*:	$751,000
Gross Profit Margin (GPM):	(395.8%)
SGA Expenses/Revenues:	(212.8%)
% Sales Increase 1992 to 1995:	infinite
% Change GPM 1992 to 1995:	not available
% Change SGA Expenses/Revenues 1992 to 1995:	not available
Total Debt/Net Worth:	5.2%
Net Profits Before Taxes 1995*:	deficit
Net Profits Before Taxes/Revenues:	deficit
Market Value/1995 Revenues*:	$118,235,000
Traded On:	NASDAQ (PERC)
Opportunity Company Addresses:	Patient-recovery time costs and discomfort following vascular surgery have been high and rising.
Elegance of Company's Solution:	Perclose's products achieve more rapid hemostasis, reduce nursing time, and allow earlier patient discharge and ambulation while improving patient comfort.

*Annualized.

the procedure. A local anesthetic is administered and a small incision made in the groin area to gain access to the femoral artery, which is punctured to create an access site for catheterization devices. The cardiologist inserts an introducer sheath into the femoral artery and places a guiding catheter through the introducer sheath to create a path from outside the patient to the arteries of the heart. The cardiologist advances a small guidewire through the inside of the guiding catheter, into the coronary artery, and across the site of the blockage. A balloon catheter is delivered over the guidewire through the inside of the guiding catheter into the artery, and across the site of the blockage. The balloon is inflated to compress the blockage against the walls of the artery, thereby enlarging the diameter of the arterial lumen and increasing blood flow to the heart muscle. At the conclusion of the procedure, the cardiologist decides if the benefits of continued anticoagulation therapy that can prevent clot formation in the coronary arteries outweigh the increased risk of bleeding at the arterial-access site. This decision influences the level of post-procedure nursing observation and the length of the hospital stay, which is typically one to three days.

Other catheter-based therapeutic coronary procedures include atherectomy and stenting. Perclose believes that the advent of atherectomy and stenting has been responsible for a significant portion of the growth in therapeutic, catheter-based coronary procedures. The emergence of these procedures has emphasized the need for improved arterial-access site management techniques because of the increased use of anticoagulation therapy and the large diameter of atherectomy catheters.

Atherectomy encompasses several types of devices that are designed to remove atherosclerotic plaque causing an arterial blockage. These procedures include directional coronary atherectomy, in which plaque is removed with a miniature cutting system; rotational atherectomy, in which a high-speed, rotating burr is used to grind plaque into microscopic particles; and laser atherectomy, in which laser energy delivered through a fiber-optic catheter is used to ablate plaque. Directional and rotational atherectomy devices often require introducer sheaths and catheters of greater diameter than balloon angioplasty catheters. Use of atherectomy devices may require more aggressive antiocoagulation therapy than balloon angioplasty.

Stents are implantable metal devices delivered on a balloon catheter and permanently deployed at a blockage site to maintain increased lumen diameter by mechanically supporting the artery. In the United States, current labeling of FDA-approved stent devices requires the use of aggressive, long-term anticoagulation therapy in order to avoid blood-clot formation at the stent site in the artery. The required anticoagulation therapy has contributed to increased vascular complications at the arterial access site, often extending the hospital stay and sometimes requiring open-vascular surgery to control bleeding. Although improved stenting techniques and new stent devices may reduce the need for aggressive anticoagulation in the weeks following the procedure, Perclose believes that anticoagulation therapy will continue to be used during stenting procedures in the United States and, in certain high risk patients, may be required for a period of time following the procedure.

Perclose has developed the Prostar and Techstar systems, which achieve rapid closure of arterial-access sites following percutaneous catheterization procedures. The systems overcome the clinical disadvantages of current closure methods and enable catheterization procedures to achieve increased operating efficiencies and cost savings. The company's products enable the physician to suture arterial access sites percutaneously, providing a means of closure that has been possible only through open vascular surgery. Since the introduction of catheterization procedures, open vascular surgery has been the definitive method used to close arterial access sites that do not respond to conventional compression therapy. Open surgery involves a significant recovery period, and increases overall treatment costs. While surgeons can close the arterial access site with one or two sutures, the invasive nature of open surgery makes it unsuitable for routine use in catheterization patients. The company's Prostar and Techstar systems are designed to provide routine, definitive closure by replicating, through a minimally invasive procedure, the results previously obtainable only through open surgery without the associated risks and costs. The ease of use of the Prostar and Techstar systems is enhanced by the design of the products, which relies on standard cardiovascular catheterization techniques.

The Prostar and Techstar systems are used in the catheterization procedure to close the arterial access site as the final step. By achieving rapid hemostasis, the Prostar and Techstar systems reduce the need for the patient to remain immobile under close observation in the coronary care unit. This minimizes pain and discomfort to the patient and allows the patient to ambulate shortly after the catheterization procedure. Early ambulation of patients also improves utilization of hospital resources.

This magnificent therapy is available today, but add the cost of a round-trip airplane ticket to Vancouver, British Columbia, or Rio de Janiero if you need it.

PHARMACY FUND, INC.

Fred B. Tarter has 25 years' experience in creating and managing successful financial ventures. In 1974 he founded and became chairman of Deerfield Communications Corporation, the grandfather of the barter business, which he sold in 1984 for $36 million. As the current chairman of Boardwalk Entertainment, he oversees a diversified program development and production company. Tarter is also involved in feature film distribution as president of The Rainbow Group, Ltd., and is a principal stockholder and board member of Screenvision, America's largest cinema advertising network. When you see an advertisement on the screen before the feature film, you're seeing a Fred Tarter production. The man finds quarters on the seats of movie theaters where the rest of us find chewing gum.

An active venture-capital investor, Mr. Tarter originally developed the idea for the Pharmacy Fund while conducting due diligence for a health-care investment opportunity and realized that the unique characteristics of third-party pharmacy insurance claims allowed them to be securitized.

The Pharmacy Fund, Inc. (PFI), is a leading financial-services company to the rapidly changing health-care industry. Through its revolutionary, patent-pending financial management system, RAPID R_xEMIT™, the company stems the heavy losses incurred by its customers due to uncollected third-party claims as well as immediately improving their cash flow and profitabilty.

According to Tarter, RAPID R_xEMIT™ "is truly unique because it streamlines the receivables process through real-time electronic evaluation, handling the management and payment of third-party prescription claims within 24 hours of a transaction.

PFI purchases electronically adjudicated claims from participating pharmacies for a small discount fee. Similar to the banking credit-card process, the system makes an overnight direct deposit into the participating pharmacy's bank account.

"The prevalent managed care trend and the overwhelming increase in third-party processors and payers, has produced an avalanche in claims, along with a very complex administrative structure," said Jeffrey M. Greene, president of PFI and former chairman of Citicorp Information Management Services. "The pharmacy industry, where 3 percent or nearly $1 billion of third-party claims are never collected, needs a solution."

PHARMACY FUND, INC.

Chief Executive Officer:	Fred B. Tarter
Principal Location:	210 E. 39th St. New York, NY 10016
Telephone:	212-557-5600
Fax:	212-679-3816
E-mail:	not available
Web site:	not available
Satellite Location:	none
Date Founded:	1993
Description of Business:	A financial-information-management system that improves cash flow and streamlines the receivables collection process.
# Employees Current:	55
% Female Employees:	44%
# Employees Projected 9/30/96:	not available
Revenues 1995*:	$45 million est.
Gross Profit Margin (GPM):	The company is privately held and is not required to publish its financial statements.
SGA Expenses/Revenues:	not available
% Sales Increase 1992 to 1995:	not available
% Change GPM 1992 to 1995:	not available
% Change SGA Expenses/Revenues 1992 to 1995:	not available
Total Debt/Net Worth:	not available
Net Profits Before Taxes 1995*:	not available
Net Profits Before Taxes/Revenues:	not available
Market Value/1995 Revenues*:	not available
Opportunity Company Addresses:	It costs pharmacists between 50 cents and one dollar to process a third-party prescription claim and 53 percent of the 2.17 billion annual claims are third-party pay.
Elegance of Company's Solution:	Relieves drug chains and pharmacists of the time-consuming task of tracking third-party claim payments, thereby lowering the costs of collecting receivables and eliminating lost claims.

*Annualized.

"Several years ago, pharmacy transactions were mostly cash. Now, third-party claims account for more than half, and soon as much as 80 percent, of the $40 billion in annual pharmacy prescription expenditures. As a result, it takes an average of 35 days for a pharmacy to receive payment for third-party prescription claims.

"Lost transactions, processing errors, bad debt, and receivables hurt cash flow and the bottom line. We estimate that pharmacies pay as much as $1.00 in transmission, reconciliation, and write-off expenses for each third-party prescription," explained Greene. "RAPID R$_x$EMIT™ makes this problem literally disappear. The system is likely to save more than $12 million annually at some large drug chain stores."

Currently, the pharmacy industry as a whole is owed over $1.5 billion in receivables at any one time, and many of the thousands of third-party administrators (TPAs) and self-insured plans are unrated. "There is no industry standard for financial control among TPAs and plan sponsors, and the rules and procedures change constantly. Companies don't completely recognize the risk involved with these receivables," said Greene.

To minimize risk, PFI uses a proprietary financial database of over 3,500 insurance companies, self-insured employers, HMOs, and Blues to evaluate a company's ability to pay. The online database is able to assess a company's overall financial and claims payment history.

RAPID R$_x$EMIT™ is transparent to the pharmacy's operation. The service is available exclusively on the National Data Corporation (NDC) network, which has access to more than 48,000 pharmacies nationwide and switches more than $22 billion in third-party prescription claims annually. NDC is also connected to virtually every processor/payer in the industry. Of the more than 1.8 billion prescription transactions covered by health insurance each year, 85 percent are processed online.

By creating strategic alliances with powerful partners in the financial and health-care industries, PFI has developed the most advanced third-party credit-based prescription-payment system in the world. Bankers Trust acts as the trustee, administrative agent, automated clearinghouse and lockbox bank, and banker for RAPID R$_x$EMIT™. PFI is just another brilliant entrepreneurial company from Fred B. Tarter, who runs toward the problems that large industries complain about with elegant solutions worth pennies on a onesy-twosey basis and hundreds of millions of dollars in the aggregate. Perhaps Tarter will take this company public and allow all of us to ride this rocket.

PHOENIX TECHNOLOGIES, LTD.

Phoenix Technologies, Ltd., is a leading maker of software that tells hardware how to understand the operating system. This software is called **BIOS** (which stands for basic input-output system). After hearing in 1990 that Microsoft wanted a piece of the BIOS business, Phoenix's first inclination was to run. Panic forced the company to develop unrelated backup businesses, including a publishing unit—just in case Microsoft stole the BIOS market. But in the process, Phoenix turned itself into a $100-million-in-sales conglomerate.

Since then, the company has taken on a more cooperative approach. It started last year by selling 80 percent of its publishing unit for a $24 million gain and its printing software unit for a $10 million loss (the publishing unit accounted for 48 percent of its sales last year).

Then, instead of surrendering to Microsoft or fighting the software giant head-to-head, the two companies agreed to co-develop **BIOS** software. It may have been the only way Phoenix could have appeased Microsoft, which has coveted the **BIOS** business.

Early fruits of the joint venture were first seen when Windows 95 was unveiled. Phoenix, not Microsoft, programmed the portion of the touted operating system known as "plug and play." Thanks in part to Phoenix's technology, devices plugged into a Windows 95–equipped computer are recognized instantly without complex setup.

What does Phoenix get out of the deal? First, it avoids a tough battle with Microsoft. There is no reason for the software giant to get into the business if it is served well by suppliers. Secondly, Phoenix gets to write the rules. Phoenix has picked up a competitive advantage in the plug-and-play **BIOS** business that didn't even exist until Windows 95 was introduced. Now, every time a customer connects to Windows 95, Phoenix ships a **BIOS** unit. In fact, it shipped $50 million worth for its fiscal year ended September 30, 1995. Phoenix has a 30 percent share of the **BIOS** market and a strategic partnership with Microsoft. That sounds like a strong position to relaunch from.

PHOENIX TECHNOLOGIES, LTD.

Chief Executive Officer:	Ronald D. Fisher
Principal Location:	2770 De La Cruz Blvd. Santa Clara, CA 95050
Telephone:	408-654-9000
Fax:	408-452-6801
E-mail:	marge_cribbin@ptec.com
Web site:	http://www.ptec.com
Satellite Locations:	none
Date Founded:	1988
Description of Business:	Leading manufacturer of software known as BIOS that tells hardware how to understand an operating system.
# Employees Current:	not available
% Female Employees:	not available
# Employees Projected 9/30/96:	not available
Revenues* 1995:	$58,974,000
Gross Profit Margin (GPM):	92.8%
SGA Expenses/Revenues:	29.1%
% Sales Increase 1992 to 1995:	not available
% Change GPM 1992 to 1995:	56.7%
% Change SGA Expenses/Revenues 1992 to 1995:	51.6%
Total Debt/Net Worth:	31.6%
Net Profits Before Taxes 1995*:	$26,935,000
Net Profits Before Taxes/Revenues:	45.6%
Market Value/1995 Revenues*:	2.5x
Traded On:	NASDAQ (PTEC)
Opportunity Company Addresses:	When a software company develops a market that Microsoft begins to covet, it has to lead, follow, or get out of the way.
Elegance of Company's Solution:	Phoenix Technologies used the potential crisis of an onrushing Bill Gates to reshape itself into a far healthier company.

*Annualized.

PHYCOR, INC.

Physician–practice management is the market's response to managed care, or health maintenance organizations (HMOs), if you prefer a personification. In nature as in economics, big attracts a counter-weight, and that phenomenon was not only predicted but acted on way back in 1988 by Joseph C. Hutts and two partners. From 1977 to 1986, Hutts had been president of HCA Health Plans, a managed-care subsidiary of Hospital Corporation of America (HCA), an aggregator/operator of hospitals. He was vice chairman and COO of Equicor, an employee-benefits company, from 1986 to 1988, when the idea for PhyCor popped into his head.

Trying to persuade the first physician group to sell their company for cash and stock in PhyCor, which would then operate their practice for them, must have been akin to the challenge faced by the first person who ate a lobster and attempted to persuade others that it tasted good. But Hutts pulled off a miracle and launched an industry that is balancing the scales against managed care.

PhyCor has acquired 27 physician practices over the last eight years. It targets multispecialty groups, of which there are about 800 in the country. Over the next five years, PhyCor is expected to acquire 100 more groups. The physician practices that PhyCor has been acquiring have had 20 or more physicians. It plans to acquire smaller and unaffiliated (with an HMO) practices in the future, giving unaffiliated physicians access to the higher patient volumes that HMOs offer. Thus, as managed care grows, PhyCor will grown in tandem, and PhyCor's operating margins should rise accordingly. The company earned 4.9 percent on revenues in 1993, 6.8 percent in 1994, and 7.3 percent (annualized) in 1995.

A multispecialty physician group or single practitioner would have to pay heed to this remarkable company; *phenomenon* is perhaps a better word. PhyCor affords doctors the opportunity to become members of the leading provider systems in their community. This dynamic health-care environment has contributed to impressive increases in PhyCor's same-clinic revenues and its clinic contribution margin. Specifically, same-clinic sales climbed from 4.1 percent in 1991 to over 15 percent in 1995. PhyCor's clinic contribution margin increased from 17.5 percent in 1990 to over 27 percent in the first half of 1995. These figures are even more impressive considering the overall pricing pressure on health-care services that currently exists in the United States. Managed care drives

PHYCOR, INC.

Chief Executive Officer:	Joseph C. Hutts
Principal Location:	30 Burton Hills Blvd. Nashville, TN 37215
Telephone:	615-665-9066
Fax:	615-665-9088
E-mail:	jc@phycor.com
Web site:	http://www.phycor.com
Satellite Locations:	27 locations throughout the U.S.
Date Founded:	1988
Description of Business:	Pioneer in the $200 billion physician–practice management industry.
# Employees Current:	not available
% Female Employees:	not available
# Employees Projected 9/30/96:	not available
Revenues 1995*:	$334,172,000
Gross Profit Margin (GPM):	not available
SGA Expenses/Revenues:	3.7%
% Sales Increase 1992 to 1995:	+264.0%
% Change GPM 1992 to 1995:	not available
% Change SGA Expenses/Revenues 1992 to 1995:	+37.0%
Total Debt/Net Worth:	40.6%
Net Profits Before Taxes* 1995:	$24,402,000
Net Profit Before Taxes/Revenues:	7.3%
Market Value/1995 Revenues*:	2.7x
Traded On:	NASDAQ (PHYC)
Opportunity Company Addresses:	The trend toward managed care has made being a physician more like being an accountant trapped in a nightmare of insurance forms.
Elegance of Company's Solution:	PhyCor began it all in 1988 when it acquired the Green Clinic in Ruston, Louisiana. It has acquired 26 more physician practices and manages all of them at a profit to them, the physicians, and the stockholders.

*Annualized.

down physician profits; PhyCor raises them. Strong operating results have enhanced PhyCor's reputation and increased the desire of many physician groups to align with it. Strong same-clinic results, along with the continued influx of new clinic acquisitions, have helped contribute to annual compounded revenue and earnings growth of 56 percent and 54 percent respectively.

What is the Microsoft of physician–practice management worth? The stock market values PhyCor at 2.7x (which is paltry in comparison to small software companies that went public during 1995 and were bid up to more than 10x revenues). When PhyCor's revenues exceed $1 billion in about five years, it may represent more physicians than Mercedes-Benz has physician drivers. The stock can go nowhere but up. Joe Hutts may push Bill Gates off the front pages and give us a new and exceptionally worthy business hero from whom we can learn business lessons.

PHYSICIANS RELIANCE NETWORK, INC.

As a result of the increasingly elderly population and exposure to carcinogens in the United States, the number of reported cancer cases has grown from 782,000 in 1980 to 1,250,000 in 1995. Concomitant with this trend, the ability to deliver cancer care is declining as oncologists are faced with capitation-based pricing and increased administrative costs—brought about by the incipient managed-care health-care provider economy. The oncologist is placed squarely between a rock and a hard place.

The outpatient-cancer-care-provider market is highly fragmented. Individual physicians and small group practices have accounted for the majority of the physicians providing outpatient cancer treatment. Physicians Reliance Network (PRN) believes that many of these providers lack the capital, management capabilities, and infrastructure necessary to address the rising business complexity, growing payer control over practice patterns, and cost pressures on physicians that require them to seek operational efficiencies.

PRN's strategy is to develop, in selected geographic markets, comprehensive oncology-care networks that provide a high quality of care in a cost-effective manner. The key elements of this strategy are to provide comprehensive services within an integrated delivery system, provide extensive support services, capitalize on growth opportunities in existing markets, expand into new markets, and provide access to clinical research.

An important component of the company's strategy is to continue to add services to its existing markets through a multistep process that begins with establishing a physician's office. It then expands the range of services that can be offered at that office by adding equipment, laboratories, and pharmacies and by recruiting additional oncologists. This increases the number of technical services that the company can provide that otherwise would be provided by a hospital or other provider. When warranted, PRN constructs a cancer center to serve one or more physician offices in a targeted market. The company currently has four additional cancer centers under development.

Physicians Reliance Network is also able to maximize the productivity of clinical equipment, such as linear accelerators and scanners. Comprehensive information systems enable the company to further control costs at a level that would be impractical for small physician groups. It is also able to exert purchasing power in its markets to obtain

PHYSICIANS RELIANCE NETWORK, INC.

Chief Executive Officer:	Merrick H. Reese, M.D.
Principal Location:	8115 Preston Rd. Dallas, TX 75225
Telephone:	214-692-3800
Fax:	214-692-9824
E-mail:	not available
Web site:	not available
Satellite Locations:	Iowa, Oregon
Date Founded:	1993
Description of Business:	Manages the practices of 146 physicians, principally oncologists.
# Employees Current:	1,375
% Female Employees:	78.1%
# Employees Projected 9/30/96:	2,750
Revenues 1995*:	$70,355,000
Gross Profit Margin (GPM):	not available
SGA Expenses/Revenues:	26.0%
% Sales Increase 1992 to 1995:	+151.9%
% Change GPM 1992 to 1995:	not available
% Change SGA Expenses/Revenues 1992 to 1995:	+16.1%
Total Debt/Net Worth:	6.8%
Net Profits Before Taxes '95*:	$6,784,000
Net Profits Before Taxes/Revenues:	9.6%
Market Value/1995 Revenues*:	+10.1x
Traded On:	NASDAQ (PHYN)
Opportunity Company Addresses:	The direct costs of treating cancer in the United States were estimated to be $35 billion in 1995 and rising annually.
Elegance of Company's Solution:	The shift to a managed-care health-care-delivery system creates an opportunity to aggregate oncologists into an integrated organization to apply counter-railing leverage.

*Annualized.

favorable prices for equipment, pharmaceuticals, and other medical supplies. For instance, given its oncology focus, PRN is often the largest purchaser of a given pharmaceutical. Consequently, the company improves operating margins while growing in sales.

PRN also controls costs and reduces patient burdens through its systems approach to internal billing and accounts receivable collection. Typically, when a patient seeks care, he or she may have to see several nonaffiliated doctors, receive various treatments from disparate entities, and visit multiple clinics. Not only is this a logistical burden on the patient, but the patient is also later forced to deal with multiple bills and forms. PRN provides one bill, not twenty, for all of its services. This billing process also enables the company to track the total costs associated with a given patient. Such data is important to develop a decision-support system necessary to operate effectively in a capitated environment.

The management team at PRN was assembled brilliantly. The CEO, Merrick "Mike" Reese, is an oncologist and so is able to communicate on a personal, experiential level with the oncological practitioners he deals with. The CFO, Randall Kurtz, was a partner with Arthur Andersen for eleven years. Dr. Von Hoff recently joined the company as its National Director of Researches; he is also the CEO of the Cancer Therapy Center's Institute for Drug Development.

Two years ago PRN didn't exist. In the fourth quarter of 1995 it has a $1 billion market value. TA Associates, the world's largest venture capital management company, bought into the business plan and funded it. There are some very bright people running this elegant enterprise.

PREMISYS COMMUNICATIONS, INC.

FedEx was the leader in using the Internet for customer service. It created a means for its customers to track their packages on the Internet for the cost of a few pennies. Other corporations got the message in a millisecond: The Internet is the best customer service medium since the door-to-door salesman. The rush to get untangled from their costly private networks and out to the public networks is driving them to Premisys.

Premisys designs, manufactures, and markets integrated access products for telecommunications service providers. The company pioneered the integrated access device equipment market with the introduction of the first of a family of IMACS products in December 1991. The IMACS products are reliable access to telecommunications services. The majority of Premisys's sales, in fact, are to the major long-distance companies. The IMACS products provide access to currently developing products such as frame relay and ATM services, in the future. The IMACS platform allows carriers to offer a variety of value-added services, switching technologies, and transmission technologies to the business customers through a single access device. The IMACS products' modular design and standards-based architecture enable carriers to offer advanced telecommunications services more quickly and cost-effectively and enhance the manageability of carriers' networks.

Premisys's products are distributed and serviced worldwide primarily through strategic distribution relationships with major telecommunications equipment vendors, including AT&T, GTE, Cox Fibernet, Time Warner, Sprint, and others. The company considers its relationships with these telecommunications equipment suppliers to be strategic in that they enable value-added elements of the public carriers' business communications solutions and, in some cases, to incorporate proprietary technology into the IMACS products. The IMACS products are sold as access components of the suppliers' communications equipment solutions. The company's strategic distribution relationships include ADC Telecommunications, Inc., AT&T Paradyne, DSC Communications Corporation, and Motorola. The company also sells its products through value-added reseller relationships and, in limited circumstances, directly to end-user customers.

Premisys was launched with $19 million in venture capital from Walden Capital; Morgenthaler Venture Partners; Burr, Egan, Deleage &

PREMISYS COMMUNICATIONS, INC.

Chief Executive Officer:	Raymond C. Lin
Principal Location:	48664 Milmont Dr. Fremont, CA 94538
Telephone:	510-353-7600
Fax:	510-353-7601
E-mail:	not available
Web site:	http://www.premisys.com
Satellite Locations:	Singapore; Hong Kong; Bristol, United Kingdom
Date Founded:	1990
Description of Business	Designs, manufactures, and markets integrated access products for telecommunications service providers.
# Employees Current:	160
% Female Employees:	not available
# Employees Projected 9/30/96:	not available
Revenues 1995*:	$39,310,000
Gross Profit Margin (GPM):	60.5%
SGA Expenses/Revenues:	24.7%
% Sales Increase 1992 to 1995:	+1,117.4%
% Change GPM 1992 to 1995:	+35.7%
% Change SGA Expenses/Revenues 1992 to 1995:	(69.8%)
Total Debt/Net Worth:	11.9%
Net Profits Before Taxes 1995*:	$9,729,000
Net Profits Before Taxes/Revenues:	24.7%
Market Value/1995 Revenues*:	24.4x
Traded On:	NASDAQ (PRMS)
Opportunity Company Addresses:	Corporations are finding that public networks, such as the Internet, are less expensive than their private networks, and they are like the wildebeest on their annual drive across the Serengeti in their need to find exits to the Internet.
Elegance of Company's Solution:	The company makes the best on-ramp to the Internet for companies that need access.

*Annualized.

Co.; and strategic capital from AT&T Paradyne Corp., its single largest customer. They put their chips on Raymond C. Lin, at the time a 36-year-old entrepreneur who had been a senior vice president of Telco Systems, Inc. Lin assembled an excellent management team and nailed down a manufacturing relationship with Fetech's Singapore facility. The company competes with Quantum Company Newbridge Networks, and with Tellabs, Nokia, and NEC.

Premisys's operating statement is a thing of beauty. GPM is rising. The SGA Expenses/Revenues is falling. Profitability is 24.7 percent and rising every year. The company's stock sells at nearly 25x revenues, but revenues are more than doubling each year. Premisys could be the next great tollgate company—maker of a have-to-have-it product—since Microsoft.

PROJECT SOFTWARE & DEVELOPMENT, INC.

Project Software develops, markets, and supports enterprise-wide client/server applications software used by business, government, and other organizations to improve the productivity of facilities, plants, and production equipment. The company's asset-maintenance management systems enable organizations to increase revenues and reduce operating costs by reducing downtime, controlling maintenance expenses, minimizing spare parts inventories and costs, improving purchasing efficiency, and more effectively deploying productive assets, personnel, and other resources.

A large organization can expend hundreds of millions of dollars annually on maintenance of factories or facilities and still lose revenues and incur costs in the hundreds of thousands of dollars for each day that valuable facilities and personnel are idled by unexpected equipment failure or protracted plant shutdowns. Competitive pressures are driving industrial companies to reduce costs and to enhance the productivity of expensive plant and equipment. The adoption of just-in-time manufacturing and other, similar quality initiatives reduces manufacturers' margins of error but makes unplanned downtime increasingly critical. In addition, equipment failures and inadequate recordkeeping can lead to increased exposure to environmental risk and employee health and safety problems.

Most companies have used manual methods of scheduling maintenance and repair tasks, managing spare parts inventories, and implementing preventive maintenance programs. However, these manual methods can be inefficient and cumbersome, provide limited capabilities for collection and analysis of statistical data about equipment performance and failures, and rely on centralized paper recordkeeping, with information accessible to only a few employees. Project Software believes that there are numerous plants, facilities, and organizations of all sizes throughout the world that could achieve substantial cost savings and competitive advantages through implementation of automated asset maintenance, planning, and cost systems.

Computerized maintenance management systems based on mainframes and minicomputers were first developed in the 1970s. However, the complexity, inflexibility, and high cost of these systems restricted their utilization to a relatively small number of large, industrial companies. Applications written for mainframes and minicomputers tend to be difficult and expensive to maintain and support and, because

PROJECT SOFTWARE & DEVELOPMENT, INC.

Chief Executive Officer:	Robert L. Daniels
Principal Location:	20 University Rd. Cambridge, MA 02138
Telephone:	617-661-1444
Fax:	617-661-1642
E-mail:	75371.1055@compuserve.com
Web site:	not available
Satellite Locations:	Australia; France; Germany; the Netherlands; United Kingdom
Date Founded:	1968
Description of Business:	Develops, markets, and supports client/server applications software that saves costs on the factory floor.
# Employees Current:	156
% Female Employees:	44%
# Employees Projected 9/30/96:	Approx. 200
Revenues 1995*:	$39,194,000
Gross Profit Margin (GPM):	73.5%
SGA Expenses/Revenues:	43.9%
% Sales Increase 1992 to 1995:	+157.7%
% Change GPM 1992 to 1995:	+12.2%
% Change SGA Expenses/Revenues 1992 to 1995:	(7.5%)
Total Debt/Net Worth:	49.0%
Net Profits Before Taxes 1995*:	$7,215,000
Net Profits Before Taxes/Revenues:	18.4%
Market Value/1995 Revenues*:	4.4x
Traded On:	NASDAQ (PSDI)
Opportunity Company Addresses:	A company may expend hundreds of millions of dollars annually on maintenance and can lose revenues and incur costs for each day that facilities and personnel are idled by unexpected equipment failure or plant shutdown.
Elegance of the Company's Solution:	The company enables customers to reduce costs and increase productivity by more efficiently scheduling maintenance activities and equipment downtime.

*Annualized.

they often use proprietary operating systems and data structures, are limited in their ability to interact with other information resources and systems in a company. Their character-based interfaces also require mastery of complex commands and procedures, discouraging access to information by workers on the shop floor.

In the 1990s, the emergence of client/server computing made possible the development of powerful applications that are capable of addressing enterprise-wide business problems in a flexible and cost-effective manner. A client/server environment permits easy access to and sharing of enterprise-wide data and applications, empowering workers throughout the organization by providing real-time access to management information. Additional computing resources can easily be added to the network in cost-effective increments as the organization grows or its computing needs evolve. A client/server environment also provides organizations with the flexibility to mix hardware, operating and network communications systems, database systems, and applications software from multiple vendors.

Many companies have found that internally developed applications using proprietary architectures, application development tools, and data structures are difficult to build, test, and debug reliably; are expensive to maintain and support; and cannot readily be adapted to changing business requirements. By licensing client/server applications from an established vendor and then customizing them as necessary to meet their own specific needs, companies with enterprise-wide computing requirements can leverage the expertise of established vendors focused on specific types of applications. Organizations can then select those hardware and software products whose price and performance are best suited to their needs.

Project Software was the first software developer to offer a client/server product combining powerful maintenance management capabilities and database connectivity with a Windows-based graphical-user interface. MAXIMO enables companies to reduce downtime, control maintenance expenses, cut spare parts inventories and costs; improve purchasing efficiency and more effectively deploy productive assets, personnel, and other resources; and increase productivity by more efficiently scheduling maintenance activities and equipment downtime. MAXIMO's statistical analysis of equipment failures enables companies to eliminate unnecessary preventive measures and concentrate on those maintenance procedures that have the greatest impact on equipment reliability.

CEO Robert L. Daniels delivers elegant numbers for his stockholders as well. GPM has risen 12.2 percent over the last four years. SGA Expenses/Revenues have fallen 7.5 percent over the same time period, suggesting greater ease in selling the product. The company's operating ratio is 18.4 percent. Daniels is bailing money. Look for some acquisitions to overcome the ineluctable boredom that comes with overachieving.

PYXIS CORPORATION

xcept for the price of its common stock—a bargain basement $14 per share in the fall of 1995—this company's management and stockholders have much to cheer about. Sales are leaping, GPM is rising, and the SGA Expenses/Revenues ratio is declining, which means that making sales is becoming easier from one year to the next. Debt is minuscule, and cash and short-term investments are $82 million or about 50 percent of net worth. Annual cash flow is approximately 50 percent of sales and is growing. There are not enough places for Pyxis to invest cash, so look for a slew of acquisitions.

Pyxis designs, manufactures, markets, and services unique, point-of-use systems that automate the distribution, management, and control of medications and supplies in hospitals and alternate-care facilities. Pyxis' systems consist of PC-controlled secure-storage units located in patient-care areas throughout the customer facility, which are linked to a Pyxis central computer in the customer's pharmacy or supply center. The Pyxis central computer communicates with the customer's management-information systems to receive patient admission data and transmit medication and supply usage data.

Pyxis' business strategy is to develop systems that provide customers the opportunity to contain costs and automate or eliminate certain tasks. Its products are designed to reduce inventory-carrying and other costs, improve billing and usage information, and increase the productivity of nurses and other staff.

The company markets its systems through its direct sales force to nurses, pharmacists, materials managers, and hospital administrators at the approximately 3,000 United States and 500 Canadian hospitals with over 100 beds. In addition, Pyxis now has placed a limited number of its systems in various alternate-care sites around the United States. Pyxis systems are customarily installed under noncancellable, multiyear capital leases under which Pyxis retains title to all equipment. By fall 1995, the company had installed its systems in more than 1,150 hospitals and seventy alternate-care sites.

In August 1995, Pyxis acquired Allied Pharmacy Management, Inc., a provider of pharmacy management services to hospitals and other health-care providers, for $30 million in cash plus the assumption of $19.4 million in Allied's long-term debt. Based in Dallas, Allied either makes so little money that Pyxis is ashamed to report that it may have overpaid for it, or perhaps it is intensely profitable and Pyxis paid an

PYXIS CORPORATION

Chief Executive Officer:	Gerald E. Forth
Principal Location:	9380 Carroll Park Dr. San Diego, CA 92121
Telephone:	619-625-3300
Fax:	619-625-6684
E-mail:	not available
Web site:	not available
Satellite Locations:	Throughout the United States
Date Founded:	1987
Description of Business:	Leading producer of systems that automate the usage of medications and inventory in hospitals and acute-care facilities.
# Employees Current:	600
% Female Employees:	37.5%
# Employees Projected 9/30/96:	700
Revenues 1995*:	$161,846,000
Gross Profit Margin (GPM):	71.1%
SGA Expenses/Revenues:	30.2%
% Sales Increase 1992 to 1995:	+350%
% Change GPM 1992 to 1995:	+2.0%
% Change SGA Expenses/Revenues 1992 to 1995:	(11.5%)
Total Debt/Net Worth:	35.1%
Net Profits Before Taxes 1995*:	$61,975,000
Net Profits Before Taxes/Revenues:	38.3%
Market Value/1995 Revenues*:	3.2x
Traded On:	NASDAQ (PYXS)
Opportunity Company Addresses:	Regulations, particularly regarding narcotics, and complex billing systems have raised the labor and inventory costs associated with dispensing medications.
Elegance of Company's Solution:	The company's systems reduce inventory costs, improve billing and usage information, and increase the productivity of nurses.

*Annualized.

embarrassingly low price. In any event, the effect of this acquisition, whose price is more than one third of Pyxis' net worth, is obfuscated in the company's financial reports and newsletter.

The principal benefit of the acquisition is the internet-working of the two products—pharmacy management and automated medication delivery systems. Each sales force can sell the other's product. A two-product-line company can cut overhead internally and discount prices to its client if they buy two services rather than one. Two of the most respected venture capital funds in the country, New Enterprise Associates and Menlo Ventures, have representatives on the company's board of directors, which provides a certain level of comfort to investors. General Electric Leasing finances the systems Pyxis leases to hospitals, thus obviating much of the credit risk, a necessary hedge in the age of a shrinking hospital market.

Pyxis has a p/e ratio of 14.0x but the key financial ratios of a 28.0x p/e company. How can management overcome its Rodney Dangerfield image in the stock market?

A diversification via acquisition into a more rapidly growing market, the acquisition of related software lines, and more complete information to stockholders would be my recommendations to senior management to push the stock up to twice its current level.

QUARTERDECK CORPORATION

hortly after Guttenberg invented movable type, which led to the printing press, an entrepreneur in Italy by the name of Guillermo Ziti began publishing books that provided instructions for the production and use of tools. The tool books set standards for their respective markets: agriculture, shipping, and industry.

Shortly after the Internet became a popular commercial marketplace, gaining access to it produced a flurry of nonstandard, rather complex steps. First, you had to find an Internet access provider, a company that offered a computerized linkup to the vast network of routers and servers. IAPs, as they are sometimes known, are not easy to find since most of them emerged after the latest yellow pages were printed.

Following the subscription to their linkup service you had to buy a dialer and a browser. The dialer connected you to the IAP's computer and the browser allowed you to explore the World Wide Web. A technical person had to advise you on their installation. That cumbersome process still exists but is being replaced by two other tools. One is to access the Web from inside the commercial online services, such as America Online, but they charge more than the IAPs, and you have to navigate through their content to get to the Web.

The newest on-ramps to the Web are software packages that combine a dialer, a browser, and the automatic setup of an account with an IAP. You install the tool in the computer and then follow a few simple steps to get on the Web and begin surfing immediately. The producers of these tools are Quarterdeck; Netscape Communications, Inc. (a Quantum Company); SPRY, Inc., a division of CompuServe (with SPRY's *Mosaic* in a box, you must use CompuServe as your IAP); Spyglass and NetCom Online Communications, both Quantum Companies.

Quarterdeck did a perfect triple somersault in the tuck position into the Internet in early 1995. It's been around since 1982, but its stock languished near $1.00 per share, producing a market value of $20 million on revenues of $26.8 million in September 1994. The board asked for the resignation of the founder and member of the management team and brought in King Lee as an interim CEO to cut overhead, slash expenses, and refocus the company toward the Internet on a hell-bent-for-leather basis. A new CEO, Gaston Bastiaens, was hired in January 1995, and he has made several strategic acquisitions and strategic partnering investments. Since that time Quarterdeck's sales have risen to approximately $64 million annualized. It has returned to

QUARTERDECK CORPORATION

Chief Executive Officer:	Gaston Bastiaens
Principal Location:	150 Pico Blvd. Santa Monica, CA 90405
Telephone:	310-309-3700
Fax:	310-314-4219
E-mail:	gbastiaens@gdeck.com
Web site:	http://www.qdeck.com
Satellite Locations:	Dublin, Ireland
Date Founded:	1982
Description of Business:	Designs, develops, produces, and markets software to make the Internet more easily accessible to users. It is rich in technology, including utility products for Microsoft Windows.
# Employees Current:	220
% Female Employees:	40%
# Employees Projected 9/30/96:	not available
Revenues 1995*:	$63,708,000
Gross Profit Margin (GPM):	75.9%
SGA Expenses/Revenues:	48.6%
% Sales Increase 1992 to 1995:	+115.8%
% Change GPM 1992 to 1995:	(13.4%)
% Change SGA Expenses/Revenues 1992 to 1995:	(20.1)%
Total Debt/Net Worth:	54.5%
Net Profits Before Taxes 1995*:	$6,435,000
Net Profits Before Taxes/Revenues:	10.1%
Market Value/1995 Revenues*:	8.0x
Traded On:	NASDAQ (QDEK)
Opportunity Company Addresses:	The Internet is a bunch of routers that connect PC users that have modems. Something is needed to make it useful.
Elegance of Company's Solution:	The company makes tools for the Internet, created by one of the most respected technology development teams in the world.

*Annualized.

profitable operations, roughly 10 percent of sales. And its stock has risen to $20 per share, giving the company a market value of $510 million.

Among its deals are a strategic alliance with Intelligence@Large, Inc., in Philadelphia, Pennsylvania. Kate Joyce, Intelligence@Large's president and Cartwright Reed, its Chief Technology Officer, have developed software to put desktop video conferencing on the Internet to enable people in chat groups to see one another. It acquired Inset Systems, Inc., whose sales were $6.5 million, to permit Internet users to view and manipulate images and graphic files on the Web. It acquired Internetware, Inc., a developer of I-ware Connect that connects LANs to the Internet. Less than a year old, InterWare's founders received 440,000 shares of Quarterdeck common stock worth more than $8 million.

On the internal development side of the firm, Quarterdeck developed Webphone to enable high-quality, two-way voice communication over the Internet. Webphone sells at retail for under $50, and it is in the parlance of the industry a "killer app." If John Guttenberg had been linked up to the Internet, upon hearing of the tool books pouring out of Italy, he would possibly have e-mailed Ziti the following message: "Killer app, dude!"

Quarterdeck has a 75.9 percent gross profit margin which has withered somewhat as a result of the company's fast and furious spate of acquisitions. But its SGA Expenses/Revenues ratio has declined by more, which indicates that the new management team has its eye on cash flow, not merely top-line performance. Following a digestion period, Quarterdeck will probably swim into the market at mid-year and gobble up another ten toolmakers.

QUICKTURN DESIGN SYSTEMS, INC.

Quickturn Design Systems, Inc., designs, manufactures, markets, and supports system-level verification solutions for the design of integrated circuits (IC) and electronic systems. The company's emulation systems are designed to improve design quality and substantially reduce time-to-market and prototype IC development costs compared with traditional verification methodologies. Quickturn pioneered the commercial application of IC and systems emulation and holds the definitive patents in this field. It is in the "Rolaids" business, giving the IC manufacturer the relief of knowing every intersection is perfect before the silicon fix.

Quickturn's System Realizer family of modular emulation systems and the Logic Animator rapid-prototyping system are used by electronic design engineers to generate a reprogrammable physical prototype, or "virtual-silicon" representation, of their electronic-circuit designs. This virtual-silicon representation is then available for concurrent verification of the entire target system, including system software and applications, and iterative design changes, all prior to silicon fabrication. The products serve the increasing complexity required to support the technology convergence of computing, telecommunications, and multimedia graphics. The company's dollar segment markets and customers include the following:

Workstations/PCs:	Apple, Compaq, IBM, NCR, NEC, Silicon Graphics, Sun
Computers:	Cray, Data General, Hitachi, IBM, Tandem
Telecommunications:	Alcatel, AT&T, BNR, DSC Communications, Hughes, NTT, Rockwell Siemens, 3 Com
Semiconductor:	AMD, IBM, Intel, LSI Logic, Motorola, Somerset, TI
Interactive Media:	C-Cube, CCL, JVC, Ball Imaging, Sierra Semiconductor, Trident
Military/Aerospace:	General Dynamics, Harris, Kaiser, Loral, Martin Marietta, TRW
Consumer Electronics:	Casio, Matsushita, Seiko, Sharp

Quickturn's products are used in some headline-making products, such as RCA's DirecTV. When RCA needed a subcontractor to design and

QUICKTURN DESIGN SYSTEMS, INC.

Chief Executive Officer:	Keith R. Lobo
Principal Location:	440 Clyde Ave. Mountain View, CA 94043-2232
Telephone:	415-967-3300
Fax:	415-967-3199
E-Mail:	not available
Web site:	not available
Satellite Locations:	Phoenix, Arizona; Plano, Texas; Marlborough, Massachusetts; Munich, Germany; Velizy, France; Reading, United Kingdom; Yokohama, Japan
Date Founded:	1987
Description of Business:	Designs, develops, markets, and supports verification solutions for the design of integrated circuits.
# Employees Current:	not available
% Female Employees:	not available
# Employees Projected 9/30/96:	not available
Revenues 1995*:	$76,520,000
Gross Profit Margin (GPM):	69.3%
SGA Expenses/Revenues:	42.1%
% Sales Increase 1992 to 1995:	+296.8%
% Change GPM 1992 to 1995:	+7.1%
% Change SGA Expenses/Revenues 1992 to 1995:	(28.3%)
Total Debt/Net Worth:	44.2%
Net Profits Before Taxes 1995*:	$7,569,000
Net Profits Before Taxes/Revenues:	10.0%
Market Value/1995 Revenues*:	1.8x
Traded On:	NASDAQ (QKTN)
Opportunity Company Addresses:	The design of an integrated circuit is akin to mapping the city of Los Angeles, putting in all of the traffic lights and then timing them.
Elegance of Company's Solution:	Quickturn's systems can emulate up to 3,000,000 such intersections before the integrated circuit is irreversibly fixed in silicon.

*Annualized.

build a demodulated error-correct receiver decoder for DirecTV, Hughes Network Systems (HNS) was the natural choice. For more than twenty years, HNS has designed, manufactured, and installed advanced networking solutions for business and government. As a global leader in satellite networks and digital communications technologies, HNS supplies nearly 20 percent of all domestic and international private, interactive KU- and C-Band satellite networks. The challenge for HNS engineers was to verify a new architecture for the product. With such a large number of required vectors, emulation became the only feasible solution. Using Quickturn's Emulation Systems, HNS *emulated a billion vectors in 16.7 minutes,* holding development time—from initial architectural exploration to working silicon—to eight months. Without Quickturn, DirecTV would not have gotten to market so rapidly.

Quickturn's year-to-year financial ratios are majestic. Sales have tripled since 1992. GPM has increased 7.1 percent and the SGA/Revenues ratio has declined a whopping 28.3 percent. The company's accounts receivable are a bit long in the tooth—112 days on hand—but its inventory days on hand are a low 32.5 days. Quickturn is an inexpensive stock, selling at a p/e ratio of 21.9x.

RALEIGH MINE & INDUSTRIAL SUPPLY

D ick Smith thought he wanted to be a teacher when he was young, and so he earned a teaching degree from Moorehead State University. But the challenges weren't there, and he took a job with Banks-Miller Supply Co., Huntington, West Virginia, in the early 1970s. "In those days, they expected a salesman to do about $350,000 a year. I did $1 million," said Smith. "Then the next year, I sold $1.5 million, and it was because I concentrated on the customers' needs." By the fourth year Smith had enough money to start his own company, Raleigh Mine & Industrial Supply Co., which acquired Banks-Miller. In fact, Raleigh has made a half-dozen acquisitions and now ranks as the leading mining-equipment distributor in the largest coal mining region of the United States.

"Don't cry for me, West Virginia," should be the new state song. The region can "poor-boy" and look for federal government support all it wants, but there are more BMWs at the Charleston, West Virginia, airport than at Orange County, California, these days. Due to the realization of the damage caused by acid rain, recent legislation has forced the electric generating plants into compliance with the clean air laws, and there has been a concomitant burst of activity in West Virginia with new mines being opened, production increased at existing mines, and expansion of coal-cleaning facilities to accommodate the increased production. In the last five years, thirty mines have opened in the company's trading area with production in excess of one million tons per year. Advances in coal-mining technology have made deep mining more cost-effective, and when compared with the costs of scrubbing the sulfur from the high-sulfur Western coal deposits, Eastern low-sulfur coal is attractive.

Many of Raleigh's customers have signed long-term contracts for its supplies and services due to the increase in their sales and enhanced profits. These contracts will give stability to the earnings of the company going forward.

Metallurgical coal has seen a dramatic increase in sales as the country has climbed out of recession and the demand for steel has grown. West Virginia's low and mid-volatile coking coal is known worldwide as the best product for making steel and is in high demand. With the recent tragedy in Kobe, Japan, and the destruction of steel reinforced buildings, we have seen an upturn in the market as the

RALEIGH MINE & INDUSTRIAL SUPPLY

Chief Executive Officer:	S. Richard Smith
Principal Location:	61 S. Mill Creek Rd. Mt. Hope, WV 25880
Telephone:	304-877-5503
Fax:	304-877-5684
E-mail:	not available
Web site:	not available
Satellite Locations:	Locations throughout West Virginia and eastern Kentucky
Date Founded:	1978
Description of Business:	Leading distributor of mining and industrial equipment.
# Employees Current:	not available
% Female Employees:	not available
# Employees Projected 9/30/96:	not available
Revenues 1995*:	$100,000,000 (estimated)
Gross Profit Margin (GPM):	The company is privately held and is not required to publish its financial statements.
SGA Expenses/Revenues:	not available
% Sales Increase 1992 to 1995:	not available
% Change GPM 1992 to 1995:	not available
% Change SGA Expenses/Revenues 1992 to 1995:	not available
Total Debt/Net Worth:	not available
Net Profits Before Taxes 1995*:	not available
Net Profits Before Taxes/Revenues:	not available
Market Value/1995 Revenues*:	not available
Opportunity Company Addresses:	The coal mines of Appalachia are humming again as the demand for steel increases worldwide.
Elegance of Company's Solution:	The role of the distributor is to be able to provide same-day or next-day delivery of the goods ordered at the best price. Raleigh is the best in its market at delivering on this premise.

*Annualized.

rebuilding of these structures begins. This forecasts growth in the market for steel products and continued growth in demand for coking coal.

The West Virginia Coal Association estimated the coal production for 1994 for Southern West Virginia at 170 million tons (final production figures will not be available until fall). Based on a conservative estimate of an expenditure by the coal industry of $2.25 per ton of mined coal for supplies, this translates into a market potential of $382,500,000. Dick Smith is carrying out a Craig McCaw strategy among the region's mining equipment distributors. McCaw consolidated the cellular phone industry and McCaw Cellular Corp. became the dominant company. Smith intends to do the same.

The primary coal mining companies in the company's service are USX Coal Company, Zeigler Coal, Cyprus Amax Coal, Peabody Coal, and A. T. Massey Coal Co. There are approximately 1,500 mining companies in the region and 30 new mining companies have come into the region in the last five years. According to Standard & Poor, the profitability of the largest mining companies in the region has increased 40.5 percent per annum from 1991 to 1994 as shown here:

TREND OF REGIONAL MINING COMPANIES 1991 TO 1994*
Sales (in millions)

	5-Company Composite		Ashland	USX	HANSON PLC	CYPRUS
	($mm)	% Change				
1994	$6,781	21	$610.1	$6,066.0	$17,660	$2,788.0
1993	5,619	(1)	498.2	5,612.0	14,601	1,763.5
1992	5,672	11	579.7	4,946.5	15,519	1,641.3
1991	5,106	n.a.	443.9	4,864.1	13,459	1,656.5

* Standard & Poor.

Raleigh has a fully automated client/server product-ordering system. Its customers are online, order from the client PCs to the company's server, and receive delivery either the same day or the next day. The roads to the mines are narrow, winding, and treacherous in the rain and snow. "But we get our trucks up the hollows, and our drivers do the unloading and are trained in being friendly and courteous," said Smith. "We may be high-tech and all that when it comes to orders," the 46-year-old natural-born salesman says, "but the face of our company is the driver and I get personally involved in training our drivers to sell Raleigh every chance they get."

"What's next for Raleigh?" I asked Smith. "We'd like to expand into the Utah coal mining market by next year and when we're at $250 million in sales, take the whole show public," he said.

SECURITY DYNAMICS TECHNOLOGIES, INC.

ew issues have created as many lines of ink in the business press as unauthorized access to computers and networks. Smut and child pornography are perhaps greater eyebrow raisers but not necessarily more difficult problems than hacking and unauthorized access. Entrepreneurs thrive on problems that are big, technical, and frightening. It represented a banquet to Ken Weiss, founder and chief technical officer of Security Dynamics Technologies, Inc. (SDTI), an internationally recognized authority on computer security and the author of the company's eleven patents.

SDTI designs, develops, markets, and supports a family of security products used to protect and manage access to computer-based information resources. SDTI's family of products employs a patent-protected combination of super-smart-card technology and software or hardware access-control products to authenticate the identity of users accessing networked or stand-alone computing resources. The company's SecurID Cards and other "tokens" and its access control products, including its ACE/Server software and Access Control Module software and hardware products, are designed to interface with a wide variety of operating systems and hardware platforms on client/server, mainframe, and mid-range systems to enable enterprise-wide security coverage. The company recently began shipping a second generation of its ACE/Server software to meet the evolving enterprise security needs of its customers.

In recent years, the task of managing access to computer-based information resources has become increasingly difficult due to a variety of factors, including:

1. the evolution of enterprise computing from centralized host-based systems to distributed environments
2. the proliferation of desktop and portable computers
3. the linking of local-area networks and wide-area networks to mainframes and mid-range systems through internetworking solutions
4. the rapid increase in remote computing applications and use of the Internet.

As a result, the number of users with direct access to information resources has increased dramatically. Sensitive data accessible from multiple locations include financial results, medical records, personnel files, research and development projects, marketing plans, and other

SECURITY DYNAMICS TECHNOLOGIES, INC.

Chief Executive Officer:	Charles R. Stuckey Jr.
Principal Location:	One Alewife Ctr. Cambridge, MA 02140
Telephone:	617-547-7820
Fax:	617-354-8836
E-mail:	not available
Web site:	not available
Satellite Locations:	none
Date Founded:	1984
Description of Business:	Leading manufacturer of computer and network security products.
# Employees Current:	138
% Female Employees:	not available
# Employees Projected 9/30/96:	not available
Revenues 1995*:	$28,795,000
Gross Profit Margin (GPM):	79.1%
SGA Expenses/Revenues:	44.4%
% Sales Increase 1992 to 1995:	+323.5
% Change GPM 1992 to 1995:	+5.9%
% Change SGA Expenses/Revenues 1992 to 1995:	(.4%)
Total Debt/Net Worth:	5.6%
Net Profits Before Taxes 1995*:	$7.596,000
Net Profits Before TaxesRevenues:	26.4%
Market Value/1995 Revenues*:	25.1x
Traded On:	NASDAQ (SDTI)
Opportunity Company Addresses:	As a result of the increase in the number of users having direct access to enterprise networks and corporate data, unauthorized access to information has become a growing and costly problem for businesses.
Elegance of Company's Solution:	The company makes four levels of security protection devices to deny access to unauthorized users.

*Annualized.

business information. Unauthorized access to information resources has become a growing and costly problem for businesses and other enterprises and continues to be identified by information system professionals as a priority in their system designs.

SDTI sells its products for the most part through marketing licenses with the leading manufacturers of hardware and software products that enable remote computing. These include network operating systems producers, Internet-related products manufacturers, and a number of remote-access products manufacturers. A large number of Quantum Companies are among SDTI's strategic partners (noted with an *). Their products rely on security protection devices in the same manner that automobile manufacturers rely on keys and lock sets.

Network Operating Systems Producers

Apple
CISCO Systems*
Microsoft
Novell

Internet-Related Products Manufacturers

Advanced Network Services, Inc. (Interlock Services)
Border Networks Technologies, Inc. (Janus)
Checkpoint Systems, Inc. (Firewall-1)
IBM (NetSP Firewall)
Raptor Systems, Inc. (Eagle)
SOS Corporation (Brimstone)
Technologic, Inc. (Firewall)
Trusted Information Systems, Inc. (Gauntlet)

Remote-Access Products Manufacturers

3Com Corp. (Access Builder)*
Ascend Communications, Inc. (Max, Pipeline)*
Attachmate Corp. (Remote Lan Node)
Bay Networks, Inc. (Lattis System 3000, 9000)*
CISCO Systems, Inc. (TACACS supported)*
Combinet Inc. (Connection Manager)
Emulex Corporation (Connect + Pro)
Gandalf Technologies, Inc. (XpressWay)
IBM (8235, Lan Distance)
ISDN Systems, Inc. (Remote Express, Drawbridge)
Kasten Chase Applied Research, Inc. (Optiva)
Microcom, Inc. (Lan Express)
Penril Datability Networks (CSX)
Rockwell (NetHopper)

Shiva Corporation (LanRover)*
TechSmith Inc. (Enterprise Wide)
Telebit Corporation (NetBlazer)
Xylogics, Inc. (Annex)
Xyplex, Inc. (MaxServer, Network 9000 Server)

SDTI's GPM is growing, and its SGA Expenses/Revenues ratio is falling. Its Operating Ratio is an eye-popping 26.4 percent. In an expanding market for access-denial solutions, stock buyers award SDTI an unusually high market-to-revenues ratio of 25.1x.

SEMTECH CORPORATION

⟨emtech's stock has languished on NASDAQ for two and one-half decades while it made a small amount of money for a large amount of toil, supplying semiconductors to the military. In the late 1980s, Semtech concluded that reduced military spending would restrict its future growth and changed its course to focus on the growing demand for semiconductors in the personal computer and telecommunications markets. As a result of this strategic change, Semtech is a significantly different company today than just two years ago. Its stock no longer languishes: It ran up from $2¼ to $31½ in 1995.

Semtech began the transition into commercial semiconductor markets in 1990 by acquiring the semiconductor division of Lambda Electronics. This acquisition provided Semtech with its IC (integrated circuit) capabilities in Corpus Christi, Texas, and Reynosa, Mexico. In 1992, the company acquired Modupower, a supplier of solid-state modules. The founder of Modupower was added to the management team to help direct the transition into commercial semiconductor markets. In October 1995, Semtech acquired Gamma, Inc., dba ECI Semiconductor, a $16 million (revenues) semiconductor manufacturer, for $20 million in Semtech stock.

Semtech has segued to the PC market by recognizing the change to lower voltages in powering ICs. For the past 25 years, most semiconductors were powered by 5 volts of direct current. Most recently, however, increased part densities within IC units have necessitated that the power supply voltage be reduced to 3.3V in order for the closely situated elements within the IC to withstand the voltage. The change to lower voltages is most prevalent in the design of microprocessors, which benefit from it through a reduction in power consumption and heat generation of approximately 50 percent. This is particularly significant in portable products. Semtech's first product introduced into this market was EZ DROPPER®. This product was sufficiently innovative to win the cover of the January 1993 issue of *Electronic Design* magazine.

The transition to lower voltage power is creating an incremental market for Low Drop Out (LDO) regulators and DC/DC converters for several reasons. 3V power may be offered as an additional output on main power supplies; however, most microprocessors will need to be powered by a local LDO located as close as possible to the microprocessor. As more motherboards become 3V, voltage drops in the wiring will be prohibitive, and localized DC/DC converters will be

SEMTECH CORPORATION

Chief Executive Officer:	John D. Poe
Principal Location:	652 Mitchell Rd. Newbury Park, CA 91320-2289
Telephone:	805-498-2111
Fax:	805-498-3804
E-mail:	not available
Web site:	not available
Satellite Locations:	Glenrothes, Fife, Scotland; Corpus Christi, Texas; Reynosa, Mexico
Date Founded:	1965
Description of Business:	Develops, manufactures, and markets power semiconductors for the computer and telecommunications markets.
# Employees Current:	279
% Female Employees:	57%
# Employees Projected 9/30/96:	450
Revenues 1995*:	$29,478,000
Gross Profit Margin (GPM):	33.9%
SGA Expenses/Revenues:	20.3%
% Sales Increase 1992 to 1995:	+146.2%
% Change GPM 1992 to 1995:	+13.4%
% Change SGA Expenses/Revenues 1992 to 1995:	(15.8%)
Total Debt/Net Worth:	30.2%
Net Profits Before Taxes 1995*:	$3,120,000
Net Profits Before Taxes/Revenues:	10.6%
Market Value/1995 Revenues*:	3.9x
Traded On:	NASDAQ (SMTC)
Opportunity Company Addresses:	With the downsizing of the military and aerospace electronics markets, this 30-year-old semiconductor manufacturer had to find new markets.
Elegance of Company's Solution:	In one of the most elegant transitions in contemporary business history, Semtech has reduced its reliance on the military market to one-third while improving GPM and cash flow.

*Annualized.

utilized. Many accessory cards, such as video circuits and modems, are also moving to 3V power, but since 3V power sources may not be available, a small LDO will be utilized. It is also becoming clear that voltages other than 3.3V will be mixed on the same board, requiring an individual LDO to supply each voltage. Semtech offers products to serve these needs and is developing products for future needs. Portable computers have very different needs, and the company is entering this market with a family of products specifically designed to maximize battery life.

Semtech manages acquisitions and transitional growth as well as any high company tech in this book. It passes my three most important tests with flying colors; to wit, rising **GPM**, declining **SGA** Expenses/ Revenues, and improving accounts receivable turnover. It has a high percentage of female to total employees, which is another catalyst for rising profitability.

SHIVA CORPORATION

hen Daniel Schwinn, 34, and Frank Slaughter, 33, selected the name of their company in 1985 shortly after they graduated from Massachusetts Institute of Technology, little did they know it was the Hebrew word for "mourning the dead." When brokers recommend the stock to some of their Jewish clients they often get the response, "I don't want to be sitting shiva over Shiva."

That isn't going to happen. In 1992, when the two entrepreneurs developed LanRover, an extremely important remote-networking software product, they recruited Frank Ingari, 46, to become the Chief Executive Officer. A former rock guitarist and head of the marketing effort for the popular Notes software at Lotus, Ingari wanted to run his own show. With an experienced CEO at the helm, the seed-capital backing of Mitchell Kapor, the founder of Lotus; and an elegant on-ramp to the information superhighway, the managers approached the indefatigable L. John Doerr of the venture capital fund Kleiner Perkins Caulfield & Byers, which invested $2 million.

Sales leaped from $23.5 million and a loss of $4.7 million in 1992 to sales of $29.5 million and a small profit of $213,000 in 1993 to $41.6 million and a profit of $2.7 million in 1994. A public offering would have been the appropriate path for Shiva in 1994, a year that began with a meager $81,000 of cash in the bank. However, 1994 was not a strong year for initial public offerings (IPOs). A mere 116 companies went public and raised $5 billion in 1994, versus 156 IPOs and $8.5 billion in 1993. But Shiva badly needed to fuel its growth, and Goldman, Sachs & Co., which has become the premier underwriter for the remote-computing industry, believed it could get the attention of new issues investors. Following a grueling two-week road show to 16 cities where Messrs. Ingari, Schwinn, and Slaughter pitched Fidelity Investments, Wellington Management, Janus Fund, and Alliance Capital, as well as dozens of brokers, they oversold the issue. Goldman raised the offering price to $15 and added 360,000 shares to the offering.

The offering came on November 19, 1995, and the stock opened at $30½, a more than 100 percent jump. The Shiva offering made Schwinn and Slaughter worth more than $30 million and Ingari $14 million. The company raised $28 million and pumped more than $5 million into marketing. Sales in 1995 will top $51 million and earnings before interest and taxes (EBIT) will come in at more than $6 million.

SHIVA CORPORATION

Chief Executive Officer:	Frank A. Ingari
Principal Location:	Northwest Park 63 Third Ave. Burlington, MA 01803
Telephone:	617-270-8700
Fax:	617-270-8999
E-mail:	support@shiva.com
Web site:	http://www.shiva.com
Satellite Locations:	Santa Clara, California; Chicago, Illinois; Windsor, United Kingdom; Sophia Antipolis, France
Date Founded:	1985
Description of Business:	Develops, produces, and sells hardware and software products, known as remote access products, that permit remote connectivity via telephone lines to local area networks (LANs) and dial-out from LANs to remote locations.
# Employees Current:	476
% Female Employees:	34%
# Employees Projected at 9/30/96:	not available
Revenues 1995*:	$51,443,000**
Gross Profit Margin (GPM):	63.8%
SGA Expenses/Revenues:	42.3%
% Sales Increase 1992 to 1995:	+118.7%**
% Change GPM 1992 to 1995:	+51.5%
% Change SGA Expenses/Revenues 1992 to 1995:	-0-
Total Debt/Net Worth:	21.6%
Market Value/1995 Revenues*:	11.5X**
Net Profits Before Taxes 1995*:	$6,078,000
Net Profits Before Taxes/Revenues:	1.8%**
Traded On:	NASDAQ (SHVA)
Opportunity Company Addresses:	The need for members of organizations whose PCs are tied to a local network to get out onto the Internet for global communications.
Elegance of Company's Solution:	By interweaving its knowledge of remote network access, PC software and technology, the company pioneered remote node access with LanRover in 1992.

*Annualized.
**Excludes the contribution from Spider.

That could change, because Shiva acquired Spider Systems Limited, Edinburgh, United Kingdom, for 2 million shares. Spider designs, manufactures, and sells digital internet-working hardware and software products, primarily ISDN tariff management systems. (ISDN is a very wide bandwidth communications system that is more common in Europe and Asia than in the United States, where it is gaining users.) Spider's sales for the year ended March 31, 1995, were $39.4 million, on which it earned $2.6 million EBIT. It will give Shiva a major marketing platform in Europe and a new product line for North America.

Shiva was beginning to run out of highway. By mid-1995 it had more than 50,000 remote access servers installed, with customers in 800 of the Fortune 1000 companies. Having the first and the best remote-access server, one that can be managed from a single desktop computer, either locally or remotely, pretty much assured its stunning success. Now, with a European sales force, Shiva is in a position to replicate its achievements abroad and move Spider's products through its domestic channels.

SKYWEST, INC.

Joseph Steinberg and Ian M. Cumming were trained by Robert Davidof, the inimitable dealmaker at Carl Marks & Co., a unique, diversified New York investment bank. Carl Marks is where you go to sell unlisted, forgotten, and dust-covered securities like Bonapartes or pre-Revolutionary rubles. Steinberg and Cumming left in the 1970s to buy the well-known but deeply troubled factor, James Talcott & Co., which was tangled in a thicket known as Franklin National Bank and controlled by an Italian felon. They studied Talcott's books and saw immense value in its assets, which had been forgotten and dust-covered for years. Out of the mess emerged Leucadia National Corp., a New York Stock Exchange gem of a diversified holding company. Leucadia surfaces from time to time as a bidder for undervalued properties.

It put its chips down on such an undervalued asset several years ago—SkyWest, Inc., a regional carrier serving the Rockies but with a current expansion program that is taking it to Honolulu and New Orleans. SkyWest has been run by Jerry C. Atkin since 1975 and, by all appearances, he is ready to burst out into major carrierville. Unless you have just returned from another planet you know that Los Angelenos have been moving to Colorado in droves and that the fastest-growing regions in America are southern Idaho and Salt Lake City. The biggest semiconductor plant in the world is Intel's in Albuquerque, and Hewlett-Packard has manufacturing facilities throughout Colorado and Oregon. Hollywood stars love Jackson Hole. Las Vegas is the fastest-growing big city in the country. And skiing the Rockies is the destination sport of millions. These markets form SkyWest's solid base. It picks up deplaning Delta passengers in Salt Lake City and flies them to and from these hot markets.

The fine print in SkyWest's 10-Qs suggest a major fleet overhaul is under way. The current plan calls for the elimination of 25 of SkyWest's 19-seat Metro turboprop aircraft in favor of the cabin-class 30-seat Brasilias over the next 18 months to two years. This represents a significant acceleration from the previous phaseout plan and is aimed directly at the least profitable segments of SkyWest's business; namely, secondary markets and those markets served from the Los Angeles hub currently using Metros. SkyWest's experience so far demonstrates that adding a Brasilia plane in a soft Metro market has improved load factors and profitability, despite the increase in plane size. The extra passengers

SKYWEST, INC.

Chief Executive Officer:	Jerry C. Atkin
Principal Location:	444 South River Rd. St. George, UT 84790
Telephone:	801-634-3000
Fax:	801-634-3306
E-mail:	not available
Web site:	not available
Satellite Locations:	not available
Date Founded:	1975
Description of Business:	A leading regional carrier serving the Rockies and Northwestern United States.
# Employees Current:	2,296
% Female Employees:	39%
# Employees Projected 9/30/96:	2,800
Revenues 1995*:	$226,908,000
Gross Profit Margin (GPM):	not available
SGA Expenses/Revenues:	14.4%
% Sales Increase 1992 to 1995:	+154.6%
% Change GPM 1992 to 1995:	not available
% Change SGA Expenses/Revenues 1992 to 1995:	(11.7%)
Total Debt/Net Worth:	35.6%
Net Profits Before Taxes 1995*:	$18,436,000
Net Profits Before Taxes/Revenues:	8.1%
Market Value/1995 Revenues*:	.83x
Traded On:	NASDAQ (SKYW)
Opportunity Company Addresses:	Notwithstanding their rapid growth, the smaller markets of the upper Northwestern United States are no longer served by the major airlines.
Elegance of Company's Solution:	The company offers interline connections to Delta passengers and its own flights in and around the Rockies and Tetons.

*Annualized.

resulting from the new Skywest interline agreement with Continental Airlines should provide added traffic and support for the new planes.

Skywest's passenger miles in 1994 were 488.9 million, up 41.2 perent from 1993. Its load factor has grown from 41.6 percent in 1992 to 50.1 percent in 1994. But passenger revenue miles dipped from $.46 to $.36 over the same period. The larger planes and longer routes are expected to reverse this ratio. Costs per seat mile have fallen from $.19 to $.16 from 1992 to 1995, indicating a management that attends to minute details.

Meanwhile, Jerry Atkin is sitting on a stash of cash: $50 million. SkyWest's funded debt is down to $32 million, while its book value is $119 million. The company could afford a $100 million cash acquisition and there are some low-price regional carriers—Mesa and Mesaba—that operate in contiguous markets.

Leucadia sifts through rubble and finds diamonds. SkyWest management is validated and mentored by one of Wall Street's top teams. At a market to revenues ratio of .83x, and a route structure built to service the Information Age, Skywest's stock is huggable.

SMITH MICRO SOFTWARE, INC.

I magine sitting at your personal computer and switching seamlessly among data, fax, and voice functions without interruption. Thirteen years ago, William Smith, a Rockwell software engineer, dreamt that he could develop software to permit this to happen. He and his wife, Rhonda, pooled their resources and began attempting to bring reality to the idea. The company was bootstrapped on the Smiths' initial investment of $22,000. They never raised outside capital but reinvested its earnings into product development, working capital, and marketing. At the time of its initial public offering in September 1995, the company owed $5.7 million and had total assets of $4.4 million. The years of struggle and dedication paid off. The Smiths raised $20.4 million personally in the IPO and continue to own 75.2 percent of Smith Micro, worth about $100 million.

The use of personal computers is growing rapidly, with worldwide shipments reaching 44.2 million in 1994, resulting in an installed base of approximately 150 million computers. Use of personal computers as communication devices has fueled demand for modems, the hardware devices that enable personal computers to communicate over telephone lines. Modem shipments increased from 10.5 million in 1992 to 12.7 million in 1993 and to 27.5 million in 1994. Both of these trends are expected to continue, with industry sources projecting that 50.4 million personal computers and 30.2 million modems will be sold in 1995.

Businesses and consumers are using personal computers and modems for an increasing number of communication applications. The ability to send and receive facsimile transmissions with a personal computer has created significant demand in recent years for modems with fax capabilities. Moreoever, modems are increasingly used to access vast information resources, share information, and transact business through online services and the Internet. According to *Interactive Age*, there are currently 20 million subscribers to consumer online services; *Information Week* reports that the number of new subscribers is increasing at a rate of 10,000 subscribers every day, with one million new subscribers added in the fourth quarter of 1995 alone. The flexibility required by an increasingly mobile workforce has fueled demand for products that facilitate remote connectivity between individuals and their corporate networks. These applications have created a demand for hardware and software products that facilitate communication between personal computer users and their information sources.

SMITH MICRO SOFTWARE, INC.

Chief Executive Officer:	William W. Smith Jr.
Principal Location:	51 Columbia Aliso Viejo, CA 92656
Telephone:	714-362-5800
Fax:	714-362-2300
E-mail:	not available
Web site:	not available
Satellite Locations:	Boulder, Colorado
Date Founded:	1983
Description of Business:	A leading provider of software that enables PC users to send and receive faxes as well as voice communications.
# Employees Current:	74
% Female Employees:	14%
# Employees Projected 9/30/96:	not available
Revenues 1995*:	$14,140,000
Gross Profit Margin (GPM):	70.8%
SGA Expenses/Revenues:	35.8%
% Sales Increase 1992 to 1995:	+322.3%
% Change GPM 1992 to 1995:	(11.7%)
% Change SGA Expenses/Revenues 1992 to 1995:	(2.4%)
Total Debt/Net Worth:	34.1%
Net Profits Before Taxes 1995*:	$3,715,000
Net Profits Before Taxes/Revenues:	26.2%
Market Value/1995 Revenues*:	9.5x
Traded On:	NASDAQ (SMSI)
Opportunity Company Addresses:	The widespread use of the fax and PC in home offices necessitates more functionality to obviate the need to phone, then get up and send a fax, then return to the PC and send an e-mail.
Elegance of Company's Solution:	Smith Micro provides easy-to-use, fully integrated PCs with fax, voice, and data communications capabilities.

*Annualized.

Modem manufacturers produce hardware to enable personal computer communication over land or wireless systems. By adopting technological advances, primarily in chip design, modem manufacturers have been able to deliver products with increasing price performance, higher transmission speeds, and increased functionality. The rapid pace of these changes, the need to support a variety of operating systems including DOS, Windows, Windows 95, OS/2, and Macintosh and the desire to differentiate products that incorporate identical chip sets presents a significant communication software challenge. Modem manufacturers generally focus on hardware and do not find it cost-effective to develop software internally to meet the evolving needs of communication software for multiple platforms. As a result, they bundle software from outside providers, among them Smith Micro, with their modems. This software is the technology that enables the modems to communicate data, faxes, and other forms of information.

The decline in Smith Micro's GPM without a concomitant decline in the ratio of SGA Expenses/Revenues would ordinarily disqualify Smith Micro from *Quantum Companies II*. However, the company is attempting to mitigate its reliance on OEMs, such as US Robotics, a leading modem manufacturer that accounts for nearly half of its sales, and begin selling direct to retail and reseller channels. Buying packaging material, creating graphic designs, and creating a brand name have been expensive, but establishing multiple-marketing channels is the right thing to do.

Look for the company's QuickLink products inside US Robotics, Practical Peripherals, Hayes, BOCA Research, Motorola, and other modems. Soon we will be able to buy the products from PC retailers and via mail order.

Smith Micro competes with the Delrina division of Symantec and with Global Village Communications, both Quantum Companies with substantial resources and market savvy. But you have to admire the gutsiness of the Smiths. Moreover, relative to the other horses in the multimedia race, Smith Micro is a relatively undervalued stock.

SPYGLASS, INC.

ometimes venture capitalists hit the nail flat, dab square on the head; Spyglass is one of those times. Bill Kaiser of Greylock and Ray Rothrock of Venrock, convinced their partners to go along with them in 1990 and 1991, respectively, and invest $3,522,000 for 60.2 percent of this browser developer, which at the time was operating in a two-room office on the campus of the University of Illinois. There weren't any revenues to speak of, and the word Internet hadn't yet been coined. Today the venture guys hold positions worth $138,600,000, an aggregate return of 40x in four years. That's an Irving Thalberg Lifetime Achievement if ever I saw one! Off the charts!

Tim Krauskopf invented Mosaic, the original software that converts the complexities of the Internet into a mouse-controlled graphic. In February 1995 Spyglass licensed Mosaic to Microsoft, Inc., for a flat $2 million, and that gave the company the validation to sign up dozens of other licensees who pay per-use fees. These include AT&T, Digital Equipment Corporation, IBM, and Quarterdeck, among others.

The story begins in 1987 when a University of Illinois student, Tim Krauskopf, working at the school's National Center for Supercomputing Applications (NCSA), developed Telnet, software to make navigating the nascent Internet easier. It worked so easily that techies around the world were downloading and copying it to surf the net. The university was unfamiliar with technology transfers, as was Krauskopf. He called a friend, Douglas Colbeth, then a vice president at Stellar/Stardust in Naperville, Illinois, to consult with his new company, Spyglass. Colbeth said, "Fine. Come on up." But none of the three employees at Spyglass had a car that could make it from Champaign to Naperville. So, Colbeth drove down.

Colbeth borrowed a licensing agreement from a friend at another computer company, and the University of Illinois found it acceptable and signed it. That stopped the pirating of Mosaic. And Colbeth's presence enabled the firm to raise venture capital. In June 1994, Spyglass relocated to Naperville.

Growth of revenues since 1992 has been more than 700 percent while growth of market value has exceeded 4000 percent. Why the buzz?

A recent survey showed that nearly two-thirds of the U.S. computer-using public is aware of the Mosaic brand name, even though the software is usually integrated into other products. Another study

SPYGLASS, INC.

Chief Executive Officer:	Douglas P. Colbeth
Principal Location:	1230 East Diehl Rd. Naperville, IL 60563
Telephone:	708-505-1010
Fax:	708-505-4944
E-mail:	dcolbeth@spyglass.com
Web site:	http://www.spyglass.com
Satellite Locations:	none
Date Founded:	1990
Description of Business:	Produces and sells Enhanced Mosaic, an Internet browser that provides graphical point-and-click access to the World Wide Web.
# Employees Current:	75
% Female Employees:	29%
# Employees Projected 9/30/96:	150
Revenues 1995*:	$6,954,000
Gross Profit Margin (GPM):	83.9%
SGA Expenses/Revenues:	42.7%
% Sales Increase 1992 to 1995:	+757.5%
% Change GPM 1992 to 1995:	+1.0%
% Change SGA Expenses/Revenues 1992 to 1995:	(-58.4%)
Total Debt/Net Worth:	12.6%
Net Profits Before Taxes 1995*:	$1,192,000
Net Profits Before Taxes/Revenues:	17.1%
Market Value/1995 Revenues*:	16.8x
Traded On:	NASDAQ (SPYG)
Opportunity Company Addresses:	If you want to surf or review catalogs on the commercial segment of the Internet known as the World Wide Web (WWW), you need a browser.
Elegance of Company's Solution:	Spyglass invented the browser.

*Annualized.

revealed that Mosaic is now used in 147 countries to access the Internet. More than 20 books have been written on Mosaic and how to use it.

Why wouldn't a company seeking to encourage access to its products or databases on the World Wide Web (WWW) include a browser in its product line? Does Hertz rent cars without steering wheels? Clearly, the need for browsers is universal. And Spyglass owns the patent and has developed an easy-to-use browser. Its future is bankable.

The WWW is the most powerful commercial component of the Internet because of the potential to sell and deliver products like music, video, and software directly to computer users. Industry figures show that the number of Internet and WWW servers, or access providers, is expanding at 20 percent a month. There are now 30 million users with Internet access and that is expected to hit 200 million worldwide within five years.

Oh, and about Krauskopf's car. He's 31 years old now and his Spyglass stock is worth $25 million. There won't be any tag days held for him.

SYSTEMS & COMPUTER TECHNOLOGY CORP.

$\int$ omebody has got to do the tough jobs. Working with administrators in universities, local governments, and utilities requires more than merely skill and a good product. Try patience, tenacity, and innovation to maintain a competitive edge. Systems & Computer Technology's accounts receivable were out 140 days in 1995 and are improving. It carries these receivables with borrowings, but that's the cost of doing business with the economy's slowest-paying organizations. Many lenders will not touch school and government paper, because the collection process is nigh infinite.

The company's skills are being appreciated increasingly within its key markets. British Gas, a key customer, is the largest utility in the world. Systems has a major outsourcing contract with Dallas, Texas, which was won in direct competition against EDS in the latter's home city. And it has more than a 50 percent market share in client/server applications in the college and university marketplace.

The June 1995 acquisition of Adage Systems provided entry into the enormous market of enterprise-resource computing. Since the closing of the deal, the company has hired ten seasoned professionals from Arthur Andersen's disbanded MacPac group. This team was highly sought after in the industry and their addition was a big coup, giving the company an instant sales force for the Adage line. A new version of its key product was recently introduced and, among other added features, it will extend the Adage system to the Windows NT platform.

As Systems gains size, market share, and stature, it is beginning to win larger deals. The company signed two large software sales to multicampus state universities and three more deals are in the pipeline. It has signed an initial contract with Continental Cablevision, the country's third-largest cable television company.

Systems may have to move more rapidly into less-expensive, client/server-based systems. A new crop of competitors, led by Buzzeo, Inc., Phoenix, Arizona is nipping at the industry leader's heels and taking away some customers, particularly in Chicago and Nashville. How Systems responds to its fleet-of-foot rivals will play out in 1996. The competitive pressure is of the better, faster, and cheaper variety usually a technology challenge. IBM, Wang, DEC, and AT&T were toppled by it. Will Systems respond with innovation or jaw-boning?

The facilities management format, invented by EDS and perfected by General Electric Information Systems, the former employer of Michael

SYSTEMS & COMPUTER TECHNOLOGY CORP

Chief Executive Officer:	Michael J. Emmi
Principal Location:	4 Country View Rd. Malvern, PA 19355
Telephone:	610-647-5930
Fax:	not available
Web site:	not available
Satellite Locations:	none
Date Founded:	1971
Description of Business:	A leader in client/server administrative software applications for the higher education markets.
# Employees Current:	1,700
% Female Employees:	not available
# Employees Projected 9/30/96:	not available
Revenues 1995*:	$169,994,000
Gross Profit Margin (GPM):	46.0%
SGA Expenses/Revenues:	24.0%
% Sales Increase 1992 to 1995:	+187.0%
% Change GPM 1992 to 1995:	+49.7%
% Change SGA Expenses/Revenues 1992 to 1995:	(20.0%)
Total Debt/Net Worth:	75.2%
Net Profits Before Taxes '95*:	$16,387,000**
Net Profits Before Taxes/Revenues:	9.6%
Market Value/1995 Revenues*:	1.8x
Traded On:	NASDAQ (SCTC)
Opportunity Company Addresses:	Higher-education institutions need special handling to reengineer their personnel and records management functions.
Elegance of Company's Solution:	The company fills this need and has taken its experience into the local government and utilities markets.

*Annualized.
**After adding back a write-off of $8,700,000 related to an acquisition.

310

Emmi, Systems' CEO, is an elegant operating model. Systems is expanding this sector of its business, which can be seen in a sharp decline in its SGA Expenses/Revenues ratio: from 30 percent in 1992 to 24 percent in 1995. The results show up on the company's bottom line.

Notwithstanding all of these plusses, Systems' stock price is relatively low by today's high-tech standards. Its market value to revenues ratio is 1.8x. There is considerable room for growth.

TIVOLI SYSTEMS, INC.

U sing the measurements for inclusion in *Quantum Companies II*, Tivoli Systems would be excluded. Its GPM did not improve over the last four years and its SGA Expenses/Revenues ratio is an incredibly high 53.1 percent. And it's rising. Its market value is more than $420 million or 11.2 times 1995 revenues. This valuation is at the high end of the curve for software companies. But the stock market is always right (eventually), so what am I missing? I asked myself.

Tivoli has one of the toughest sells imaginable. It has to wean its customers (like the ubiquitous "Helen" who has been at the company for 45 years running inventory control or accounts payable and who has some mean-looking bumper sticker on her desk saying "Can't you see I'm busy? Get a life!") from using the company's mainframe computer. It has to convert them to a server, which ties into the company's LAN; but they don't trust the server, they don't trust the salesman who brought it into their lives like cholera, and they certainly don't trust senior management—their bosses—who are persuaded to make the change.

Tivoli was founded on the belief that client/server systems present such dramatically new and different challenges that any successful solution must make a significant break from past approaches. The company identified the need for an industry-standard infrastructure on which to build systems-management applications and filled this void by developing its Tivoli Management Framework (TMF). Through the innovative application of object-oriented technology, the TMF provides a common foundation on which to build highly integrated systems-management applications that mask the complexity of large scale, multivendor UNIX and PC networks. TMF is the basis of the company's comprehensive product architecture for systems management, called the Tivoli Management Environment (TME), now in its second generation (TME 2.0).

In addition to TMF, the TME includes a wide range of applications that are built on top of and are tightly integrated with the TMF. The company believes that no other currently available product offers the scalability (accommodating installations of thousands of clients and servers) and heterogeneity (accommodating disparate UNIX and PC platforms) provided by the TME. In addition, TME 2.0 provides key client/server systems management applications such as software distribution, client and server configuration management, and event monitoring and correlation. A broad array of tool kits allow customers

TIVOLI SYSTEMS, INC.

Chief Executive Officer:	Franklin H. Moss
Principal Location:	9442 Capital of Texas Hwy. N. Arboretum Plaza One, Suite 500 Austin, TX 78759
Telephone:	512-794-9070
Fax:	512-418-4992
E-mail:	laura.moore@tivoli.com
Web site:	not available
Satellite Locations:	none
Date Founded:	1989
Description of Business:	Develops, markets, and supports systems-management software for the client/server computing market.
# Employees Current:	262
% Female Employees:	21%
# Employees Projected 9/30/96:	450
Revenues 1995*:	$36,427,000
Gross Profit Margin (GPM):	77.9%
SGA Expenses/Revenues:	53.1%
% Sales Increase 1992 to 1995:	7.8x
% Change GPM 1992 to 1995:	(1.3%)
% Change SGA Expenses/Revenues 1992 to 1995:	+5.7%
Total Debt/Net Worth:	26.6%
Net Profits Before Taxes 1995*:	$2,472,000
Net Profits Before Taxes/Revenues:	6.8%
Market Value/1995 Revenues*:	11.2x
Traded On:	NASDAQ (TIVS)
Opportunity Company Addresses:	Critical corporate data has traditionally been kept on mainframes. However, corporations are moving to enterprise-wide remote computing. Can the critical data be operated on much smaller servers?
Elegance of Company's Solution:	It assists management in moving data off their mainframes by offering superior management information systems on servers.

*Annualized.

and third parties to develop new systems management applications and to customize existing applications. Tivoli uses a consultative-selling process complemented with a broad array of services to assist customers in rapidly deploying and effectively using these solutions. They also wait about 83 days to receive payment on their sales and have the slowest-turning receivables of any software company in this book. But this ratio improved from 135 days in 1994, which indicates that Helen is reluctantly starting to say "yes" somewhat sooner.

VERITY, INC.

alk about sharing the risk of a venture with an "unsuspecting" public market: Take a look at Verity. Two venture capital funds—Olympic and U.S. Venture Partners—and three strategic partners—Advanced Decision Systems, Adobe Systems, and Thomson-CSF Ventures— pump $35.7 million into a software development company over seven years and they lose all of it. So, they clean house, bring in a new CEO, and change most of the key personnel. With losses of $5.8 million on revenues of $15.9 million, the investors find an underwriter that believes it can sell 2,500,000 shares of stock to the public at $12. Two of the investors ask to lighten up, and they sell 830,000 shares in the same offering. The underwriter values the company at $120 million. It is October 1995. *The stock market immediately runs the stock up to $43!* What's going on here?

Verity believes that growth in the volume and variety of available information—on enterprise networks, online services, the Internet, CD-ROMs, and other information—has made it increasingly important for individual businesses, government agencies, and information publishers to be able to search, filter, and disseminate information according to their particular criteria. Its Topic family of products is designed to address these needs by providing rapid and timely search, retrieval, and categorization of archived textual information, as well as real-time monitoring and filtering of information selected from dynamic text files. Users are able to conduct personalized searches across Topic-indexed information stored within multiple sources and formats. Verity's Topic technology has been deployed within the company's own suite of applications and also as an embedded feature within broadly distributed third-party software applications, including Lotus Notes and Adobe Acrobat.

The company originally developed its core Topic technology for use by large government agencies, such as the Central Intelligence Agency and the National Security Agency, to perform complex, customized search and retrieval applications. In the past two years, Verity has enhanced and expanded its Topic family of products and now offers or has under development a number of products designed to address the markets for enterprise, CD-ROM, online, and Internet dissemination of electronic information.

The "search-engine" librarian at the public library in your town earns about $20,000 a year to find reference books for you. Depending upon

VERITY, INC.

Chief Executive Officer:	Philippe F. Courtot
Principal Location:	1550 Plymouth St. Mountain View, CA 94043
Telephone:	415-960-7600
Fax:	not available
E-Mail:	bford@verity.com
Web site:	http://www.verity.com
Satellite Locations:	Westport, Connecticut; Highland Park and Oakbrook Terrace, Illinois; Boston, Massachusetts; Waterford, Michigan; Sugarland, Texas; Acwarth and McLean, Virginia; Canberra, Australia; Benelux, the Netherlands; Epson, United Kingdom; France; Germany
Date Founded:	1988
Description of Business:	Develops and markets search-and-retrieval software used on enterprise networks.
# Employees Current:	180
% Female Employees:	24%
# Employees Projected 9/30/96:	250
Revenues 1995*:	$17,853,000
Gross Profit Margin (GPM):	80.6%
SGA Expenses/Revenues:	71.6%
% Sales Increase 1992 to 1995:	(7.3%)
% Change GPM 1992 to 1995:	+12.4%
% Change SGA Expenses/Revenues 1992 to 1995:	+24.5%
Total Debt/Net Worth:	272.5%
Net Profits Before Taxes 1995*:	deficit
Net Profits Before Taxes/Revenues:	deficit
Market Value/1995 Revenues*:	22.8x
Traded On:	NASDAQ (VRTY)
Opportunity Company Addresses:	You know the data is somewhere in the system. How do you find it? Dum-da-dum-dum.
Elegance of Company's Solution:	Perhaps Verity should name its products "Dragnet" and "Joe Friday," because they search and retrieve specific content items lodged on enterprise networks or the Internet.

*Annualized.

the complexity of your question, it may take her or him one minute, one hour, or one day. But the service is free and the librarian will be there rain, snow, or shine.

Topic will find the reference for you in seconds and you don't have to leave your home or office. The market values this service at about $900 million. It will doubtless move up. The librarian versus Topic comparison pretty clearly delineates the perceived value of live, on-demand topic searching.

Virtual I.O, INC.

Linden Rhoads met C. Gregory Amadon in 1991 when she joined his rapidly growing Seattle company, Cellular Technical Services, Inc. (CTS). She was quickly promoted to market development manager for this developer of real-time fraud-detection software for cellular carriers. CTS went public in 1993 at $4 per share and rose to $48 within 12 months. But the challenge wasn't there for Rhoads or Amadon, the latter a video buff and former member of the White House press corps.

They formed Virtual I.O to solve the problem of putting an enormous amount of data and entertainment onto a personal display the size of a human palm. Eyeglasses would replace the palmtop. 3-D would replace 2-D. With their impeccable track records Rhoads and Amadon raised approximately $20 million from strategic partners Logitech, Thomsom-CSF Ventures, TeleCommunications, Inc., and Planar Systems.

Virtual i-glasses are an eight-ounce headset that connects to PCs, laptop computers, televisions, VCRs, laser disc players, and video game systems. They create the effect of a very large virtual screen in front of the viewer, displaying three-dimensional images in an immersive, full-color environment, and providing PC game players with head-tracking capabilities that enable them to maneuver in computer-simulated environments. Virtual i-glasses also can be used to view television and video programming in 2- and 3-D. The product sells for about $799 at computer retail stores. Many major software developers including Microsoft, IBM, Electronic Arts, and Lucas Arts Entertainment currently support Virtual i-glasses.

The company launched its first product to dentists. The small, lightweight product lets dental patients watch TV and video programming on a virtual screen that appears to be 80 inches in size, 11 feet in front of them. Virtual i-glasses not only help patients feel more relaxed and entertained during procedures but also give dentists more time to focus on their work without the need to verbally comfort nervous patients. The product is currently distributed by Patterson Dental, the nation's largest provider of dental products, which expects to sell 10,000 units in 1995.

Two versions of Virtual i-glasses have been introduced to the consumer market. The first version connects to personal computers and enables users to enter, and interact in, fully immersive, 3-D gaming environments and virtual worlds. This is accomplished using stereo-

Virtual I.O, INC.

President:	Linden Rhoads
Principal Location:	1000 Lenora St. Seattle, WA 98121
Telephone:	206-382-7410
Fax:	206-382-8810
E-mail:	vio@vio.com
Web site:	http://www.vio.com
Satellite Locations:	none
Date Founded:	1993
Description of Business:	Leading manufacturer of virtual-reality headsets for the consumer market.
# Employees Current:	200
% Female Employees:	40%
# Employees Projected 9/30/96:	400
Revenues 1995*:	not available
Gross Profit Margin (GPM):	The company is privately held and is not required to publish its financial statements.
SGA Expenses/Revenues:	not available
% Sales Increase 1992 to 1995:	not available
% Change GPM 1992 to 1995:	not available
% Change SGA Expenses/Revenues 1992 to 1995:	not available
Total Debt/Net Worth:	not available
Net Profits Before Taxes 1995*:	not available
Net Profits Before Taxes/Revenues:	not available
Market Value/1995 Revenues*:	not available
Opportunity Company Addresses:	The flat panel display on a palm-top-size device simply cannot provide a large amount of information to a worker or enough exciting entertainment to a consumer.
Elegance of Company's Solution:	With an eyeglass display the viewer is able to see more images in 3-D, enter and interact in, and fully immerse him or herself in 3-D gaming environments and virtual worlds.

*Annualized.

scopic 3-D displays and a head-tracking device that lets users look up, down, around, and even behind themselves.

The company's second consumer product connects to TVs, VCRs, and traditional video gaming platforms to create a private, personal big-screen effect for its user. Like the dental product, the virtual screen inside the headset appears 80 inches in size, 11 feet in front of the viewer in full stereo sound. The product also delivers a stereoscopic 3-D viewing experience when used with content produced in 3-D.

As prices come down to the $300 to $400 range, consumers will flock to this new device, and it will become an important travel, training, and mechanics' visual repair manual as well. The Rhoads-Amadon team may be the greatest combo since Gates and Allen or Hewlett and Packard, and Rhoads isn't even 30 years old.

VISIO CORPORATION

T he ingredients in the recipe for this beautifully crafted company are essentially three: stir in Jeremy A. Jaech, the 40-year-old cofounder of Aldus Corporation and the technical leader for the original development of PageMaker; Kleiner Perkins Caulfield & Byers, the most highly regarded venture capital fund in the United States, and Technology Venture Investors, the venture capital fund that backed Bill Gates when many fund managers thought Seattle was too far away to send their money and monitor it; and $6,545,000 in venture capital from the two funds.

As soon as Visio broke into the black, its board began thinking "exit strategy," and it called on Alex Brown & Sons to raise $39.5 million for the company at $16 per share in November 1995. The underwriters permitted insiders to sell $5.9 million of their shares at the IPO. Not too bright—the stock soared to $27½.

The tasty dish made from these three validating ingredients is the leading supplier of business drawing and diagramming software. Visio software, introduced in 1992, enables business and technical users to create drawings and diagrams using a simple "drag and drop" approach. Customers use the software for creating drawings and diagrams ranging from simple diagrams such as space plans, electrical schematics, and network designs. Visio's flexible product architecture and powerful graphics engine meet a broad range of business drawing and diagramming needs and help organizations realize savings on purchasing, training, and support. The company's mission is to become the single standard for creating, storing, and exchanging drawings and diagrams in business.

Drawing and diagramming—the visual representation of concepts, processes, and relationships—can be as important to businesses as words and numbers for communicating and exchanging ideas, abstract concepts, and relationships such as organizational structures and technical schematics. Traditionally done by hand using rulers, templates, and graph paper, or delegated to specialists such as graphic artists or drafters, business drawings and diagrams are increasingly created using software products. Just as the advent of personal computers made electronic word processing and spreadsheet preparation possible for the general user, the widespread acceptance of easy-use graphical user

VISIO CORP

Chief Executive Officer:	Jeremy A. Jaech
Principal Location:	520 Pike St. Seattle, WA 98101-4001
Telephone:	206-521-4500
Fax:	206-521-4501
E-mail:	not available
Web site:	http://www.visio.com
Satellite Locations:	Dublin, Ireland; Munich, Germany; Paris, France
Date Founded:	1990
Description of Business:	Leading supplier of drawing and diagramming software.
# Employees Current:	157
% Female Employees:	37.6%
# Employees Projected 9/30/96:	200
Revenues 1995*:	$34,224,000
Gross Profit Margin (GPM):	82.2%
SGA Expenses/Revenues:	57.8%
% Sales Increase 1993 to 1995:	+479.2%
% Change GPM 1993 to 1995:	(2.4%)
% Change SGA Expenses/Revenues 1993 to 1995:	(22.6%)
Total Debt/Net Worth:	37.8%
Net Profits Before Taxes 1995*:	$3,206,000
Net Profits Before Taxes/Revenues:	9.4%
Market Value/1995 Revenues*:	9.4x
Traded On:	NASDAQ (VISIO)
Opportunity Company Addresses:	Drawings and diagrams can succinctly communicate abstract concepts, but to date, drawing and diagramming software has been very expensive and limited in utility.
Elegance of Company's Solution:	Visio has introduced easy-to-use, more functional, and less expensive drawing and diagramming software.

*Annualized.

interfaces has created a similar opportunity for personal computer software to replace traditional paper-based drawing and diagramming for general business users.

Most of the drawing and diagramming software available, such as PageMaker, was introduced for narrowly defined drawing needs, for specialists, or as secondary features of office suite products. For example, single-purpose products were created for specific tasks such as the flow charting, organizational charting, or network diagramming. Users were confronted with a variety of products, each with a different user interface, and the drawings and diagrams they produced were often difficult to integrate into word-processed documents, spreadsheets, or presentation materials. Illustration, page layout, and CAD software has also been created for graphics artists, designers, and drafters. These specialty products generally do not address the needs of nonspecialists who wish to create, share, or modify drawings and diagrams. The result has been a market highly focused on specific users and fragmented among many applications.

Visio was designed with an open architecture and ease of customization, and the company is seeking to develop relationships with third-party solution providers, system integrators, and software developers who can create specific content for Visio products.

An outstanding product that solves real problems. Proven entrepreneurs and managers. Relationships with gatekeepers to the primary channels. Validation from two of the most esteemed venture capital funds in the country. These are the ingredients of a vibrant winner.

WONDERWARE CORP.

This elegant company trades on NASDAQ at a market-to-revenue ratio of 5.2x and a p/e ratio of 25.0x. It probably deserves more both because it has selected a very big problem to solve and it is delivering its solution very profitably around the world. A little background is needed to get the picture.

In the 1960s, electronic equipment and computers were generally believed to be unsuitable for the manufacturing environment, primarily because of their insufficient reliability for mission-critical production management and control tasks. Pneumatic controls and electromechanical devices were the preferred methods for controlling production equipment. However, as improvements were made in the capability and reliability of analog and digital electronics, production-control tasks were increasingly assumed by controllers employing integrated circuits and early microprocessors. In the 1970s, the programmable logic controller (PLC) emerged from Allen-Bradley and Siemens. PLCs were thought of as "hard hat" computers, designed to function in the hostile environment of the factory floor and be programmed by electricians. PLCs found early acceptance in discrete manufacturing segments, such as the automotive industry.

Parallel with this trend, distributed control systems (DCSs) from manufacturers including Foxboro and Honeywell evolved to provide computerized control capabilities for "continuous" processes, such as oil refining and chemical production. Both PLCs and DCSs were based on proprietary hardware and software technology. Today, these and other computer-based control systems are widely used throughout both the discrete and continuous-process manufacturing industries.

Initially, the operator interface for PLCs was provided by dedicated panels of buttons, lights, and indicators known as operator interface panels. For DCSs, this interface capability was typically provided by special-purpose devices or proprietary-graphics consoles supplied by the DCS vendor. Because of their proprietary, closed-architectures, and primitive operator interfaces, these approaches were generally expensive, inflexible, difficult to program, limited in capability, and unable to communicate easily with other systems.

On the plant-management side of manufacturing, computers began to replace the manual recording of production data and other hand-written reports in the 1960s. In the 1970s mainframe and minicomputer venders, such as Digital Equipment, Hewlett-Packard,

WONDERWARE CORP.

Chief Executive Officer:	Roy H. Slavin
Principal Location:	100 Technology Dr. Irvine, CA 92718
Telephone:	714-727-3200
Fax:	714-727-3270
E-mail:	not available
Web site:	not available
Satellite Locations:	Amsterdam, the Netherlands; Munich, Germany; Singapore
Date Founded:	1987
Description of Business:	Designs, develops, produces, and supports software-development tools for the industrial automation market.
# Employees Current:	327
% Female Employees:	not available
# Employees Projected 9/30/96:	477
Revenues* 1995:	$45,006,000
Gross Profit Margin (GPM):	95.1%
SGA Expenses/Revenues:	50.1%
% Sales Increase 1992 to 1995:	+297.3%
% Change GPM 1992 to 1995:	+4.6%
% Change SGA Expenses/Revenues 1992 to 1995:	(12.3%)
Total Debt/Net Worth:	8.9%
Net Profits Before Taxes* 1995:	$12,386,000
Net Profits Before Taxes/Revenues:	27.1%
Market Value/1995 Revenues:	10.5x
Traded On:	NASDAQ (WNDR)
Opportunity Company Addresses:	Data needs to be captured from programmable logic controllers on the factory floor and transmitted to management quickly and efficiently.
Elegance of Company's Solution:	PCs running the company's software can interface with the electromechanical production-control equipment.

*Annualized.

and IBM, identified manufacturing industries as potentially significant markets for their hardware and software products. These companies developed applications—such as materials-resource planning, cost accounting, inventory control, and production scheduling—that offered improved functionality but were closed and tedious to program, cumbersome to use, and difficult to integrate with other systems.

As PLCs, DCSs, and computer systems became increasingly prevalent in the manufacturing environment throughout the 1980s, several serious problems became apparent. Most of these systems were proprietary and built on platforms that lacked the ability to communicate outside their own environment. For example, PLCs, while greatly improving control of individual processes, created multiple "islands of information" that were generally unable to communicate or share data with other systems throughout the manufacturing enterprise. Software for a manufacturing operation typically had to be developed or customized to satisfy the unique requirements for that operation. As a result, high initial cost and high cost of ownership characterize the application of computer hardware and software to each facet of the manufacturing enterprise.

With the advent of low-cost, high-performance, standard personal computers and open operating environments, such as Microsoft Windows, the economics of the mass market can now be brought to the factory floor to solve the problems inherent in the traditional automation solutions.

Wonderware's overall business strategy is to offer manufacturing enterprises innovative, easy-to-use, and open-software solutions that exploit advances in hardware, software, and communications technologies. Its products are intuitive, object-oriented software tools for the industrial automation market. Wonderware's products run on Windows, and the proliferation of Windows in the manufacturing environment has fueled the company's recent growth and favorably positioned Wonderware as Windows continues to penetrate the industrial-automation market.

Its early commitment to and focus on Windows has enabled the company to develop a high degree of expertise in developing Windows applications. For example, recognizing a need for easy communications among Windows applications on networks, Wonderware developed its NetDDE connectivity products. This technology has been licensed to Microsoft for inclusion in Windows and Windows 95 and has the Microsoft endorsement, which is worth a lot on the factory floor. In that environment, brand names stand for reliability. With year-to-year leaps in sales, Wonderware's ratio of SGA Expenses/Sales has been declining. The result is a NPBT/Sales of 27.1 percent in 1995, up from 23.8 percent in 1992. Given all this good news, the stock market values this small company at $250 million! I think it's worth that, and more.

XING TECHNOLOGY CORP.

L et's say you live in Allentown, Pennsylvania, and you really miss live television (or even radio) broadcasts of football and basketball games of your alma mater, Boise State University. Suffer no more. The Internet is here.

Let's say you have moved to Tibet but really miss the Evening News with Tom Brokaw. Suffer no more. You can see Mr. Brokaw anywhere on the planet via the Internet and on demand for less than $5 a day. NBC uses the StreamWorks server-plus-software product developed by a small central-California company located in a strip shopping center next door to Levitz Furniture Co.

Xing Technology Corp. produces enabling technology not unlike the RCA Digital Satellite System for delivery of programming. It enables publishers, recording artists, movie studios, radio and television broadcasters, and other content producers to market their content over the Internet, thereby establishing a new commercial channel with unlimited cash flow potential. Similar broadcasts of audio/video content over private enterprise networks for general communications or training are also enabled.

StreamWorks, the company's product suite, is proprietary and transmits very high quality sound over 28.8 modems and very high quality video at 30 frames per second over double ISDN lines (128 kbps). Radio and television broadcasters have been ordering it at a rapidly increasing rate as they familiarize themselves with its features as an on-ramp, or tuner, to the Internet. These features include the ability to:

- broadcast anywhere so long as the listener/viewer is on the Network
- capture the name, gender, address, and other demographic information of all listeners/viewers in real-time
- advertise and sell product to listeners/viewers
- conduct market research or poll the listeners/viewers about the broadcasters' content
- offer games, contests, and other forms of interactive communication with listeners/viewers.

Customers include NBC, Reuters, CompuServe, International Telecommunications Union, E-Z Communications (owner of twenty-one radio stations), Time Warner, Telecom Finland, Swiss News Agency,

XING TECHNOLOGY CORP.

Chief Executive Officer:	Howard R. Gordon
Principal Location:	1540 West Branch St. Arroyo Grande, CA 93420
Telephone:	805-473-0145
Fax:	805-473-7440
E-mail:	hgordon@xingtech.com
Web site:	http://www.xingtech.com
Satellite Locations:	none
Date Founded:	1989
Description of Business:	Proprietary software that enables the bit streaming of live and on-demand audio, music, and video over private networks and the Internet.
# Employees Current:	40
% Female Employees:	25%
# Employees Projected 9/30/96:	90
Revenues* 1995:	$10,000,000 (estimated)
Gross Profit Margin (GPM):	The company is privately held and is not required to publish their financial statements.
SGA Expenses/Revenues:	not available
% Sales Increase 1992 to 1995:	not available
% Change GPM 1992 to 1995:	not available
% Change SGA Expenses/Revenues 1992 to 1995:	not available
Total Debt/Net Worth:	not available
Net Profits Before Taxes* 1995:	not available
Net Profits Before Taxes/Revenues:	not available
Market Value/1995 Revenues:	not available
Opportunity Company Addresses:	An alternate channel that permits a football fan living in a foreign city to listen to or watch his favorite team play or enables a singing group that can't get a sponsor to record on the Internet.
Elegance of Company's Solution:	The company provides such a channel to tens of millions of Internet users for the cost of a local phone call.

*Annualized.

Bloomberg, The Tribune Company, KOOL-FM, KOA (Denver), MCI, and more. They each pay Xing between $10,000 and $16,000 for a complete, ready-to-operate StreamWorks system. This includes live encoders, server, and decoding software.

Xing was founded in 1989 by Howard R. Gordon, who has been the company's President, CEO, and Chief Technical Officer since that time. With the exception of a $2 million strategic capital investment from Sumitomo in January 1996 and a $100,000 promissory note with warrants that funded in September 1995, the company has not raised any outside capital but, rather, has grown via OEM product sales and engineering contracts. It has licensed audio and video compression and broadcast technologies to Microsoft, Intel, Bellcore, NTT Japan, Fujitsu, Samsung, Hewlett-Packard, and IBM. Beginning in 1994, the company began shipping OEM versions of the MPEG encoder and decoder. To date, approximately 100,000 units of this product have been distributed through this channel.

What put Xing on the map was its selection by Microsoft and NBC to provide the technology for their new 24-hour all-news channel. With these endorsements, Xing will be as important to broadcasting over the Internet as Technicolor is to movies.

YAHOO CORP.

Yahoo Corp. provides a topic-oriented directory that classifies Web sites in 14 different subject categories, which are each divided into subcategories. To complement its topic-oriented search capabilities, Yahoo recently agreed to include Open Text Corp.'s Web Index to provide text-indexing search capabilities as well. Additionally, Yahoo provides various popular subcategories including "What's cool," "What's new," "What's popular," and "Headlines"—an hourly updated service that provides news about sports, politics, and business. Yahoo has significant strategic relationships with MasterCard, MCI, Reuters NewMedia, and Worlds, Inc.

Created in April 1994, Yahoo began as a hobby of two Stanford University electrical egineering Ph.D. students, David Filo and Jerry Yang, who saw the need to help people navigate through the overwhelming content of the Internet and gather meaningful information. In April 1995, Filo and Yang took a leave of absence from Stanford to make Yahoo an even more intuitive and efficient guide. They now work on Yahoo full-time along with a senior management team and support staff of 94 people. BellSouth, the owner of L. M. Berry and R. R. Donnelley, the two leading Yellow Pages publishers in the country, certainly let this opportunity slip away from under their leather desk chairs.

The advantages of advertising on the Internet are well-known: The Internet offers a degree of interactivity unmatched by other media; it has a highly desirable demographic of well-educated, computer-literate people; and it has the potential of being the most "trackable" of all media, whereby advertisers have the capability of understanding the individual who views their advertisement.

For millions of Internet cruisers a week Yahoo is home base for their online adventures. Today Yahoo is the world's most intuitive, up-to-date, and efficient guide for information and online discovery. More than a simple directory or search engine, Yahoo's free online guide satisfies a key need of consumers and working professionals to navigate through the Internet and gather information for both business and pleasure.

In September 1995, Yahoo recorded over 100 million page views to its service, growing at roughly 10 percent monthly. Yahoo estimates that at least three million users use Yahoo a month; most Yahoo users visit the service at least several times a week. The company has consistently ranked among one of the top three most-trafficked sites in the world.

YAHOO CORP.

Chief Executive Officer:	David Filo
Principal Location:	110 Pioneer Way Mountain View, CA 94041
Telephone:	415-934-3230
Fax:	415-934-3248
E-mail:	not available
Web site:	http://www.yahoo.com
Satellite Locations:	none
Date Founded:	1994
Description of Business:	Offers the most popular directory on the World Wide Web with approximately 300,000 visitors per day.
# Employees Current:	25
% Female Employees:	6%
# Employees Projected 9/30/96:	50
Revenues 1995*:	not available
Gross Profit Margin (GPM):	The company is privately held and is not required to publish its financial statements.
SGA Expenses/Revenues:	not available
% Sales Increase 1992 to 1995:	not available
% Change GPM 1992 to 1995:	not available
% Change SGA Expenses/Revenues 1992 to 1995:	not available
Total Debt/Net Worth:	not available
Net Profits Before Taxes 1995*:	not available
Net Profits Before Taxes/Revenues:	not available
Market Value/1995 Revenues*:	not available
Opportunity Company Addresses:	"You can't tell the players without a scorecard," and that idiom from the baseball park applies to the World Wide Web.
Elegance of Company's Solution:	Yahoo publishes the most complete directory of Web sites.

*Annualized.

Yahoo differs from other Internet advertising opportunities in that it offers highly targeted areas for advertisers. The demographic profile of Yahoo's users provides a broad view of Internet users in general.

Gender	
Male	83%
Female	17%
Age	
Under 18	7%
18–24	20%
25–35	34%
36–44	20%
45–54	14%
55+	5%
Education	
High School or Less	24%
Bachelor's Degree	40%
Graduate Degree	29%
Other	4%
Marital Status	
Single	47%
Married	44%
Living with Partner	9%
Profession	
Student	23%
Professional/Managerial	42%
Academic	8%
Technical	19%
Other	8%
Income	
Less than $20,000	20%
$20,000–$34,999	23%
$35,000–$49,999	21%
$50,000–$79,999	22%
$80,000–$100,000	7%
Over $100,000	7%

Data obtained from a survey taken on Yahoo from June 30, 1995, to July 18, 1995, with over 60,000 respondents.

While the home is the primary access point for 55 percent of Yahoo's users, the vast majority (85 percent) have some access from the home. This portends the emergence of the Web as a mass-market phenomenon, not just a curiosity that people access after hours. Acquiring a home account is a proactive choice that most current Web users have made.

Fifty percent of respondents state they primarily access the Internet/Web via direct-dial through an Internet service provider. Forty percent access through their employer or educational institution's continuous access. Eight percent report their primary access is through a commercial online service. With this base of support Yahoo will be a $100 million-plus revenues company by 1997. That day should come at about the time Filo and Yang would have been earning their Ph.D.'s.

ZYGO CORPORATION

When you study the recent and historical financial statements of Zygo Corp., you see a company so vastly improved over the last three years that its takes your breath away. Gross profit margin leapt 402 percent from 1993 to 1995. SGA Expenses to Revenues have plummeted 22.3 percent. Sales have almost doubled and the Operating Ratio climbed from 3.1 percent to 12.3 percent. If there is a piece of soot caught in the eye, it is in a slower turn of both accounts receivables and inventories. But Gary K. Willis, CEO, who joined the company from the top spot at Foxboro Corp. in 1992 has whipped Zygo into a lean, mean instrument-measuring machine.

Zygo operates in a single-business segment, electro-optics, and offers products that fall into two general categories: instruments and accessories and precision optical components. The company selects market segments that have significant growth potential and in which it can expect to: become a leading manufacturer; achieve and maintain a leadership position by using distinctive technologies to provide products offering high performance and quality; and maintain its position through customer-specific applications-oriented engineering and marketing. The company invests about 9 percent of sales in research and product development to enable it to compete effectively in its market areas.

Zygo markets and sells its products worldwide (roughly 45 percent of sales are to international customers) through a direct sales force and through independent distributors and sales representatives. Products are sold to a broad range of end users, including major corporations and government facilities. Zygo competes on the basis of product performance, applications engineering, customer support, reputation, and price.

Almost all of the company's instruments and accessories have the common characteristic that they employ a laser or white-light source to make noncontact measurements. Using light to achieve measurements requires specific techniques; a primary technique used in many of the company's instruments is the interference of light. A number of different generic instruments are based on interference of light and therefore are called interferometers. These interferometers are used to measure the surface shape, surface roughness, or distance and position of an object, or to provide information about the object's effect upon light transmitted through it.

ZYGO CORPORATION

Chief Executive Officer:	Gary K. Willis
Principal Location:	Laurel Brook Rd. Middlefield, CT 06455
Telephone:	860-347-8506
Fax:	860-347-8372
E-mail:	not available
Web site:	not available
Satellite Locations:	none
Date Founded:	1970
Description of Business:	Designs, develops, manufactures, and markets high-performance noncontact electro-optical measuring instruments.
# Employees Current:	227
% Female Employees:	24%
# Employees Projected 9/30/96:	275
Revenues 1995*:	$32,233,000
Gross Profit Margin (GPM):	55.8%
SGA Expenses/Revenues:	20.3%
% Sales Increase 1992 to 1995:	+142.0%
% Change GPM 1992 to 1995:	+40.2%
% Change SGA Expenses/Revenues 1992 to 1995:	(22.3%)
Total Debt/Net Worth:	30.0%
Net Profits Before Taxes 1995*:	$3,956,000
Net Profits Before Taxes/Revenues:	12.3%
Market Value/1995 Revenues*:	3.9x
Traded On:	NASDAQ (ZIGO)
Opportunity Company Addresses:	The need to be ultraprecise in the manufacture of electro-optic products and components.
Elegance of Company's Solution:	Zygo's products employ lasers to make noncontact measurements of surfaces, shapes, distance, and position.

*Annualized.

One type or class of interferometric measurement instruments is used by companies and laboratories to measure, align, and inspect optics and optical assemblies. In industries that make or use ultraprecision parts, such as the electronics industry, such measurement products are used to inspect read/write heads, assemble CD-laser pickups, and examine recording media. To be able to measure parts of various shapes and sizes it is necessary to offer instruments of various apertures ranging from an instrument with a beam size of almost a meter to one that is effectively a microscope. Zygo has a significant share of the market for these measurement products.

Zygo has a number of competitors, with Wyko Corporation (Tucson, Arizona) being the most significant one. Zygo's stock price has increased ten-fold in 20 months, with another ten-fold move facing it in what promises to be a future as bright as its laser lights.

PART THREE

INDEXES

GEOGRAPHIC INDEX

Alabama

Medpartners, Inc.   213

Arizona

Cycare Systems, Inc.   129
Employee Solutions, Inc.   147

California

Adaptec, Inc.   39
Advanced Digital Imaging, Inc.   42
Advent Software, Inc.   45
Altera Corporation   48
Applied Materials, Inc.   60
Arbor Software Corporation   66
@Home   75
Aurum Software, Inc.   175
Auspex Systems, Inc.   78
Authentic Fitness Corp.   81
Best Internet Communications,
    Inc.   90
CISCO Systems, Inc.   111
Clarify, Inc.   114
Cybercash, Inc.   126
Diamond Multimedia
    Systems, Inc.   138
DSP Technology Inc.   141
Future Labs, Inc.   159
Geoworks, Inc.   163
Global Village Communications,
    Inc.   166
Information Storage Devices, Inc.   72
Legato Systems, Inc.   193
Lexi International, Inc.   196
Logic Devices, Inc.   199
Lumisys Inc.   202
Macromedia, Inc.   205
Maxis, Inc.   211
Mercury Interactive Corp.   216
Netcom Online Communications,
    Inc.   222
Net Count, LLC   224
Netscape Communications Corp.   227
Neurex Corporation   236
Orthopedic Technology, Inc.   242
Pacific Pioneer Corp.   248
Perclose, Inc.   257

Phoenix Technologies, Ltd.   264
Premisys Communications, Inc.   272
Pyxis Corporation   278
Quarterdeck Corporation   281
Quickturn Design Systems, Inc.   284
Semtech Corporation   294
Smith Micro Software, Inc.   303
Verity, Inc.   315
Wonderware Corp.   324
Xing Technology Corp.   327
Yahoo Corp.   330

Colorado

CIBER, Inc.   108

Connecticut

Ameridata Technologies, Inc.   57
CUC International, Inc.   123
Gartner Group, Inc.   161
Zygo Corporation   333

Florida

Interim Services, Inc.   184
Parkervision, Inc.   251

Georgia

Pediatric Services of
    America, Inc.   254

Illinois

Spyglass, Inc.   306

Iowa

Featherlite Mfg. Inc.   153

Massachusetts

Applix, Inc.   63
Aspen Technology, Inc.   69
Avid Technology, Inc.   84
BBN Corporation   87
Cascade Communications
    Corp.   99
CMG Information
    Services, Inc.   117
FTP Software, Inc.   156
Inso Corporation   178
Kronos Inc.   190

Project Software & Development, Inc. 275
Security Dynamics Technologies, Inc. 290
Shiva Corporation 297

Michigan
Network Express, Inc. 230

Missouri
Jack Henry & Associates, Inc. 187

Nebraska
Data Transmission Network Corp. 135

New Hampshire
Cabletron Systems, Inc. 96

New Jersey
Computer Horizons Corp. 120
IDT Corp. 169

New York
Cheyenne Software, Inc. 105
MapInfo Corporation 208
Network-1 Software & Technology, Inc. 233
Ovid Technologies, Inc. 245
Pharmacy Fund, Inc. 261

North Carolina
Broadband Technologies, Inc. 93

Oregon
Merix Corp. 219

Pennsylvania
Cephalon, Inc. 102
Interdigital Communications Corp. 181
Systems & Computer Technology Corp. 309

South Carolina
Datastream Systems, Inc. 132

Tennessee
Phycor, Inc. 266

Texas
American Oncology Resources, Inc. 54
Occusystems, Inc. 239
Physicians Reliance Network, Inc. 269
Tivoli Systems, Inc. 312

Utah
Skywest, Inc. 300

Virginia
America Online, Inc. 51
EZ Communications, Inc. 150

Washington
Edmark Corporation 144
InControl, Inc. 172
Virtual I.O, Inc. 318
Visio Corporation 321

West Virginia
Raleigh Mine & Industrial Supply 287

COMPANY INDEX

*3Com Corp. 290
*Acxiom Corporation 39
Adaptec, Inc. 39
Advanced Digital Imaging, Inc. 42
Advent Software, Inc. 45
Altera Corporation 48
America Online, Inc. 51
*American Medical
    Response, Inc. 42
American Oncology
    Resources, Inc. 54
Ameridata Technologies, Inc. 57
Applied Materials, Inc. 60
Applix, Inc. 63
Arbor Software Corporation 66
*Asanté Technologies, Inc. 45
*Ascend Communications, Inc. 48
Aspen Technology, Inc. 69
@Home 72
*Atmel Corporation 51
Aurum Software, Inc. 75
Auspex Systems, Inc. 78
Authentic Fitness Corp. 81
Avid Technology, Inc. 84
*Bay Networks, Inc. 54
BBN Corporation 87
Best Internet
    Communications, Inc. 90
*Better Education, Inc. 57
Broadband Technologies, Inc. 93
*C-Cube Microsystems, Inc. 72
Cabletron Systems, Inc. 96
*Cambridge Neuroscience, Inc. 63
*Cambridge Technology
    Partners 66
Cascade Communications
    Corp. 99
*Catalina Marketing Corp. 69
Cephalon, Inc. 102
*Cerner Corporation 75
Cheyenne Software, Inc. 105
*Chipcom Corporation 78
CIBER, Inc. 108

*Cirrus Logic, Inc. 81
CISCO Systems, Inc. 111
Clarify, Inc. 114
CMG Information
    Services, Inc. 117
Computer Horizons Corp. 120
*Computer Network
    Technology Corp. 84
*Corel Corporation 87
*Corrections Corporation
    of America 90
CUC International, Inc. 123
Cybercash, Inc. 126
Cycare Systems, Inc. 129
Data Transmission
    Network Corp. 135
Datastream Systems, Inc. 132
*Davidson & Associates, Inc. 93
*Decision Quest 96
Diamond Multimedia
    Systems, Inc. 138
*Digital Link Corp. 99
*Dionex Corporation 102
*DNX Corporation 105
DSP Technology Inc. 141
*Ecoscience Corp. 108
Edmark Corporation 144
*Education Alternatives, Inc. 110
Employee Solutions, Inc. 147
*Ensys Environmental
    Products, Inc. 113
*Envirotest Systems Corp. 116
EZ Communications, Inc. 150
Featherlite Mfg. Inc. 153
*Fore Systems, Inc. 119
*Frontier Insurance
    Group, Inc. 123
FTP Software, Inc. 156
Future Labs, Inc. 159
Gartner Group, Inc. 161
GeoWorks, Inc. 163
Global Village
    Communications, Inc. 166

* Company profiled in *Quantum Companies*, published by Peterson's Pacesetter Books in 1995.

*GTI Corporation   126
*Harmony Brook, Inc.   129
*Hauser Chemical
    Research, Inc.   132
*Health Management
    Associates, Inc.   134
*Healthdyne Technologies, Inc. 137
*Heart Technology, Inc.   140
*Hemosol, Inc.   143
*Homecare Management, Inc.   146
IDT Corp.   169
InControl, Inc.   172
*Information America, Inc.   150
Information Storage
    Devices, Inc.   175
*Informix Corporation   153
Inso Corporation   178
*Integrated Health
    Services, Inc.   156
Interdigital Communications
    Corp.   181
Interim Services, Inc.   184
*International High Tech
    Marketing Inc.   159
*Invision Systems Corporation 162
Jack Henry & Associates, Inc. 187
*Just for Feet, Inc.   165
Kronos Inc.   190
*Landstar Systems, Inc.   168
Legato Systems, Inc.   193
Lexi International, Inc.   196
*Life Resuscitation
    Technologies, Inc.   171
Logic Devices, Inc.   199
Lumisys Inc.   202
Macromedia, Inc.   205
MapInfo Corporation   208
Maxis, Inc.   211
*Medicenter, Inc.   173
*Medicus Systems Corp.   .   176
Medpartners, Inc.   213
*Medrad   179
*Megahertz Holding Corp.   181
Mercury Interactive Corp.   216
Merix Corp.   219
*Mitek Surgical Products, Inc. 184
*Molten Metal Technology   187
*Mothers Work, Inc.   190
*National Health Corp.   193
Netcom Online
    Communications, Inc.   222

Net Count, LLC   224
*NetFrame Systems, Inc.   196
Netscape Communications
    Corp.   227
Network Express, Inc.   230
Network-1 Software &
    Technology, Inc.   233
Neurex Corporation   236
*Neurogen Corp.   199
*Newbridge Networks Corp.   202
*Nextel Communications, Inc. 205
Occusystems, Inc.   239
*On Assignment, Inc.   208
*Orbital Sciences Corp.   211
*Orthogene, Inc.   214
Orthopedic Technology, Inc.   242
Ovid Technologies, Inc.   245
Pacific Pioneer Corp.   248
*Parametric Technology Corp. 217
*ParcPlace Systems, Inc.   220
Parkervision, Inc.   251
Pediatric Services of
    America, Inc.   254
Perclose, Inc.   257
Pharmacy Fund, Inc.   261
*Phenix Biocomposites, Inc.   223
Phoenix Technologies, Ltd.   264
Phycor, Inc.   266
Physicians Reliance
    Network, Inc.   269
*Pleasant Company   225
Premisys Communications,
    Inc.   272
*Progressive Corp.   228
Project Software &
    Development, Inc.   275
Pyxis Corporation   278
*Qualcomm, Inc.   231
*Quantum Health Resources,
    Inc.   234
Quarterdeck Corporation   281
Quickturn Design
    Systems, Inc.   284
*Quorum Health Group, Inc.   237
Raleigh Mine & Industrial
    Supply   287
*Res-Care, Inc.   240
*Research Management
    Consultants, Inc.   243
*Roper Industries, Inc.   246
*Ryka, Inc.   249

Security Dynamics	
Technologies, Inc.	290
Semtech Corporation	294
*Sentinel Systems, Inc.	251
*Shaman Pharmaceuticals,	
Inc.	254
Shiva Corporation	297
Skywest, Inc.	300
Smith Micro Software, Inc.	303
Spyglass, Inc.	306
*SRX, Inc.	257
*Stores Automated	
Systems, Inc.	260
*Sunrise Medical, Inc.	263
*Swift Transportation Co., Inc.	266
*Sybase, Inc.	269
*Synaptic Pharmaceutical	
Corp.	272
*Synopsys, Inc.	275
*Systemix, Inc.	278
Systems & Computer	
Technology Corp.	309
*Tecnol Medical Products, Inc.	281
*Tetra Tech, Inc.	284
*The Body Shop	
International PLC	60

*Thermo Electron Corp.	287
*Three-Five Systems, Inc.	293
Tivoli Systems, Inc.	312
*Transmedia Network, Inc.	296
*Tresp Associates, Inc.	299
Verity, Inc.	315
Virtual I.O, Inc.	318
Visio Corporation	321
*Vivra, Inc.	302
*Vivus	305
*Wall Data Inc.	308
*Whole Foods Market, Inc.	311
*Wholesome & Hearty	
Foods, Inc.	314
Wonderware Corp.	324
Work/Family Directions	317
*Workstation Technologies,	
Inc.	320
*Xilinx, Inc.	323
Xing Technology Corp.	327
*Xircom, Inc.	326
Yahoo Corp.	330
*Zebra Technologies Corp.	329
*Zia Metallurgical Processes,	
Inc.	331
Zygo Corporation	333

INDUSTRY INDEX

Apparel

Authentic Fitness	81

Biotechnology

Cephalon, Inc.	102
Neurex Corporation	236

Consumer Electronics

Virtual I.O, Inc.	318

Digital Video

Advanced Digital Imaging, Inc.	42
Avid Technology, Inc.	84
Macromedia, Inc.	205

Education Software

Edmark Corporation	144

Employee Leasing

Employee Solutions, Inc.	147
Interim Services, Inc.	184

Health Care

Pediatric Services of America, Inc.	254

Information Management Systems

Cycare Systems, Inc.	129
Data Transmission Network Corp.	135
Ovid Technologies, Inc.	245
Pharmacy Fund, Inc.	261

Insurance

Pacific Pioneer Corp.	248

Integrated Circuits

Altera Corporation	48
Applied Materials, Inc.	60
Information Storage Devices, Inc.	175
Logic Devices, Inc.	199
Merix Corp.	219
Quickturn Design Systems, Inc.	284
Semtech Corporation	294

Internet Services

BBN Corporation	87
Best Internet Communications, Inc.	90
CMG Information Services, Inc.	117
CUC International, Inc.	123
Network-1 Software & Technology, Inc.	233
Quarterdeck Corporation	281
Security Dynamics Technologies, Inc.	290
Shiva Corporation	297
Smth Micro Software, Inc.	303
Spyglass, Inc.	306
Verity, Inc.	315
Xing Technology Corp.	327
Yahoo Corporation	330

Measuring Instruments

Zygo Corporation	333

Medical Devices

InControl, Inc.	172
Lumisys, Inc.	202
Orthopedic Technology, Inc.	242
Perclose, Inc.	257

Mining Equipment

Raleigh Mine & Industiral Supply	287

Network Devices

Auspex Systems, Inc.	78
Cabletron Systems, Inc.	96
Cascade Communications Corp.	99
CISCO Systems, Inc.	111
Diamond Multimedia Systems, Inc.	138
Global Village Communications, Inc.	166
Parkervision, Inc.	251

Online Services

America Online, Inc.	51
@Home	72

Physician Practice Management

American Oncology
　Resources, Inc. 54
Medpartners, Inc. 213
Occusystems, Inc. 239
Phycor, Inc. 266
Physicians Reliance
　Network, Inc. 269

Software

Adaptec, Inc. 39
Advent Software, Inc. 45
Applied Materials, Inc. 60
Arbor Software Corporation 66
Aspen Technology, Inc. 69
Aurum Software, Inc. 75
Cheyenne Software, Inc. 105
Clarify, Inc. 114
Datastream Systems, Inc. 132
Inso Corporation 178
Jack Henry & Associates, Inc. 187
Kronos, Inc. 190
Legato Systems, Inc. 193
MapInfo Corporation 208
Maxis, Inc. 211
Mecury Interactive Corp. 216
Network Express, Inc. 230
Phoenix Technologies, Ltd. 264
Project Software &
　Development, Inc. 275

Phyxis Corporation 278
Systems & Computer
　Technology Corp. 309
Tivoli Systems, Inc. 312
Visio Corporation 321
Wonderware Corp. 324

Systems Integration

Ameridata Technologies, Inc. 57
CIBER, Inc. 108
Computer Horizons Corp. 120
DSP Technology, Inc. 141

Systems Software

GeoWorks, Inc. 163

Telecommunications

Broadband Technologies, Inc. 93
EZ Communications, Inc. 150
Interdigital Communications
　Corp. 81
Premysis Communications, Inc. 272

Telemarketing

Lexi International, Inc. 196

Transportation

Featherlite Mfg. Inc. 153
Skywest, Inc. 300